UNDER FIRE

The Blitz diaries of a
volunteer ambulance driver

Other books by Naomi Clifford

THE DISAPPEARANCE OF MARIA GLENN
WOMEN AND THE GALLOWS 1797-1837
THE MURDER OF MARY ASHFORD

UNDER FIRE

The Blitz diaries of a
volunteer ambulance driver

Naomi Clifford

**CARET
PRESS**

9 Durand Gardens
London SW9 0PS
caretpress.com

First published by Caret Press 2021

ISBN 978-1-9196232-0-7

This book is dedicated to
June's descendants, and
to everyone swept along by
events beyond their control

Contents

	MAP	*viii*
	ABBREVIATIONS	*x*
	PICTURE CREDITS	*x*
	ACKNOWLEDGEMENTS	*xi*
1	June Spencer	*1*
2	Goodbye to All That	*9*
3	Ritzkrieg and Sitzkrieg	*22*
4	At the Ready	*40*
5	Summertime	*59*
6	Without Turning a Hair	*76*
7	A Battleship on High Seas	*95*
8	Like Wolves	*112*
9	Searching for Escape	*124*
10	Beautiful Dolls	*137*
11	Disaster	*152*
12	The Stars Go Out	*165*
13	A New World	*177*
14	Love, Possibly	*190*
15	The Menagerie	*202*
16	Final Destinations	*214*
	BIBLIOGRAPHY	*231*
	INDEX	*235*
	SPONSORS	*240*

1 **Lindsey House**, June Spencer's home from 1940 to 1942.

2 **The boatyard below Cheyne Walk**, where A.P. Herbert moored the *Water Gypsy*.

3 The location of **AS22**, in a yard behind Danvers Street.

4 **Beaufort Street**, where a street shelter was bombed on 8 September 1940.

5 **Paultons Square**: crews from AS22 liked to drink at the Black Lion.

6 **Chelsea Old Church**, destroyed on the night of 16 April 1941.

7 **Church of the Holy Redeemer** in Upper Cheyne Row, bombed on 14 September 1940.

8 **ARP post** at Cook's Ground School.

9 **Decontamination Unit** at Manresa Road.

10 **Sloane Square** station, bombed on 12 November 1940. Peter Jones is on the opposite corner.

11 **Chelsea Royal Hospital**, a frequent target of the Luftwaffe, was bombed multiple times.

12 **King's Road**, location of AS23.

Lots Road power station is near to the river, to the west of the map.

Victoria station is to the east of Sloane Square.

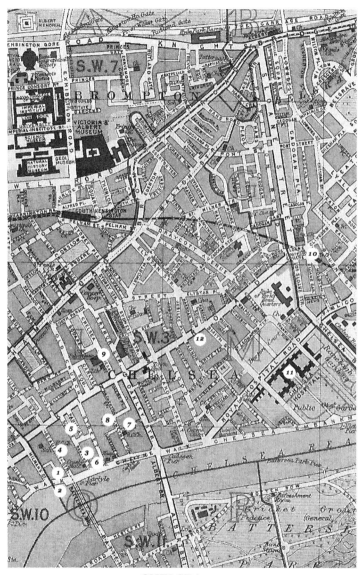

CHELSEA 1940

ABOUT THE TEXT

In 1940 £1 was worth approximately £40 in 2021 values. A skilled tradesman might earn £8 for five days of his labour.

Extracts from June's diaries have been corrected for spelling and punctuation. Where text is omitted I have used three-dot ellipses.

June Spencer (given name Elizabeth June Spencer) should not be confused with the radio actress June Spencer.

ABBREVIATIONS

AA	Anti-Aircraft
AFS	Auxiliary Fire Service
ARP	Air Raid Precautions
AS	Ambulance Station
ATS	Army Territorial Service
FANY	First Aid Nursing Yeomanry Corps
FAU	Friends Ambulance Unit
FO	Foreign Office
LCC	London County Council
LAAS	London Auxiliary Ambulance Service
MoF	Ministry of Food
PEP	Political and Economic Planning
PWE	Political Warfare Executive
RAF	Royal Air Force
RES	River Emergency Service
TS	Territorial Station
WAAC	War Artists' Advisory Committee
WAAF	Women's Auxiliary Air Force
WRNS	Women's Royal Navy Service (Wrens)
WVS	Women's Voluntary Services

PICTURE CREDITS

ACKNOWLEDGEMENTS

First and foremost, heartfelt thanks to June Spencer's family: Fenella Gatehouse, for lending me June's diaries, and her partner Simon, for his enthusiasm and encouragement; Jamie Buchanan, for combing the manuscript for accuracy and for the loan of photographs in his collection; and Andy Buchanan, for his useful comments.

Few of those who knew June during the war years are still with us. However, some of their descendants are. Thanks are due to the family of Patience Clifford, as well as to the relations of June colleagues in the ambulance service: Pauline Nagle, Pamela Radford, Frank Enefer, Alexander MacTavish. Sybil Gilliat-Smith's story was told with the invaluable assistance of Andrew Sim of Sim Art. Special thank-yous to Jane Cook for her encouraging sessions, which helped me find give a direction for the book and to Karen Robinson for her help and advice on publishing. The patience, calm and nuanced suggestions of my agent Hedda Archbold and the team at HLA Agency are evidenced in the finished book.

I finished writing the manuscript of the book during the time of Covid lockdowns, but before that had spent long periods in the National Archives, British Library, Westminster Archives, London Metropolitan Archives and Kensington & Chelsea Libraries, where I was assisted by the wonderful staff.

The biographical details of many of the inhabitants of Lindsey House and others of whom June wrote would not have been known but for the expert genealogical research of my brother Paul Klein. Speaking of family, I recall long hours in my little study, left in peace to decipher June's scrawls, and from time to time let off dog walking duty—impossible without the consideration of Tim, Lily and Izzy Clifford, and of course Beeper the dog herself.

Finally, thanks to all the contributors who helped crowd-fund this project on Kickstarter. They all played a part in bringing June's unique story into the light.

June Spencer

IF YOU STAND by the Thames at the southern end of Battersea Bridge and look across the water, you will see to the left the seven red-brick Brutalist towers of the World's End estate. In comparison, the centuries-old dwellings of Chelsea surrounding them are like dolls' houses, tiny and exquisite. Now trace the embankment rightwards. There, behind a collection of barges and small jetties, sitting back from the rest of the surrounding houses, is the top part of Lindsey House on Cheyne Walk. In 1940, in a room at No. 97 on the fourth floor, June Spencer sewed, drank tea, gossiped, made lifelong friends and wrote her diary.

June's room became her refuge. After the stress and tedium of her ambulance-driving shifts, it represented safety and independence, even as bombs shivered the floors and blew out the windows. The building belonged to the charismatic antiquarian and merchant seaman Richard Stewart-Jones, who also owned nearby houses in the row, including No. 96, known by many as Whistler's House because the artist had once lived there.

In Chelsea June observed some of the high dramas of the times. Think of her sunbathing in the back garden on 7 September 1940, the air sultry and motionless after days of high temperatures and full sun, looking up at a sky filled with hundreds of small black planes 'not bigger than pinpricks'. It was the moment she and millions of other Londoners realised that the much-feared aerial assault on their city had begun.

Now cross to the other side of the bridge road and continue along by the river, past the new-builds, towards the corner of Battersea Park and look across the river once more. Above the trees you will see the solid brick tower of Chelsea Old Church. Imagine a dark night in April 1941. Echoing across the water you might hear the shouts of the demolition men as they topple walls, or of the heavy rescue teams as they appeal for silence so that they can listen for the cries of survivors, the penny whistles of the ARP wardens, the insistent whine of raiders still overhead; you might see the small dark figures of firemen, stretcher parties, first aiders, doctors, nurses and the ambulance crews lit by feeble headlights. Somewhere in the mix, is June, hurriedly returned from a night in the West End, holding up the skirt of her pink and black evening gown as she clambers over rubble. She is talking to her ambulance colleagues who tell her that the ambulance station has been wrecked and that the death toll at Chelsea Old Church includes five firewatchers.

While you stand by the river, conjure now another scene. This one takes place just over a year later. It is daytime. A bitter wind zips through tall leafless trees in Battersea Park. See June, buttoned into her thick navy Ambulance Service coat, cycling across the bridge, her eyes dark with anger. Her life has been turned upside-down, by the absence of bombs accompanied by the maddening possibility of more at any time. The days ahead promise only constant boredom and constant vigilance. She understands that to survive she must cut a new path in life.

You can carry out a similar exercise anywhere in London, half-seeing the unsung and the long-forgotten in their khaki or dark blue uniforms, their aprons or their cloth caps going about their chores and duties, your imagination positioning them amongst then-blasted hollows and gap-toothed streets. The temptation is to beatify those who lived through wars, who endured the front line or the home front, who were said to never complain and cheerfully carried on regardless. Their lives and experiences seem extraordinary to us now, but in truth they were no different to any other generation past or future: we all, as humans, must cope with the obstacles life throws in our path. If we assume that they were built of sterner stuff and were able to emerge unscathed from the war, at least mentally, we would be wrong. It's just that they learned to manage in a certain way. And there is always a cost.

The writings of June Spencer, debutante, nightclubber,

ambulance driver, dress designer, civil servant, Wren and climber-over-obstacles, bears witness to this.

June Spencer was born in 1916 into a comfortably-off upper middle-class family and grew up in a large house at Odsey Corner, a hamlet near the picturesque village of Ashwell in Hertfordshire, twelve miles from Cambridge. As a child she was sporty and adventurous, good at games rather than at lessons. She loved horse-riding, golf and tennis, which she played well into her eighties. When she was ten, her father, recognising her physical confidence, taught her to drive. She took to it instantly and was celebrated in her family for accurate and spirited reversing. Early on she also showed artistic talent. After she left school, having developed a love of sewing and craft, she trained at a dress-making school in Knightsbridge.

In most respects June's life followed the standard trajectory for a young woman of her class: boarding school, jaunts in Paris, skiing trips to Austria and parties with the appropriate people in London. In May 1938 she was presented to the King and Queen at Buckingham Palace, her curtsey in front of the Royal couple being, in effect, an announcement of her availability for marriage to a suitably rich and well-connected man.

June may have been brought up amongst privilege, but this did not mean she was a stranger to hard work. She provided herself with a modest personal income by designing and making fashion belts which she sold to the London department stores Fortnum & Mason and Peter Jones. She also made clothes, for herself, family members, friends and servants. She had absorbed the idea that there were new possibilities for women and throughout her life she was resourceful, independent-minded and organised.

❖

In 2016 June's daughter Fenella Gatehouse first showed me the chunky quarto-sized lined notebooks in which June wrote her diary from late 1939 to early 1943. Fenella knew that I liked to investigate the stories of 'ordinary', hitherto unknown women, and I was ready for a new project, so this seemed perfect. When

I opened the first notebook, my impression was that reading the diaries through would not take long. June wrote in italic script; it all looked satisfyingly regular. There were only a few crossings-out and arrowed-in additions.

I could not have been more wrong. Although the handwriting looked neat, it was often illegible. June used a pencil; sometimes a soft, blunt one, in which case one letter would elide into the next, and at other times a hard, pointed one, turning her writing into a scrawl of pale spindly spiders. It was difficult to know which was worse. Fenella later told me that although June was left-handed she had been forced at school to use her right hand and that this might account for her deceptively neat-but-illegible script.

It did not help that her spelling was unreliable. Some words were easy to interpret—bicycle was always *bycicle*, were was always *where*—but when it came to the names of people, restaurants and places June would just make a stab at a phonetic version. Even so, I felt sure that I would, in time, learn June's quirks, and to some extent that was what happened, although there are still a few words and names that remain, to me, indecipherable.

It was quickly clear that the only way to get to grips with the diaries was to transcribe them in their entirety. It would not be enough merely to over-read them and extract the most interesting passages. If I did that, I risked missing tiny nuggets of fact or juicy asides and would fail to take in the full scope of June's world.

After I was able to make sense of most of the script, I had something to work with. June loved to write but she was not a writer in any professional sense. Her words, dashed down in a few minutes, flowed out of her. From the pages emerged the names of June's myriad friends and acquaintances, many of them well known at the time although perhaps now primarily to the older generation: the actress Constance Cummings and her playwright husband Benn Levy, the maverick MP and writer A.P. Herbert, artists Tom Dugdale, Harry Morton Colvile (with whom June was romantically involved), Augustus John and Anthony Devas, as well as numerous politicians and luminaries, Kenneth Lindsay and Graham Spry among them, connected to Political and

Economic Planning, the forerunner of the Policy Studies Institute, which aimed to plan Britain as a better place. It was a surprise, although not a big one, to discover that June was acquainted with Mary Wesley and was a visitor at Boskenna, the estate in Cornwall Wesley used as an inspiration for her novel *The Camomile Lawn*.

As I read June's words I came to understand that they give an insight into how a young woman coped with the searing events of war, whether they occurred on her doorstep or across seas. June was not a typical Londoner, if such a thing could ever exist—after all, she came from a posh family and was a debutante—but her wartime experiences, and her responses to them, an ability to show coolness, stoicism and even cheerfulness in spite of the constant chance of harm or death and to hide deep-seated fear and anxiety, were common to millions.

Part of the trick to maintaining *sang froid* was to stay busy. Throughout June's long life her calendar was chock-a-bloc and never more so than when she was in her early twenties and associating with a host of other young people, all of whom were leading lives as hectic as her own. During the Blitz, despite being kept awake by the Luftwaffe or dog-tired from night shifts, she had seemingly boundless reserves available for parties, drinks, balls, nightclubs, exhibitions, cinema and theatre trips, outings to the country, shopping expeditions, days at the races and meals out, not to mention hours crafting her belts and designing and sewing complex outfits for her friends.

Every few weeks she would head back to her family in Hertfordshire for respite from London, but even here there was always something to do: visiting her aunts and grandmother or helping out at the Red Cross canteen her mother ran, walking the dog, rat-catching or more sewing, making and painting. She was never one to sit contemplating her navel. Creativity provided an escape from the world around her and overcoming a design dilemma or a technical challenge in order to emerge with a stunning gown, coat or frock could lift her out of her immediate surroundings and give simple satisfaction in a job well done.

No wonder her handwriting was a mess—she was never at

rest, always on the go. In any case, she was clearly not writing for posterity and probably did not care if no one else could read her words. June's matter-of-fact style was not exceptional; few diarists offer evocative detail, even when recording events they know will go down in history. When she made her almost daily entries, listing out what she had done that day, June may have assumed that she would be the only person to read them and that as long as she could interpret her own scrawl it was fine. Indeed, it was fine and she *was* able to understand her own writing. In her eighties, she visited primary schools and talked to groups of children about her experiences in the Blitz, reading to them from the pages in those lined notebooks.

June wrote throughout her life. The volumes covering her teenage years and the start of the war on 3 September 1939 have been lost and there was a long break after 1943 when she joined the Women's Royal Naval Service and met 'Buck' Buchanan, a dashingly handsome RAF pilot, but she resumed writing later and continued through the birth of her three children, her divorce and into old age.

Why did she write them? As I mentioned, they may have been partly for herself, an *aide-memoire* for use at some point in the future when she wished to recall exactly what she had done on a particular day. Certainly many entries were mundane, merely lists of places visited and people with whom she had lunched. This example is typical:

> *Monday 24 June 1940* Borrowed a bicycle. Had tea with
> Peter B. in the Kings Rd. Bicycled down to the West End.
> Supper with the Donnellys.

Given the perfunctory nature of much of the writing, why are June's diaries as a whole so fascinating? The most obvious answer is that they add to the body of eyewitness accounts of the London Blitz—and surely we can never have enough of these. Also, the role of the London volunteer ambulance driver may be well known but the details of their work are not. There are few published diaries of those who served in the London Auxiliary Ambulance Service (LAAS). May Greenup's memories of her experience at Station 39 in the West End of London, which were compiled in detail by her niece Angela Raby in *The Forgotten Service*, and Tracy Shaler's *Frenchy: I Wanted to Get Back at Hitler*, which tells the story of Jewish refugee Jeannette Marx who served with the LAAS in the East End of London, are probably the best known. The novelist Rose Macaulay wrote candidly of her experiences driving for the LAAS in Camden, north London in which she described waiting for people to be excavated from dust and rubble before rushing them to hospital, but her most vivid accounts are themselves buried in the archives.[1]

June's diaries also paint pictures of worlds long disappeared: the wartime West End night scene; Chelsea's villagey mix of artists, writers, aristos and those once called 'common people'; the hive of activity at the extraordinary Lindsey House in Cheyne Walk; and the continued difficulties of life on the home front after the Blitz of 1940–41 ended.

The world is not short of memoirs of Chelsea during the war, of course. The teenage Joan Wyndham's *Love Lessons* detailed her enthusiastic search for sexual experience while bombs dropped around her. Both Frances Faviell and Theodora Fitzgibbon moved in some of the same social circles as June and wrote memoirs. There are also the writings of the ruins inspector A.S.G. Butler and the diaries of June's friend the architectural historian James Lees-Milne. More recently, Donald Wheal recalled his early life living in the Guinness Trust estate at World's End at the western end of Chelsea and provided a welcome balance to the many accounts of the privileged.[2]

1. In 1939, aged 59, Emilie Rose Macaulay (1881–1959) signed up to serve with the LAAS as a part-time driver. She wrote about her work in letters to her sister Jean (*Letters to a Sister*) and in the magazine *Time and Tide* (5 Oct 1940). See Lara Feigel's *The Love-charm of Bombs*.
2. See bibliography for details of these publications.

June's diaries are decidedly not confessional. Although my thinking is that she probably saw herself as the primary reader, I also have a feeling that she might also have been writing with her mother, or someone like her, in mind, perhaps to prove her independence from the family or to reinforce her separation from the relative comfort of life in Hertfordshire. But she may have also feared that her mother would actually read them, which could explain why she gave no hint of sexual encounters—she wrote of romance but never of physical intimacy—and gave only fleeting indications of her emotional life. June said almost nothing about being dumped by her boyfriend Harry Colvile and when another love-sick admirer berated her for refusing his advances, she did not mention the insulting letter he sent her afterwards. Another explanation for June's silence on personal matters may be that from childhood she was trained to be stoic. Not emoting was the norm for her class and time. She could not let the side down by making unnecessary fuss—to do so was selfish and harmful. Feelings, especially negative ones, were to be suppressed.

June's reticence extended to the scenes she witnessed on duty with the auxiliary ambulance service. She was warned by her superior officers to self-censor, as expansiveness might break confidentiality or her diaries might fall into the wrong hands. Whether for these reasons or from a natural feeling of reserve, she did not describe in detail, as some did, the corpses and body parts, the trapped victims, the distressed and shocked survivors, and said little about the destruction of the beloved buildings of London. With some notable exceptions, the diary entries were clipped and peremptory, the effects of war kept at arm's length.

The veneer June laid over her words hides much. On the surface her diaries paint unique vignettes of life in Britain, mainly London, in the Second World War—but they are more than this. At their heart June's words tell us, sometimes through vanishingly small clues, that wartime optimism, self-sacrifice and bravery were only part of the story.

Goodbye to All That

Thursday 26 October 1939 Called by Eliza [the maid] at 7.30. Listened to the news at 8. Nothing fresh. Weather cold—the first frost. Painted in my room most of the morning. Dusted out the messy drawers. After lunch to Hitchin with Janet, had tea with Granny, who was very well. The Jonsons were there. Did an hour's Red Cross at the Hospital, back to dinner. Daddy in town. Finished *Paint & Prejudice* by C.R.W. Nevinson and started *Oil Paint & Grease Paint* by Laura Knight.[1] George Turnbull rang up, also Mrs Edgcumbe.[2]

ON THE DAY June opened the new volume of her diary, newspaper front pages carried stories of Air Marshal Hermann Goering's latest threats. 'The moment has come when the war which Britain wanted must shower down on the British Isles themselves,' he warned.[3] This was generally interpreted to mean that the Nazis intended to bomb and gas civilians. June did not write in her diary about Goering or the war, except to say that she listened to the BBC news. Instead, she enumerated the things she had done that day. A simple list took only a few minutes to do and brought reassurance that life would go on as normal.

June's earlier diaries have not survived so we cannot know her precise reaction to the outbreak of war. We could think of her at 11 in the morning of Sunday 3 September 1939, in that

---

1. Christopher Richard Wynne Nevinson (1889–1946) joined the Friends Ambulance Unit during the First World War and was later appointed a war artist. Dame Laura Knight (1877–1970) was the first woman elected to full membership of the Royal Academy.
2. George Grant Turnbull (1912–1998); Mrs Edgcumbe (1877–1964) was born Lilian Agnes Arkwright.
3. *Daily Herald*, 26 Oct 1939, p.1C.

over-worn scenario, seated around the wireless, with her brother David and sister Janet and their parents Arthur and Helen,[4] listening to Prime Minister Neville Chamberlain announce that 'this country is at war with Germany' but she was just as likely to have been up in London nursing a hangover after a good party or out tramping through the woods near her home at Odsey Corner with Steve, the family dog.

Like everyone else, she had known for months that war was approaching. This realisation came with Hitler's annexation of Austria in March 1938 and the subsequent crisis over the seizure of the Sudetenland; Chamberlain's desperate attempts to stave off war with the Munich Agreement did little to allay fears. In the summer of 1939, after the German invasion of Czechoslovakia, June and her sister studied for the Red Cross first aid exam. Arthur volunteered as an air raid warden and Helen enrolled in the Women's Voluntary Service, helping out at a mobile Red Cross canteen in Hitchin, their local market town. The family built an air raid shelter in the garden.

Local authorities had been drawing up civil defence plans since 1935 and the recruitment of stretcher-bearers, firefighters, demolition workers and ambulance drivers had begun. Thirty-eight million gas masks had been distributed in anticipation of attacks from the air. Everyone was familiar with the meaning of the acronym ARP – Air Raid Precautions – even if they could not at this stage imagine quite how important they were to be.

June and her family learned, from bulletins broadcast on the radio, the different permutations of the warning sounds made by air raid klaxon. On their trips to London they saw doorways filled with sandbags, trench shelters and street-level concrete boxes built in readiness for bombs, which most people assumed would start falling the instant war broke out.

On the day that the prime minister warned of the 'days of stress and strain' ahead and called on the nation to pull together,

---

4. David Hitchcock Spencer (1914–2004); Janet Rosemary Hitchcock Spencer (1920–2012), later Winn Roberts; Helen Beryl Hitchcock Spencer (1889–1988), née Wright; Arthur Lincolne Hitchcock Spencer (1870–1950).

the blackout, the order to eliminate light on the ground and make the job of the German bombers more difficult, was already two days old. Even so, and despite this being the least unexpected war in history, it was a shock when the moment actually arrived.

❖

The village of Ashwell has a chocolate-box appeal: the streets are pristine, the houses painted regularly and the lawns beautifully kept. There are Tudor half-timbered terraces and upright Georgian townhouses. There are thatched roofs. About fifteen hundred people live there now, a figure that has not changed much over the past two hundred years.

At the centre of the town's small grid of streets is the fourteenth-century Church of St Mary, complete with a churchyard studded with ancient graves. There, on 12 July 1912, 41-year-old Arthur Spencer, his right eye sporting a rakish black patch (the result of a boyhood practical joke that had backfired), the son of a business-minded Hitchin engineer, and 23-year-old Helen Wright, the youngest of seven children of a solicitor from the same town, were joined in wedlock. Afterwards the couple lived a few miles southeast of Ashwell at Odsey Corner, the house Arthur had commissioned in 1909 in preparation for family life. The location was exceptionally well chosen, within walking distance of Odsey Grange, where his widowed mother Mary lived, and close to Ashwell and Morden railway station, an easy commute to the London office of W.H. Spencer & Co., the boilermaking firm he had inherited from his father.

Odsey Corner was an attractive, unimposing and practical family home (it is still standing and is Grade II listed), designed in the Arts and Crafts style by Geoffry Lucas,[5] with three pitched red-tiled roofs, a large chimney stack and pink pebbledash walls. With its wooden beams, modest proportions and leaded windows there was something of the cottage about it, while the polished oak floors and solid fixtures and fittings also spoke of comfort,

5. Thomas Geoffry Lucas (1872–1947) was noted for his work in the garden city movement.

both physical and financial, and a judicious balance between necessity and design. The lawns and flowerbeds were neatly divided by yew hedges and the kitchen garden was well stocked with vegetables and fruit trees. On one side the estate was flanked by trees, shielding it from the road to the station, and on the other by extensive grounds bordering on open fields.

David was born eighteen months after Arthur and Helen married, followed by June (christened Elizabeth June) in September 1916 and Janet Rosemary in 1920. June's arrival just under seven weeks after the death of her mother's oldest brother Edmund,[6] a captain in the King's Shropshire Light Infantry, from wounds inflicted two days earlier at the Battle of the Somme, must have been a cause for bitter-sweet celebration.

The Spencer children had a happy and settled childhood. Collectively the family was warm and affectionate, fond of their pets, kind to their servants – a cook and two housemaids as well as a family nanny – and helpful to their neighbours, with a wide circle of friends and family in the area and in London. June was an active child, but early in life suffered from mastoiditis, a recurrent infection of the honeycombed bone behind the ear, which left her partially deaf. The treatment was simply to lie in a darkened room, which must have been an excruciating lesson in patience for someone who was so clearly a 'do-er'. Because of her illness she was initially taught at home but eventually, in her teenage years, boarded at Overstone, an 'experimental' girls' private school outside Northampton, which believed in encouraging pupils to think imaginatively rather than to rely on formal learning. Here she excelled at sport and art.

At this time studying for a university degree was an aspiration for a few young women: those who were obviously academically gifted, exceptionally determined and not particularly keen on getting married. It was deemed far more important that girls, as young unmarried women were termed, were 'agreeable', knew the laws of hospitality and showed good manners at all times. Being

6. Edmund Lancelot Wright (1883–1916) left a widow and seven-month-old son, Lancelot.

'clever' was seen as a passion-killer whereas being 'bright' was not. Girls who had 'gumption' and forbearance, without acting the martyr, were admired, as was having a special talent, particularly in the arts. At eighteen, her artistic skills already formally recognised (while at school she had been entered in the Royal Drawing Society's examination and was awarded honours), June was leaning towards a career in clothes design and decided to take a course in dressmaking in London.

June was taught by Hélène Venturette, a Frenchwoman whose business was based in the upper floors of 21 Beauchamp Place in Knightsbridge, a few streets south of Harrod's department store. At the time, the area was crammed with services to women's fashion: dressmakers, milliners, corsetières and women's tailors and outfitters. The London Post Office directory for 1934 lists twenty-five dressmakers in Beauchamp Place alone, of whom five were court dressmakers.[7]

Madame Venturette was so impressed by June's work that she asked her to stay on as an assistant. Dressmaking was beginning to emerge as a feasible occupation for girls of the 'educated classes', perfect for keeping them busy in those tricky years between school and marriage. For centuries, seamstressing was a badly paid occupation for working-class women, carried out in cottage workshops or garrets or more latterly in crowded factories and sweatshops, while a facility for what was called 'work', which might include embroidery and other refined forms of needlecraft, was prized amongst genteel women. In the early twentieth century, dressmaking acquired a new glamour, encouraged by small schools in the West End, whose graduates could claim that they had studied art and dress designing rather than 'trained to be a dressmaker'. For June, designing and creating clothes was never merely a hobby. There was no certainty she would marry – in her own family, her aunt Ethel Hitchcock Spencer, a watercolour artist who had exhibited at the Royal Academy, was a perfect exemplar of the single life. If June did not find a husband

7. Court dressmakers produced bespoke fashion in London and clothes suitable for formal functions. After the war they were replaced by *haute couturières*.

she would need to be able to hold down some sort of job, if for no other reason than for her own satisfaction.

Between working for Madame Venturette and the beginning of the war, June pursued a life typical of her class: trips to Paris and Austria, where she visited Kitzbühel and skied down the Hahnenkamm (considered to be one of the most challenging runs in the world), a few chaste romantic friendships, and regular spells in London, sometimes staying at Lindsey House, a seventeenth-century mansion on the river at Chelsea belonging to the eccentric and charismatic Richard Stewart-Jones, or at a flat in Mayfair owned by family friends the Dorrien Smiths.[8]

Although she must have been planning it for years, it was probably from late 1937 that Helen Spencer started actively to prepare her eldest daughter for presentation at court. In this anachronistic ritual, which was performed for the last time in 1958, hundreds of young women announced their arrival on the upper crust marriage scene by curtseying to the King and Queen at a ceremony at Buckingham Palace. It was not quite a cattle market but it was viewed as a helpful opportunity for families to size up the new stock of young women available for courting and marrying. Women dominated the whole complex process but in what seems an irony now were described purely in terms of their relationship to a man: 'The wife of', 'the daughter of', Mrs John Smith and so on.

At 21, June was somewhat older than most of the other girls, who were generally aged 17 or 18, and this may have helped her through what promised to be an exciting, albeit stressful, few months. Debutantes had not just the presentation to enjoy, or endure as the case may be, but a whole season of parties, gatherings and events at which they would be looked over and judged. Many, although probably not June, were overawed by the whole process and became obsessed with their own inadequacies.

8. Richard Llewelyn Stewart-Jones (1914–1957). The Dorrien Smith family has a long association with the Scilly Isles.

Some were tongue-tied at crucial moments and sought tearful refuge in the ladies' toilets.

Although the aristocracy and upper echelons of the British upper classes dominated the presentation, girls did not have to be especially wealthy or high-born to take part. Being relatively poor was not necessarily a barrier – as long as the girl came from a 'good' family. Looking back at the time of her own debut in 1937, Madeleine Turnbull, whose brother George was for a while June's boyfriend, said, 'It was infinitely more prestigious to come from a family of ancient lineage and be poor as church mice than to be jumped up and enormously rich; so the latter were secretly scorned.'[9] Even here, if the girls behaved acceptably, were not brash or attention-seeking, their regrettable antecedents could be ignored. In the main, however, most came from titled or upper-class families or, increasingly, from the ranks of the solidly upper middle class as did the Hitchcock Spencers.

June's paternal grandfather William Hitchcock[10] was the only son of an Islington cloth merchant who had done well in business, eventually owning an engineering works; her maternal grandfather Frederick Wright was a well-off provincial solicitor. The Spencers' closest friends were other established Hertfordshire families: Colonel Eustace and Barbara Hill,[11] Phyllis and Wolverley Fordham, the Raikes, the Serocolds and the Seebohms. Most of the men had military or commercial careers, and the women tended to be active in do-gooding, heading local committees for charitable causes. A few of them, like the Spencers themselves, had Quaker ancestors.

June's beauty was considered reason enough for putting her on display. Many people had an unashamedly Darwinian approach to marriage and reproduction. This was an age when women's

9. Madeleine Mary Turnbull (1919–1989), later Sandilands, quoted in Lambert, p.85.
10. William Hitchcock (1831–1897) was the son of William Hitchcock (1799–1860), whose mother Catherine asked him to add the name Spencer to the family name, as she was the last of this particular Spencer line.
11. Norah Le Grand Eustace Gribble (1886–1970), later Hill, was also known as Barbara.

looks were considered a marker of 'breeding' and when the upper classes thought nothing of comparing women to pedigree racehorses. June's English rose appearance – immaculate skin, soft brown hair, blue eyes, excellent figure – helped her make friends and attract potential suitors and gave her enough outward confidence and poise to do well in social situations.

In the run-up to the presentation itself there was much to be done. June practised her royal curtsey many times; the action was more difficult than it sounds, involving a low, slow, sweeping dip, with the left knee locked behind the right, while keeping the body straight, the head erect and hands to the side. She also designed and sewed her own court dress. Most of the other debutantes and their mothers or sponsors had theirs made for them, by Marshall & Snelgrove, Harrod's, Worth, Hartnell, Debenham & Freebody or Harvey Nichols, or by one of the dressmaking companies specialising in formalwear, such as Jacqmar of Grosvenor Street or Venturette, where June herself trained, or by their favourite independent dressmaker. June's decision to sew her own was perhaps less to do with saving money – a dress might cost £100[12] – than taking on the challenge to display her needlework skills.

In 1938 the fashion was for white or pastel shades, with off-the-shoulder necklines and skirts styled as modern versions of Victorian crinolines. Most of the gowns were decorated with flowers, feathery fronds or large leaves, perhaps in seed pearls or diamanté. Diana Sanders wore a gown of white net embroidered with silver and a train of silver lamé, made by Marythé in Dover Street; Rolline McMurrough Kavanagh a frock of Watteau pink slipper satin with a train of pink satin and net, made by Rose Stratton. The sponsors, the older women who accompanied the debutantes and 'presented' them to the King and Queen, were entitled to wear stronger colours: Mrs John Fortescue chose a gown of gold lamé draped over the shoulders with jade green satin, with a train of jade lined with gold; her daughter Rosemary

12. Anon. (1974). 'Reminiscences of a Court Dressmaker: Miss Emily Phillips interviewed by Janet Arnold in January 1974.' *Costume*, Vol. 8, No. 1, pp.22-25. The total cost of coming out was around £2,000.

June in the court dress she made herself,
photographed by Douglas of St James's.

was in a frock of white tulle with a full skirt and diamanté and silver flowers.[13]

June decided on a shimmering sheath of pale yellow moiré shot with gold and a train of matching ruched tulle. Her friend 'Eve' Streatfeild,[14] who was also presented in 1938, chose an altogether more conventional costume, a Harrod's gown of white slipper satin, full skirt and wide sash of silver lamé and a train of satin lined with white chiffon forming a cowl around the shoulders.[15]

Because the rule was that a sponsor had to have been a debutante herself, June was not presented by her mother but by family friend Barbara Hill, who was also that year presenting her

13. The list of those presented at court in May 1938 is from *The Scotsman*, 12 May 1938, p.12B; see also *The Times*, 12 May 1938, p.10F.
14. Yvonne Streatfeild (1919–2020) lived near the Spencers in Hertfordshire.
15. *Scotsman*, 12 May 1938, p.12B; *The Times*, 12 May 1938, p.10F.

own daughter Vivien, known to all as Robin.[16] Mrs Hill probably got together with Helen to network with other mothers in the area before the big day, lining up invitations to balls, lunches and teas for the girls or planning their own. These peripheral social events were important for their daughter's future marriage prospects, although young men were always in short supply for the dances; brothers and cousins and their friends were actively pursued and sometimes strong-armed into attending. According to his sister, George Turnbull was 'always being rung up by hostesses who literally begged him to come to their dinner-parties. He was rather grand about it all, and refused any but the most exotic or interesting invitations.'[17]

A few days before the presentation, Mrs Hill, Robin and June came up to London for shopping, final dress fittings and to have their hair done. At about nine o'clock on the evening of Wednesday 11 May 1938, the girls, wearing their court dresses, complete with the traditional three ostrich feathers of the Prince of Wales in their hair, and draped in borrowed fur and diamonds, sat with Mrs Hill in a chauffeur-driven limousine parked in The Mall with the other Rolls-Royces, Bentleys and Humbers. Outside on the pavement crowds of the 'hoi-polloi' peered into the windows and passed loud judgment on the beauty or otherwise of the occupants. The Season, whose stiff conventions were taken so seriously by those participating, was regarded by ordinary people as a source of free entertainment, a series of idiosyncratic rituals on which, they were told, the edifice of society depended. The waiting limousines with their silk and satin-clad cargoes were a perfect illustration of the pyramidical social order, with the King at the pinnacle and the labourers, coalminers, housemaids and cleaners at the bottom which, even with the disruption caused by the First World War, was broadly the same as it had been for centuries.

Eventually, Mrs Hill's chauffeur was beckoned to drive slowly through the gates of Buckingham Palace and to wait until it was time for the women to disembark. Finally they were ushered into

16. Vivien ('Robin') Eustace Hill (1920–2017), later Parkinson.
17. Quoted in Lambert, p.52.

the Palace itself and led to an antechamber, where they sat on gilt chairs until called in to the great White and Gold Throne Rooms. Here, seated on a dais hung and canopied in crimson velvet and emblazoned in gold, attended by the Lord Chamberlain, the King, George VI, wearing the scarlet tunic of a field marshal, and Queen Elizabeth, resplendent in a silver lamé gown embroidered with silver pearls, sequins and diamanté with a silver train, the famous Koh-i-noor diamond glittering at her throat, received a line of some three hundred women.

Led in by Mrs Hill, June first passed before the dais, dropped her curtsey to the King and took three steps to the side to do the same before the Queen. Receiving a nod and smile in return, she got up and walked carefully backwards out of the room, swishing her train so that she would not fall over it (she was not allowed to pick it up). After Robin had completed the same sequence, they lined up in the corridor with Mrs Hill until the last presentation was made and the National Anthem was played. They followed the King and Queen into the Banquet Hall for a Champagne buffet supper, where they ate delicacies off plates embellished with the crest of George III, drank iced coffee and greeted people they knew. Eventually, when it was time to leave, they went downstairs and waited for their cars to arrive to take them to the photographers Lafayette's in Bond Street or Douglas in St James Place, which stayed open all night for the occasion. Here, more crowds in search of a glimpse of quasi-moviestar glamour greeted them.

The next morning, *The Scotsman* listed June among the best dressed. *The Daily Telegraph* also approved, noting that her yellow gown was 'filled to the last inch by Miss Spencer's splendid figure.'

Every year, in the wake of the royal presentation, came numerous balls – the Hibernian in Edinburgh, Oxford Commemoration and Cambridge May Balls, as well as regimental and charity dances – lunch and cocktail parties, polo matches, Hurlingham, Ascot, Goodwood, Henley, Cowes, country house weekends and the Royal Horticultural Society's Flower House in the grounds of the Royal Hospital at Chelsea. The most spectacular, and arguably most bizarre, event of the Season was the Birthday Ball in aid of Queen Charlotte's Maternity Hospital, held a week after the court presentation in the vast art deco ballroom of Grosvenor House Hotel on Park Lane. This opened with the cake ceremony, in which two hundred and fifty hand-picked debutantes (referred to as 'maids of honour'), wearing their court gowns and tiaras, filed down the twin staircases into the ballroom and separated as if they were a choreographed Red Sea, in order to create an aisle down which a huge white cake was carried. In 1938, a Movietone reporter, perhaps trying to conjure up a story where there was none, described the scrum for slices of cake as 'maidenly refinement degenerating into ungainly competition.'[18]

The richest parents would host coming-out balls or dinner-dances for their daughters, either at their own country residences or, more usually, in London. As most of the upper classes no longer owned town houses big enough to hold balls, they rented London venues such as Claridge's, the Savoy, 6 Stanhope Gate or 23 Knightsbridge. The huge ballroom in Richard Stewart-Jones's house, 96 Cheyne Walk in Chelsea, big enough for two hundred people, was also used. There is no record that June's parents held a dance for her but June was certainly invited to many.

The balls were formal, traditional affairs, supervised by hawk-eyed mothers and aunts. The rules were strictly defined. The role of the girls was to wait to be asked to dance by the young men. There was no possibility that they might take the initiative themselves. Instead they must look demure, clutch their dance cards and wait anxiously for an invitation. Most had few friends of the opposite sex, except for their own brothers and cousins. Some parents took active steps to keep them cloistered, insisting they be chaperoned to and from dances and delivered to dinner parties by the family chauffeur; some were forbidden to use public transport alone, even during the day. There were examples of astonishing

18. *Debutantes' Ball* (Movietone, 5 Dec 1938, Story No. BM33292).

sexual ignorance, and it was not unknown for girls to believe that kissing could lead to pregnancy. It is hardly surprising that some were eager to shake off the parental shackles, but they could not do so openly. Former debutantes have described returning to their homes after a coming-out dance, changing their clothes surreptitiously and then sneaking out to a taxi in which waited a keen young chap. June's parents were more relaxed than most and it is not difficult to imagine her drinking and dancing with the daring crowd, at The 400 or the Embassy,[19] and after she and her friends had snaked around the nightclub in a tipsy conga in the early hours, the management diplomatically encouraging them out into the street to pile into cabs home.

If the aim of coming out was to network with the 'right' sort of people and bag a husband, June was only partly successful; she emerged with numerous friends and an address book stuffed with contacts, but no engagement. She saw no need to gallop up the aisle. In 1938 she refused Lieutenant 'Buzz' Lloyd, an ebullient officer in the Royal Engineers, who wrote to her regularly from his posting in Waziristan[20] and pressed her to marry him. 'I've been miserable for a week and I simply must hear how you are and what you are doing,' wrote Harry Knight, a sweet-natured captain in the Scots Guards, after she had also turned him down.[21]

June knew she wanted more from life than marriage, children and endless housekeeping. It was for good reason that she gave her occupation in the 1939 Register of England and Wales, a census taken at the start of the war, not as 'unpaid domestic duties' as many daughters living at home did but 'dress designer'. Creativity was part of her identity and dress designing and making was an occupation that in later life stood her in good stead.

---

19. The 400 was in the basement of 28a Leicester Square; the Embassy was in Old Bond Street.
20. Waziristan is now part of Khyber Pakhtunkhwa in Pakistan.
21. Harold H. Knight (?–1941), adopted son of Ian Standish Monteith Hamilton (1853–1947) and Jean Miller, Lady Hamilton (1861–1941). 'Buzz' Lloyd is unidentified.

Ritzkrieg and Sitzkrieg

Friday 24 November 1939 To London after lunch. Staying
the night with Lady Turnbull for a military dance at Buckhurst
[in Essex]. George Turnbull, Virginia Cunard[1] and I drove out
to a gun station for dinner in the officers' mess.

THE ATMOSPHERE OF fearful anticipation and righteous belli-
gerence dissipated in the months after Chamberlain's announcement of war. Gas masks were forgotten or discarded; sandbags
split and sprouted. The civilian population felt the emergency
they had been warned of was a damp squib. 'It almost seemed
as though the Government had conspired to make it a Bore
War,' complained the journalist Hannen Swaffer in *The People*
in October 1939.[2] Even the BBC, which had cancelled outside
broadcasts and was playing records instead, was dull.

London was tiresome and silent. Places of entertainment—
dance halls, nightclubs, theatres—had been shut down
completely two days after the declaration of war, the government
fearful that bombs falling on such buildings would produce
mass casualties. Within days, a campaign to reverse the order
was underway. Tom Harrisson, the head of Mass Observation,
a survey of aspects of everyday life in Britain, complained that
the closures were 'bad for morale'[3] and a *Spectator* editorial
described them as 'an incalculable loss to the good spirits... of
the nation.'[4] West End hotels also actively resisted the ban. On

1. Virginia Beatrice Cunard (1912–2002), later Barrington.
2. 8 Oct 1939, p.7C.
3. M-O A TC Propaganda and Morale 1939-44, 43-2-A: 'Typed extracts
re propaganda and the MoI: 7.9 TH' (1939); See footnote 4.
4. *The Spectator*, 3 Sep 1939, p.2; footnotes 3 and 4 quoted in Nott (2017).

14 September the Berkeley[5] reopened its dance floor 'in response to mass requests'. 'Dancing will make people forget their worries,' said the management. By early December the government had recognised that dancing was essential for morale and, at least partially, rowed back on its regulations: dance halls outside London were no longer required to close by 11pm.

Bore War was just one of many terms given to the eight months of apparent inaction after September—there was also the more well-known Phoney War, as well as Twilight War, Strange War and Sitzkrieg, a play on the German word *Blitzkrieg*, meaning 'lightning war'—something the Nazis had used to devastating effect in their assault on Poland.

All of the epithets reflected the frustration and anxiety felt by a waiting and fearful population desperate for the government to take the initiative against the enemy. When the Allies did so, trying to blockade German ports, they became involved in a deadly game of hide-and-seek with German U-boats, resulting in terrible losses. In September the aircraft carrier HMS *Courageous* was sunk by U-boats with the loss of five hundred lives and in October the battleship HMS *Royal Oak* suffered the same fate at Scapa Flow in the Orkneys, when six hundred perished. On land the strategy seemed to be to meet Hitler's aggression with a timid defensiveness. The RAF was sent on missions over Germany but dropped propaganda leaflets rather than bombs. The French push into the Saar was successful to begin with but by October had stalled—there was no follow-through. As for the expected German invasion, the Allies were content to wait and see, putting their faith in the Maginot Line, a string of forts along the French–German border, and in the thick forests of the Ardennes. They predicted that this combined impermeability would force the enemy into invading through northern Belgium and thereby into a trap. That confidence was to prove misplaced.

5. The Berkeley is located at the corner of Piccadilly and Berkeley Street.

*June in the fields near Odsey Corner
with the family dog Steve.*

As June pondered her next step in life, she kept herself busy. She painted and sewed and started a business making a line of embellished belts that she hoped to sell to department stores in London. There were parties, trips to London, drinks and dinners. After her friend and sister debutante Robin Hill became engaged to Reay Parkinson, a sub-lieutenant in the Royal Navy,[6] June offered to make her wedding dress. She played with her baby godson, Robin's nephew Gurney,[7] went to the cinema in Cambridge and the races at Newmarket, took Steve the dog for walks and collected berries in the woods. She visited her wider family: her maternal grandmother Ann Wright, who lived in Hitchin with her three unmarried daughters, Madeleine, Mary and Ann, a hospital secretary; and Aunt Ethel who lived at the

6. Reay Parkinson (1917–1979).
7. Michael Gurney Sheppard (1938–2003), son of Cynthia (known as Sukie) Eustace Hill (1916–2008) and Daniel Gurney Sheppard (1908–1988).

Hitchcock Spencer family home, Odsey Grange, cared for by the family nanny, Ellen Burrows.[8] In the early months of the war June's diary entries were, in the main, lists of her activities; she only diverted from that when recording the vivid shades of the passing seasons. 'Glorious orange and cerise colours against grey autumn sky,' she noted on 1 November, 'Marvellous yellows and red and orange colours,' on the 12th.

On 24 November June travelled to London to join her boy-friend George Turnbull and Virginia Cunard, a nurse in the Voluntary Aid Detachment, for a military dinner. It meant driving eleven miles in the blackout from the Turnbulls' family home in Regent's Park Terrace to Buckhurst Hill in Essex. Under the regulations, the car could use only one headlight, which was masked with cardboard to reduce its beam to a narrow slot. The sidelights were disabled and the red rear lights and reflectors painted over. It was easy enough to drive through Camden Town, Holloway and Harringay; street lights were screened to give a 'subdued moonlight' effect and there was residual light from pedestrians' feeble flashlights, by which the driver could just see the kerbsides, now painted white. Even so, there was a spike in accidents. The writer Rose Macaulay, who was a part-time driver for the London Auxiliary Ambulance Service in north London, wrote of cars crashing into street refuges, pedestrians and each other.[9]

The risks of accidents increased as the landscape turned suburban and even more so in the countryside. At a roundabout in Watford, not far from June's home, a driver was seriously injured after colliding with a bollard while following the white markers in the road, and another man ended up in Hitchin Hospital with severe head injuries after being hit by a lorry while walking along Baldock Road. In the absence of enemy bombers, he and other victims of blackout accidents may have wondered what was the point of it all.[10]

8.   Ellen (Nellie) Lizzie Burrows (1888–1974).
9.   Macaulay, *Life Among the English*, p.47.
10. *Hertford Mercury and Reformer*, 15 Sep 1939, pp.4E, 2E.

The 'gun station' June referred to in her diary on 24 November was a heavy anti-aircraft emplacement at Buckhurst Hill, manned by the Royal Artillery, in which George Turnbull had recently been commissioned a second lieutenant. The station was a sea of mud and a sentry had to push George's car to the officers' mess, which turned out to be a rough wooden hut. Despite this, June pronounced the dinner 'marvellous' and she and her friends were unfazed by the five phoned-through air raid warnings.

After this outing June did not see George for another six weeks, when he took her to dinner at the Berkeley in London. They were not in love—they seem to have been content to escort each other to social events—and sometimes he infuriated her. In February, she wrote that on a drive back to London after another formal dinner, this time at Aldershot, he said or did something to so enrage her that she 'nearly knocked [him] out with my shoe. A rather unhappy ending to the day.' She waited five days to send a letter apologising. Despite their ups and downs, she and George remained friends and she wrote to him when he went on active service and dined with him in London whenever he was on leave.

A few days after the evening at Buckhurst Hill, June was back in London for dinner and dancing at the Café de Paris.[11] This time she stayed the night, as she often had on trips to town, with Richard (Ric, as he was known to his friends) Stewart-Jones in Cheyne Walk. This may have been when she first became friendly with siblings John and Penelope Gough, who boarded there.[12]

In early December, June drove the Spencers' car to Tewkesbury in Gloucestershire, a journey of three and a half hours, to spend a long weekend with Pen, whose father, the Reverend Edward Pountney Gough, was canon of the Abbey. It snowed hard on her return journey. The fields and villages, laden with thick white blankets, must have seemed a million miles from war.

For June, day-to-day life was relatively unchanged. There

11. The Café de Paris was at 3–4 Coventry Street.
12. Penelope Mary Gough (1910–1993), later Pipe-Wolferson, and John S. Gough (1913–?); Rev Canon Edward Pountney Gough (1877–1945).

were the usual social rounds in Hertfordshire, sewing of course (she made a red flannel dress for Eliza, the family's maid, a yellow leather jacket for herself and some hessian belts), as well as shopping trips to London's West End, where the atmosphere was grim and the weather horrible: thick fog and very cold. She stayed with Ric at Lindsey House, but on this occasion his sister Diona (known as Di),[13] with the Stewart-Joneses' nanny in tow, was also visiting. It was not a comfortable time. 'Nanny in a bad mood as usual,' wrote June of the fearsomely protective Christiana Sams, or 'Sambi' as the Stewart-Joneses called her.[14] She and June rubbed each other up the wrong way from the start, and over the ensuing months, when they came to live under the same roof, their acrimonious relationship came to a head in a way that was to leave June's self-esteem permanently bruised.

News from abroad was disappointing. June wrote of the *Graf Spee*, a German battleship which in the first weeks of the war had destroyed nine Allied vessels and was finally halted by British cruisers when it was scuttled by its captain in Montevideo harbour. It did not feel much like a victory.

Despite the sameness of life and the non-appearance of a German attack on the British home front, Christmas 1939 was measurably different. Church bells were not rung for fear of alarming the neighbourhood that an invasion was in progress, carol singers did not call and midnight services were cancelled because stained glass windows could not be blacked out. In rare reveals of her emotions, she complained on 9 December that she was 'feeling very despondent' and ten days later she and her sister Janet were 'feeling low'.

Christmas morning at Odsey Corner was bitterly cold. According to June, everyone was 'slightly on edge' although things improved after church and lunch with Aunt Ethel at the Grange, where the family listened to the King's speech on the radio. Slowly, hesitantly—June noted that his stammer was particularly bad at the beginning—George VI gave thanks to those who were

13. Diona Stewart-Jones (1909–1975), later Murray.
14. Christiana Sams (1875–1963).

'prepared to sacrifice everything', appealed for unity across the Empire and expressed faith in the rightness of the British cause. 'A new year is at hand,' he said. 'We cannot tell what it will bring.'

On the first day of the new year, June echoed his thoughts:

> This is the new year—how much will happen in it? The whole world is in the biggest crisis it has ever known. We are at war. France, Germany, Russia, Finland, China, Japan. Here we are, living at Odsey Corner, in perfect peace. How much will we do? How far will we go in 1940?

> *Tuesday 9 January 1940* Met Mummy at 3. We shopped and had tea at Bertaux in Greek Street. Went back to Lowndes Street with Ma, who had a terrific cold. Out to dinner with George Turnbull. Berkeley, Savoy and then to The 400... Great fun.

In daylight it would have taken June and George about twenty minutes to walk from Lowndes Street to the Berkeley. The Savoy was another half hour through St James's and down the Strand, and The 400 was a ten-minute hop to Leicester Square. In the blackout, the journey took at least twice as long, maybe longer. On a moonless cloudy night, when the world became a thick inky well, almost nothing could be seen. It was forbidden even to strike a match. For walkers, London became a landscape of pitfalls and obstacles, of sounds, smells and dim glimmering lights: the ghostly blue interior of a blacked-out bus spied through the open platform as it passed; the distant clanking of a tram; the drumming of rain on windows; the wafts of drains and restaurant kitchens; the narrowed beams of feeble headlights; the tap-tap-tap of heels behind you.

June would have been aware of the hazards of walking after sundown[15] but the pleasures of a night out, with its implied two fingers up to Hitler, outweighed the dangers. June may have

15. The spike in accidents was followed by a long dip because there were fewer cars on the road, the result of petrol rationing and of the bombs.

consulted the calendar for the brightest moonlit nights, but it was more likely that she took measures to protect herself. As long as she could lay her hands on much sought-after batteries, she would have held a small torch downwards while she felt her way, like a Braille reader, around the shadowy streets. She may also have dressed specifically for the blackout. Oxford Street department store Marshall & Snelgrove advertised a smart off-white mackintosh for women ('suitable also for uniform wear') with a generous pleat 'to allow free movement'.[16] Men were encouraged to wear a light-coloured coat or carry a newspaper or white handkerchief to make themselves more visible. In a special demonstration staged in Hyde Park after dark, the Men's Wear Council asked members of the public to show the advantages of wearing white by modelling bandolier belts, gas mask boxes, walking sticks, umbrella tips, ladies' hat bands and handbags and covers for bowler hats, while walking towards a car lit only by its sidelights.[17]

June and George took taxis, at least between some of the stops on their tour of the West End on 9 January. It was safer and faster than walking and relatively cheap if they split the rides with strangers. No one did this before the war but now traditional British reserve had shifted, at least a little. '[Sharing taxis] has been developed into a sport,' said one young woman interviewed by *The Sketch*, the weekly bible of high society, 'and when you can't bag one, perfect strangers offer you lifts, or commissionaires act as liaison, so that you can double up with people going your way.'[18] 'It seemed all class dislike had gone, the few people in the streets were all your friends,' June said years later, remembering the 'all in it together' feeling the national crisis had brought. The feeling was, in the end, fleeting, but there was certainly a new informality between people of differing backgrounds, which did not go away entirely; social rules about who was or was not fit to consort with were melting.

16. *The Bystander*, 15 Nov 1939, p.33.
17. *The Manchester Guardian*, 23 Sep 1939, p.8E.
18. *The Sketch*, 18 Oct 1939, p.24.

Dress rules were also relaxed. Before the war an evening out required a complete change of clothes. The war did not stop women putting on long gowns, gloves and jewellery, and perhaps a fur in cold weather, doing their hair and wearing full make-up. Men still wore dinner jackets. It was not thought strange to get on the Tube or a bus done up to the nines and indeed June often did so, even during the worst of the Blitz. The addition of a gas mask, either carried over her shoulder in its utilitarian cardboard box or actually worn, undermined the whole 'look' or gave it an amusing, ironic twist, depending on your point of view.

The real difference now was that evening dress was no longer *de rigueur*. Uniform, daytime frocks and even workwear were also acceptable. One debutante spoke of finishing her shift at an aircraft factory in suburban Cricklewood and jumping straight on the Bakerloo line to Green Park, still wearing her boiler suit, to catch a drink at the Ritz.[19] A willingness to dress informally was visible proof that you were 'doing your bit'.

Despite the blackout-induced friendliness and new leeway in dress code, to some of those peering upwards, nothing much had changed. In fact, they discerned among the upper classes a strengthened resistance to social change. The satirist Michael Barsley, who lived in what he archly called 'Lesser Kensington', used the term Ritzkrieg[20] to describe a 'private war' prosecuted by toffs who wanted to retain power and its spoils for themselves for ever. His articles for the *New Statesman* included crude comic stereotypes such as Colonels Blimp and Bogus, Major-General Garrison-Harrison and debutante Lucy Rolls-Voyce.

Barsley's bitterness was not without cause, particularly when it came to the privileges of wealth, such as eating out. Food supplies were severely affected by attacks on British merchant fleets and rationing for butter, bacon and sugar was introduced

19. De Courcy, pp.148–9. The Ritz is on Piccadilly, next to Green Park station.
20. The origin of the term Ritzkrieg is unclear. A piece in the *Daily Record* (20 June 1940, p.7E) headed 'Luxury Conflict' reads: 'Some people still do not realise what war means. We're preparing, in fact, for a sort of Ritzkrieg.' Barsley's articles in the *New Statesman* were published in October 1940. His book *Ritzkrieg: The Old Guard's Private War* appeared in 1940.

on 8 January 1940; everyone was issued with a ration book, which had to be registered with specific retailers. By 11 March meat was rationed, with tea and margarine following in July. Rich restaurant diners, however, were free to order whatever they liked.

In the West End, Quaglino's, for instance, which was owned by Italian brothers John and Ernesto[21] (who were interned as enemy aliens after Italy allied with Germany), continued uninterrupted. *The Tatler* magazine waxed lyrical on 'the abundance of that huge menu' including 'poissons, rôtis et grillades': 'Have them at the table. Have them at the bar. Take a glass of wine (by the glass) with this and that.' The magazine's photographer delighted in capturing men in uniform and glamorous young women, in keeping with the current ethos, in 'not quite glad rags', at tables replete with champagne buckets and set for fine dining. Prunier's in St James's got into the spirit of things with its 'blackout dinner' of four courses for ten shillings and sixpence. Alcohol was not in short supply. There was plenty of wine, including German bottles that had been stockpiled in the months before war was declared, and pubs had good stocks of beer, although sometimes there was a dearth of glasses and customers were encouraged to bring their own.[22]

'There may have been days when a good Porterhouse or Chateaubriand were hard to come by, and the Brie was a little on the wet side. But a little cajoling on the part of an obsequious Italian waiter, and the substitution of Surrey chicken or a good saddle of mutton or double Gloucester might work wonders,' wrote Barsley. Later in the war, restaurants were restricted to offering menus of up to three courses at a maximum price of five shillings but this did little to deter the well-off.

Barsley's views on this world of string-pulling and privilege was tempered a little by his simultaneous conviction that this old order was, after all, doomed: 'recently... many important saddles

21. Giovanni or John and Ernesto Quaglino, immigrants from Piedmont, founded their restaurant in Bury Street, St James's in 1929.
22. *The Tatler*, 4 Oct 1939, p.5, 17 Apr 1940, p.92; *The Bystander*, 21 Feb 1940, pp.12–13.

are now occupied by quite ordinary people *without titles*. We, the People, are delighted. They, the Best People, are not.'[23]

By early January 1940 the West End was once more buzzing. People had adjusted to the blackout; workarounds had been found. A writer for *Vogue* magazine saluted the revival of social life, even if it had to hold its metaphorical nose a little. 'We no longer sit at home, breathless, behind heavily curtained windows, listening to the silence, each other's point of view, or the endless broadcast news-bulletins. Theatres are opening again, at odd times, and in odd places, it is true—but still, entertainment we must and shall have. Elegant stalls-audiences trooped out to the fringes of London, to suburban theatres, such as Golders Green... Cinemas play to capacity at 2.30pm, and open their doors at 10am, and no one feels depraved to be attending premieres... before lunch, or before breakfast, for that matter.'[24]

Initially thousands of workers had been laid off and managements pleaded with local authorities to be excused paying rates. The lockdown had meant that the hotel and boarding house trade had struggled to stay afloat. Gradually, confidence returned. Some hotels were saved by being entirely requisitioned by the army or other government agencies. 'At the present time there is more life in London than anywhere else in Great Britain,' said Frank Fisher, manager of The May Fair Hotel, delighted with the upturn and the failure of the Nazi bombers to materialise.[25] The bars and restaurants of high-end hotels such as The Savoy became hotspots of late-night socialising where the respectable, and the less so, hob-nobbed with cabinet ministers, journalists, refugees, spies and foreign dignitaries. The Dorchester became a home from home for diplomats.[26]

London hotels, in fierce competition with each other,

23. Barsley, p.v.
24. *Vogue* (US), Oct 1939, p.62.
25. *The Sphere*, 10 Feb 1940, p.34.
26. The Dorchester, 53 Park Lane.

advertised their safety benefits. The Savoy converted its Abraham Lincoln Room and the adjoining Pink and Green Rooms into air-conditioned, steel-reinforced, gas-proof and sound-proof dormitories equipped with backgammon sets, maids, valets, waiters and nurses. Two hundred beds were installed in curtained bays, with a separate provision for self-confessed snorers and special compartments for VIPs. A young woman interviewed in *The Sketch* fizzed with enthusiasm about Grosvenor House and its 'ground-floor corridor with little gold chairs... and some small rooms for the fainting sort, with beds and couches all ready.'[27] Some hotels tried to attract the upper classes into permanent residency. After their servants left to serve in the forces or to go into better-paid factory work, many of the grander families shut up their London homes, with some members opting for the benefits of life in a hotel where there was no queuing for rations nor the bother of inexpertly cooking your own meals.

June wrote of numerous evenings out in the West End before, during and after the Blitz of 1940–41. A simple tally of keywords in her diaries shows how much she loved going out: the Berkeley occurs seventy-seven times, the Ritz thirty-two, The 400 twenty-eight, the Embassy twenty-one, the Grosvenor fifteen. She also frequently mentioned the Junior Carlton, the Café de Paris, L'Apéritif, Quaglino's, Scott's, Hatchett's and many others.[28] Why was it so important to her, and thousands like her, to go out on the town? Why did she not stay at home at Odsey Corner and spend her evenings tatting rugs by the fire for the good of the country? There was as yet no real danger from the air, despite Goering's threats, and some people, Winston Churchill among them, did not really believe that Hitler would indiscriminately bomb British civilians.

June's evenings out were about gossip, laughter, sharing tables with new people, waving across rooms to interesting

27. *The Sketch*, 18 Oct 1939, p.86.
28. Grosvenor, 86 Park Lane; Junior Carlton, 30 Pall Mall; L'Apéritif, 102 Jermyn Street; Scott's Restaurant, specialising in seafood, was in Coventry Street, near Piccadilly Circus; Hatchett's, 67a Piccadilly.

acquaintances, the possibility of finding a life's companion, and dancing. One of June's friends described her as burning at 'low wattage' during this period of her life, friendly but diffident. But dancing, whether at a village hop, in a nightclub or to gramophone records at home, energised her. It lit her up. She often wrote in her diaries of dancing although it was always in passing and she never expanded on the pleasure it gave her; her notes were characteristically terse, along the lines of 'Elizabeth and I went to the Embassy where we danced for the rest of the night. Quite mad' (29 December 1939) and 'Enjoyed my dancing immensely' on a night in the West End in the middle of heavy bombing (21 February 1941).

June was not the only one to appreciate the emotional relief that dancing could bring. It surged in popularity during the war, and not just in the exclusive nightclubs of the West End. Across the country, people responded to the pressures of life by going to dance halls. There were some compromises. At the Coronation Ballroom in Ramsgate, long dresses were banned—they were liabilities in the event of an emergency—and the management took the precaution of holding practice evacuations, with the band playing a 'quick march step' to encourage a rapid exit. Dances were also ways to raise money for good causes and June went to many such events in the villages near her home in Hertfordshire.

For June, dancing was a way to relieve anxiety about the future but perhaps there was also something about the intimacy of the venues that drew her. The exclusive Embassy Club in Old Bond Street, where Reginald Foresythe and His Band[29] played, and the Café de Paris, two floors beneath the pavement, offered a womb-like comfort. At the Café de Paris June danced to the music of Ken 'Snakehips' Johnson[30] and George Melachrino[31] in the famous ballroom based on that on board the *Titanic*,

29. Reginald Foresythe (1907–1958), jazz pianist, arranger, composer and bandleader.
30. Kenrick Reginald Hijmans Johnson (1914–1941), bandleader and dancer.
31. George Melachrino (1909–1965), born George Miltiades, musician, composer of film music, and musical director.

with twin staircases sweeping down to the small dance floor. The 400, a private members' club in Leicester Square catering to the upper classes, was much more exclusive — and astonishingly tiny. It managed to cram an eighteen-piece orchestra and hordes of dancers into its compact space and to serve food as well, and it kept going to four in the morning. There were always queues to get in, even during the Blitz, with bombs dropping all about.

London trips punctuated June's life but most of the early part of 1940 was spent with her family at Odsey Corner, where she kept to her normal domestic routine. She went skating, vaselined her hair, walked the dog on Gallows Hill, arranged some guitar lessons for herself and, above all, sewed: apart from the wedding dress for her friend Robin, she made a dress for Janet, curtains and lampshades, underwear and her decorated belts. In January she went to London to buy a wedding trousseau for Robin, who was suffering from a cold, and to meet up with another friend, Jo Ainsworth,[32] a volunteer driver for the LAAS in Chelsea, who had arranged to come back to Odsey Corner with June to spend a few days of leave.

June paid close attention to the news and sometimes made notes on it in her diary but the war still felt like a distant threat. The dramatic rescue on 16–17 February of nearly three hundred British prisoners of war, originally captured by the battleship *Graf Spee* and later taken off the *Altmark* as it passed through neutral Norwegian waters, was a passing cause for hope, but other news, such as the Finnish capitulation to Russia, the meeting of Hitler and Mussolini at the Brenner pass on the Austrian border and Germany's occupation of Denmark, was deflating. 'Listened to the everlasting news at twelve,' wrote June disconsolately on 4 March. The capture of the strategically important port of Narvik was a bright point in an otherwise disastrous campaign, which ended in the withdrawal of the Allies from Norway.

32. Josephine Bernard (1915–2011), later Ainsworth, later West.

*June's boyfriend George Turnbull, a second
lieutenant in the Royal Artillery.*

She buried negative thoughts in a blizzard of outings, to films, hastily arranged weddings, racing at Newmarket, fundraising village dances and *thés dansants*, trips to London for nights out with George Turnbull at the Berkeley or the Grosvenor, always followed by dancing and after which she was sometimes, she wrote, 'extremely worse for wear'. She knew George would soon be deployed away from London—'How I shall miss him when he goes'—and distracted herself with yet more socialising.

All around her, people were signing up for the forces or volunteering as auxiliaries and for ARP duties. She knew she would have to do something for the war effort, but how could she combine it with her career as a designer, just as she was beginning to find success? Both Fortnum & Mason and Peter Jones had now given her orders for belts. Her brother David joined the Royal Field Artillery in early April and two weeks later her sister Janet joined the Women's Auxiliary Air Force—although this proved to be a disaster. Within days Janet was describing the base in Liverpool as a 'concentration camp' and before two weeks were up had left the service and was back at Odsey Corner. What were June's options? Although aiding the war effort was not yet compulsory—that did not happen until late 1941 when women aged twenty to thirty were conscripted—she was young and unattached and had no reason not to help.

On 10 May, after a night out with George at the Berkeley followed by an officers' party in London and dancing at The 400, at the Green Park Hotel (unusually she had been unable to find a bed with friends) June awoke to 'big news': 'Hitler strikes the Low Countries. Belgian, Dutch and French towns bombed. The war has really begun at last,' she wrote. The Germans had drawn the French and British forces into conflict around the French border with Belgium while their tank divisions, protected from above by the Luftwaffe, simultaneously punched through the narrow roads and thick forests of the Ardennes. Neville Chamberlain resigned the same day, having lost the confidence of the House of Commons after the Norway disaster. Winston Churchill became prime minister.

On 21 May June and George, who was consoling himself after being medically rejected for foreign service, had a night out at The 400. 'Great fun. Very empty,' she wrote, adding 'I could hear guns on the French coast.' The Sitzkrieg was well and truly over. A few days later, June wrote out the words of the National Anthem in her diary:

O Lord our God arise
Scatter our enemies
And make them fall
Confound their politics
Frustrate their knavish tricks
On Thee our hopes we fix
God save us all

❖

There were no presentations at court in May 1940, nor indeed until after the war was over. June's sister Janet was one of those who lost out, although the Spencers hosted a compensatory 'tea party for debs' at Odsey Corner on her behalf. Some of the nation's would-be debutantes made do with the Queen Charlotte's Birthday Ball as a substitute. *The Tatler* profiled a handful of these 'charming blossom buds of spring', some of whom had volunteered to work for the 'national cause'.[33]

June must have cast her thoughts back to two years earlier, when she was thinking about which direction her life would glide and wondered how she had taken such a carefree existence for granted. Daily the news from France grew worse. The British Expeditionary Force failed to hold back the Nazis, let alone push them eastwards, and on 26 May it was ordered to withdraw. It was the start of Operation Dynamo, the evacuation which evolved into 'Dunkirk' and came to involve over eight hundred small boats sailing from Britain to rescue stranded servicemen. The next day June's diary entry read simply: 'These are the gravest days in all the history of the world as we know it.' She had just learned that her friend Lisel had been informed that her husband Richard Anthony Raikes, a second lieutenant in the King's Royal Rifle Corps, was missing.[34]

June knew the country was in for the long haul and she also knew she must now do something. She called in at the Sloane Square office of Universal Aunts, a quirky company providing private carers and escorts for unaccompanied children. There was plenty of work taking them to the US and Canada, but nothing came of the interview. She may have consulted the National Service handbook, first published in 1938, whose fifty pages outlined the requirements and age limits for service in the Land Army, the Observer Corps and Civil Defence services.[35] Her friend

33. *The Tatler*, 22 May 1940, pp.300–1.
34. Richard Anthony Raikes (1909–1940), a lieutenant in the 60th Rifles, missing presumed killed at Calais. Lisel Helen Josepha Lasch, who was born in Cologne in 1911, remarried in 1946.
35. *National Service: A Guide to the Ways in Which the People of This Country May Give Service* (1939). London: HMSO.

Jo Ainsworth was already working as a driver for the LAAS and during one of her trips to London June may also have talked about her dilemma to Katharine Scott, an architecture student who lived at Lindsey House and who was also a volunteer ambulance driver.[36]

On 4 June Churchill made his famous 'We will fight on the beaches' speech and the following day June was told that her friend David Sewell, a 22-year-old second lieutenant in the Royal Armoured Corps, whom she had last seen in February in Cambridge, had been killed in action in Belgium.[37] Finally, she decided on a course of action.

She would join the army.

36. The 1939 register lists Anne Katharine Sibella Scott (1912–2008), an architecture student, and her sister Mary Margaretta (1910–1960), 'Amateur Musician Society', at Lindsey House. Anne, known as Katharine, later married Jocelyn Morton (1912–1987), a textile manufacturer, who lodged at Lindsey House at the same time. Her brother Philip, and a cousin, Joan, also lived there.
37. David William Berre Sewell (1918–1940).

At the Ready

Thursday 6 June 1940 Went to see about driving an ambulance
at the ATS recruiting office. Had lunch in Bywater Street with
Mintie, Peter, John, Jo & Pat and Pip D.M. Had tea again
there later and then to Cheyne Walk to a sherry party given
by Esther Darlington,[1] and supper in Chelsea.

JUNE DID NOT join the Auxiliary Territorial Service, the women's
section of the British Army. Perhaps there were no vacancies for
drivers or perhaps she had second thoughts when the recruiting
officers told her that she would not be able to choose her own
job and might end up in a dull office. Disappointed, she returned
to Hertfordshire by bus the next day, only to learn that another
family friend, Piers Edgcumbe, a second lieutenant in the
Royal Armoured Corps, had been killed during the retreat from
Dunkirk.[2] On the Sunday she, Janet and their parents drove over
to the Edgcumbes' parish church at Essendon for the memorial
service. 'It was so desperately tragic. Shall never forget it for as
long as I live,' wrote June. After supper, as the air cooled, she
walked alone on Gallows Hill. Nature was a consolation. 'The hill
is a mass of flowers and everything is too heavenly. The birds, the
smells, the breeze, the flowers. There never was such a summer.'

A few days on, she was back in London, staying at the Dorrien
Smiths' flat in Curzon Street. She had made another decision.
'Went off to join the London County Council ambulance drivers.
Passed my test driving round London in a very ancient bus,' she
wrote on 11 June. There were more tests the next day but, in reality,

1. Esther Mabel Darlington (1910–1993).
2. Piers Richard Edgcumbe (1914–1940) is listed on the war memorial at
St Mary the Virgin Church, Essendon.

there was little chance of her failing. The bar was not high—she had only to navigate the streets near County Hall in Waterloo for a bit, steer her vehicle around obstacles in a yard and try not to spill the water in a bucket in the footwell–the basic test for recruits. There was an acute shortage of ambulance drivers in London and, because so few people were coming forward, standards had been lowered as far as possible.

The call for Air Raid Precautions (ARP) and emergency services volunteers had gone out well before war was declared, with clergymen, mayors, MPs and even cabinet ministers stumping the country appealing for people to come forward. The Air Raid Precautions Act of 1937 made local councils responsible for collecting the casualties of bombing raids. Across Britain there was a patchwork of ambulance providers–in some places the local fire brigade did the work—but in London there was a centralised provider, the London Auxiliary Ambulance Service (LAAS).

London County Council estimated that twenty thousand volunteers were needed to staff the LAAS,[3] which would work alongside the regular ambulance service and other related organisations such as the St John Ambulance, the Red Cross and the Friends Ambulance Unit, which also had roles such as training in first aid, organising first aid stations, leading stretcher parties and ambulance convoys, caring for those in air raid shelters and running their own ambulances. The volunteers in these services were predominantly male. It was different in the LAAS. From the start, it was envisaged that it would be not only staffed by women but also managed by them, except at the very top–but recruiting them proved to be problematic.

The Times reported in February 1939 that London County Council was 'begging' women to put their hands up.[4] Five months later, to drum up interest in the LAAS, it had organised a week-long tour of the London boroughs, with a parade of ambulances, auxiliary vehicles and ambulance-buses accompanied by crew

3. *The Times*, 10 Mar 1939, p.18C. Civil Defence Services vastly overestimated expected casualties.
4. *The Times*, 8 Feb 1939, p.9G.

members with placards and loudspeakers. They were not greatly successful. Only one in ten families had a car, and compared to men, few women held driving licences. Most women were, in any case, too busy working and caring for their families to take on additional civil defence responsibilities.

Local newspapers carried advertisements for 'women who can drive a car and have a little spare time,' promising that training could be fitted around existing engagements.[5] 'Here's a job for women motorists—the London Auxiliary Ambulance Service. Go to it!' exhorted cinema newsreels.[6] The service was not offering much in the way of financial reward. Part-timers were not paid at all and the full-timers working forty hours a week in eight-hour shifts received only the £2 a week standard wage given to all ARP women. When full-time men were recruited to make up the numbers they were paid the ARP rate of £3 5s (£3.25), a standard gender differential which most women accepted without a second thought.[7] For those not in receipt of allowances or trust funds, the pay from ARP work was an essential part of their family finances. This was probably true of Chelsea ambulance driver Isabelle Thornton, a chauffeuse before the war, whose income would have disappeared with the blackout and petrol rationing.[8]

When war was declared in 1939 the ambulance service recruits were on high alert. Barbara Emary, a 31-year-old film continuity

5. *Chelsea News*, 3 Mar 1939, 3F.
6. *Appeal for Stretcher Bearers and Ambulance Drivers* (1939) and *Call for Woman Workers at London Auxiliary Ambulance Service* (1940). (Reuters, Gaumont British Newsreel). Both films are available at britishpathe.com.
7. If injured on duty women in the civil defence services received two-thirds of the compensation to which a man was entitled. The British Federation of Business and Professional Women and the London and National Society for Women's Service and other women's organisations objected to this situation. Women MPs from all parties combined in the Woman Power Committee to press for equality for women, but success was patchy and support difficult to rouse. Apart from the lifting of the marriage bar and less reluctance to hire married women generally, women's employment status did not improve. See Harold Smith, 'The Problem of "Equal Pay for Equal Work" in Great Britain during World War II,' *The Journal of Modern History* (1981), Vol. 53, No. 4, pp.652–72.
8. Isabelle Thornton (1901–1989).

secretary who volunteered early for the LAAS, found herself on 1 September 1939 on full-time duty at an auxiliary station in Kensington. 'The minute the war started everybody had to report for anything which they'd been rehearsing for or training for, such as ambulance driving and so on,' she remembered. After a few weeks of the Phoney War she was released back to her job and until the end of the war worked part-time at the ambulance station. In the West End Rose Macaulay initially worked alternating weeks of nine-hour night and day shifts. Her first task was to drive patients home from St George in the East Hospital in the East End which was being emptied in preparation for raid casualties.[9]

At first, the service was in a permanent state of flux, with people leaving to pursue other avenues, especially the part-timers for whom it was often a stopgap before joining the military or something better presented itself. The novelist Mary Wesley complained that ambulance work was boring: all she seemed to do was scoop up drunks at night and fill sandbags during the day. She was relieved to be offered a job on a team trying to break German and Russian Morse code and swiftly accepted. Chelsea artist and art teacher Sybil Gilliat-Smith decided her energies were better suited to escorting children to safety overseas and enrolled with Children of the Overseas Reception Board (CORB), which sent children who lived in areas that were especially vulnerable to air attack overseas, mainly to Canada.

Women had a long and much-lauded history of driving in wartime, both on the home front and abroad. In London, during the First World War, women drove for the Motor Transport Volunteers, the Women's Reserve Ambulance (Green Cross Corps), an outfit that attended the scene of the first major Zeppelin attack on London in September 1915, and the Military Transport Section of the Women's Legion, as well as chauffeuring troops on leave and driving mail vans. Women were also at the centre of the frontline ambulance service in France and Belgium, but to get there they had had to face down the opposition of the British

9. Macaulay, *Letters to a Sister*, p.83. The hospital, which closed in 1956, was in Raine Street, Wapping.

Army, which preferred women to confine themselves to more traditionally feminine roles, such as nursing. Eventually there were women ambulance units in the Voluntary Aid Detachment motor ambulance convoy, the Women's Auxiliary Army Corps and the First Aid Nursing Yeomanry Corps, whose staff were nick-named FANYS. Most of the FANYS, who were often from aristo-cratic or upper-class families, paid their own way, providing their own uniforms and kit, and sometimes also ambulances. For these women, service was not compulsory or a way to ensure a salary but a badge of honour.

For June, who had seen her sister join the Women's Auxiliary Air Force and then beat a hasty retreat, the ambulance service perhaps represented a middle ground between the dreariness of the exclusively female support services such as the Women's Voluntary Service, which was dominated by women of her mother's generation, and the military services with their fearfully strict discipline. Working for the ambulance service meant not only would she be able to continue with her dressmaking and design activities but she would also have, for the first time, an opportunity to live her life independently.

Thursday 13 June The fighting is even more tense 23 miles from Paris. 6,000 of our men were taken prisoner. I rose at 7 and got to my ambulance station in Danvers Street at 7.30. Collected my tin hat, gas mask and uniform and learned the streets leading to all hospitals etc. Came back by the afternoon and went to bed, too tired to do anything else well. It was a warm day. London seemed very quiet. It was so great to be alone. The evening was very still and gramophones drifted up to my window: Handel, Beethoven, Delius. I read *Rebecca*.

Within two days of her interview at County Hall, June was serving her first shift at Ambulance Station 22 (AS22) in Danvers Street, around the corner from Ric Stewart-Jones's Lindsey House in Cheyne Walk. He had promised her a room when one was available and while she waited she remained in the Curzon Street flat. In daylight it was a half-hour walk to the ambulance station—longer in the blackout of course—so the sooner she moved to Chelsea the better.

Although June described her first day of work in typically spare terms, there was much to learn in her new job. She would have been taken around the station and inducted into its routines and rules: signing in, filling in the logbook, when to take breaks and practice blackout driving and how to check and clean the vehicles and equipment. She was given her LAAS armband and black 'tin' hat (officers wore white ones) and told to memorise the local area by walking the streets (petrol was reserved for call-outs). She was shown the gear to put on for active service: a rubber one-piece suit, a special helmet with rubber flaps, and heavy rubber waders and gloves to protect her from being drenched when the fire service hosed down buildings. No wonder she was exhausted at the end of it.

There was not yet a proper uniform. Recruits had to provide their own slacks, tunics, shoes, jumpers, gloves, stockings and warm winter coat. Some women chose to mimic ARP uniform by wearing plain navy blue and men often favoured army-style fatigues. Eventually, in order to keep up morale and as a sop to the widespread feeling that the LAAS was a 'Cinderella' service, London County Council gave women navy peaked skiing caps with detachable earflaps and flimsy cotton gabardine overcoats. These were derided and given the nickname 'Flit coats' because they resembled those in an advertisement for a brand of pesticide. Men wore standard blue ARP boiler suits. Thick navy overcoats and sturdy footwear were not issued until late 1941.

Friday 14 June Paris was completely evacuated and was in enemy hands by the end of the day. I scrubbed out my ambulance with Tulip Finlayson. Her husband is missing but I didn't know it. She is a marvellous person...

Wrote to David. Bed early and read. Very hot day. I watched the

[barrage] balloons going up through my window. They are so
near now. What will it be like when it's all over, if I am still here?

At Danvers Street, the rota was divided into eight-hour shifts.
Early shifts started at 7.30am and were over by mid-afternoon,
giving June enough time to get back to the flat, change her clothes
and perhaps meet a friend for tea at the Ritz. If she was on the
afternoon shift she could shop in the West End beforehand and
go on to a party or out dancing at The 400 after it finished. Night
shifts started at 11.30pm.

She would often look in at Lindsey House to take breakfast
or lunch with one or other of the many young people lodging
there or to sunbathe in the garden. She was still restless, and not
fully confident that the ambulance service was the right place for
her. Only two weeks after starting she was making enquiries at
CORB about accompanying evacuated children to Canada, but
nothing came of it. The service was overwhelmed with volunteers
and could afford to pick and choose from fully qualified medics
and teachers.

Gradually June settled in and got to know her new colleagues.
Auxiliary ambulance stations the size of AS22, which was based
in a former motor garage, generally had a mix of full and part-
timers. Who were they? It is not easy to say. Research into the
LAAS is hampered by the lack of staff records, which were almost
all destroyed after the service was disbanded at the end of the
war. Some names emerged from June's diaries; a few I found
by searching newspapers and magazines; and most I gleaned
by trawling the 1939 Register of England and Wales for the
Borough of Chelsea. This was a simplified census carried out in
early October 1939 in which wartime service was noted—'LCC
ambulance driver', 'LCC Womens volunteer ambulance driver'
and 'auxiliary ambulance driver' are typical entries. Occasionally,
the precise place of work, for example, 'Station 22' or 'King's
Road station', was recorded but not often and not consistently.
There were several ambulance stations in Chelsea, so it is often
difficult to say accurately whether an individual was at AS22 with

June or not. Nor is it possible to be sure who worked part-time and who full-time. In all, I found more than 180 people who were employed as LAAS drivers or attendants in the borough. In the main they worked at AS22, AS23 on the King's Road or the Territorial Station in Riley Street (TS3).

Of those 180, women outnumbered men three to one. With a mean age of 34 they were also five years younger than the men. At 18, Vivien Lush was the youngest; 53-year-old Katherine Parker was the oldest.[10] The men's ages ranged from Peter Bulmer Howell, a 20-year-old Oxford student, to Augustus Cave-Clark, a retired farmer and First World War veteran, who was 64.[11] By looking at their civilian occupations and digging a bit further into their family backgrounds, I found that the recruits were pre-dominantly middle or upper class. This was no surprise. Chelsea, although home to a diverse population, was one of the wealthier boroughs in London.

Nearly half the women on the list did not have to earn a living outside the home; twenty-eight of them lived on private means, among them June's friends Jo Ainsworth (who was married) and Daphne Catt; widows Moira Hale and Muriel Vereker; and Gerda, Coral and Blenda Morgan, three middle-aged unmarried daughters of the late Master of Jesus College;[12] six women described themselves as housewives; seven had 'no occupation'.

Magazines loved to feature posh women 'doing their bit' as ambulance drivers. In October 1939, *The Sketch* published a photo of Lady Burghley, a volunteer ambulance driver, in well-cut sailor's trousers and a neat cable-knit sweater, her steel helmet

10. Officially recruitment was focused on the 18 to 50 age group but there were exceptions at either end.

11. Vivien Lush (1921–1975), a buyer for Marks & Spencer, volunteered with her mother Gladys Blagden (1896–1971); Katherine ('Kitty') Parker (1886–1971), later Eisdell, was a noted composer and pianist. Peter N. Bulmer Howell (1919–2015) served in the Rifle Brigade later in the war, and afterwards became an actor; Augustus Cave-Clark (1875–1947).

12. Daphne Catt, later Fournier, later Barnett (1919–2004); Moira Hale (1900–1984); Muriel Vereker (1891–?), later Carroll, later Cavendish; the Morgan sisters were Gerda Myfanwy Hyde (1888–1966), Coral Georgina (1890–1967) and Blenda Ava Rhadegund (1892–1973).

slung across her shoulder, about to step into her LCC ambulance.[13] The journalist expressed mild astonishment that such a person would consent to taking part in physical work: 'She will seize a broom and sweep out a garage with as much efficiency as if she were used to it.' It was a sentence that could have come from the satirist Michael Barsley, who created the characters Kitty Kensington and Lucy Rolls-Voyce to illustrate well-born women 'ladying it' by volunteering for the Women's Voluntary Service or the various auxiliary services.[14] Despite the derision or toadying admiration of some commentators, it is worth remembering that without the contribution of women like June and indeed Lady Burghley, the ambulance service, understaffed at the best of times, would have collapsed.

Several of the women serving in Chelsea had directly relevant experience of ambulance driving. During the First World War, Geraldine Hedges,[15] aged 49 in 1939, had been a driver for Elsie Inglis's Scottish Women's Hospitals ambulance units, serving on the Russo-Romanian front in terrible conditions. In more recent years, she was a noted racing and rally driver, and owned a car dealership in Chelsea. There were also two women who gave their occupation as 'ambulance driver' and who may have been seconded from the regular service.

There was a good sprinkling of professionals, which showed how possibilities were opening up, at least for middle-class women. Nadine Dagmar Beddington, Barbara Köllerstrom and Jessica Albery were architects; Elizabeth Doll was an architect's draughtsman and Katharine Scott, who lived at Lindsey House, an architecture student. Doreen Anderson, Joan Secretan, Ann Strauss, Marjory Nicol-Smith, Joyce Sanderson and Irene Briggs were artists. Margaret Wheaton was a doctor. Diana Howard was a freelance journalist and Dorea Stanhope wrote for the left-wing *Time and Tide* magazine, and was a qualified pilot. Guida Mary

13. *The Sketch*, 18 Oct 1939, p.1; Lady Burghley (1904–1984) was born Mary Theresa Montagu-Douglas-Scott.
14. Barsley, pp.27, 37.
15. Geraldine Care Hedges (1890–1968).

Fletcher was a German and French translator.[16] A handful, such as Lois Mary Brown and Margaret Bridges, worked as private secretaries. Kathleen Ash was a housekeeper-companion. The volunteers also included a nurse, a children's nurse, a drapery manageress, two estate agents, a masseuse, a café owner, a model and two dressmakers.[17] Tulip Finlayson,[18] who had scrubbed out the ambulances with June and whose husband was missing in action (he was later discovered to be a prisoner of war), was a knitting pattern model.

Among those we know served at AS22 with June were Richard Patrick Russ, better known as Patrick O'Brian, the author of the Aubrey–Maturin series of maritime novels, and his partner Mary Tolstoy, the estranged wife of Count Dimitri Tolstoy. O'Brian later claimed to have joined the ambulance service after being rejected for active service and while this may have been true and it is clear that he was not physically afraid—driving through the blackout under a rain of bombs could be fully as hazardous as anything on the front line—it was more likely that he volunteered for the LAAS so that he and Mary could be together and that he could continue writing. In London, they were free agents. O'Brian's

16. Nadine Dagmar Antoinette Sarah Beddington (1911–1990), architect; Barbara Köllerstrom (1902–1978), later Cole (changed by deed poll), architect; Jessica Mary Albery (1908–1990), architect; Elizabeth Honor Doll (1916–?), architectural draughtsman; Katharine Scott (see footnote page 39); Doreen Gordon Forster Anderson (1906–1971), artist; Joan Henrietta Secretan (1912–1999), later Radcliffe, later Goring, portrait artist; Anne Sadelbia Mary Nichols (1902–1988), later Strauss (Lady Conesford), sculptress; Marjory Catherine Nicol-Smith (1913–1978), later Mortada, mural artist; Joyce Mary Sanderson (1899–1980), advertising designer; Violet Irene Savile, later Hamilton Gay, later Briggs, later Worsfold (1899–1987); Margaret Helena Banks (1902–1958), later Wheaton, medical practitioner; Diana Louise Norwood (1911–2003), freelance journalist; Dorothea ('Dorea') Scudamore-Stanhope (1903–1968), journalist and investment consultant; Guida Mary Fletcher, later Crowley (1915–2011), French and German translator.
17. Lois Mary Gordon Brown (1905–1983), private secretary; Margaret Bridges, later Molnar (1911–1976), secretary; Kathleen Ash, later Delefortrie (1916–2004), housekeeper companion.
18. Peggy Mary Clotilde Pagot-Chester (1914–2004), later Finlayson, later Harley. Her husband the Canadian actor, producer and director Wallace Stuart Finlayson (1911–1990) used the stage name Wallace Douglas.

*The ambulance crew at AS22 in Danvers Street included a wide
social mix although the middle and upper classes dominated.*

estranged wife and two children lived in Suffolk and Tolstoy's
two children were cared for by their grandparents in Devon. Mary
was a 'fearless but highly dangerous driver', according to her son
Nikolai and, although she did not mention it in her diaries, June,
who loved dogs, was probably charmed by Mary's habit of driving
her ambulance with her black long-haired dachshund Miss Potts
on her lap. June got to know the couple well and had much in
common with Mary who, like her, was *sportif*.[19]

O'Brian's male ambulance colleagues were generally aged 30
to 50 and included a number of men, mostly in their forties and
fifties, whose trade gave them relevant expertise in mechanics.
There were nine chauffeurs, two taxi drivers, a lorry driver, a
train guard and a motor mechanic. There were also men who
had been rejected for military service for medical reasons, were
in protected professions, or were conscientious objectors who
had been ordered to do ambulance work by the courts. A handful
of men in their twenties were waiting to join the military, such

19. Tolstoy, pp.140-50. Frieda Mary Wicksteed, later Tolstoy (1915–1998);
Richard Patrick Russ aka O'Brian (1914–2000). Interestingly, among the list of
ambulance workers I found in the 1939 Register was Eric B. Maturin, a possible
inspiration for the name of O'Brian's fictional physician Stephen Maturin.

as advertising agent Michael Lumley, and there were also a few well-off businessmen, including Tom Burroughes, the managing director of a family billiards table business (who was also, in 1939, a sometime boarder at Lindsey House).[20]

For a good many, service in the LAAS was the first time they worked in the same space, on an equal footing, with people from the opposite end of the social scale. It was the same in other civil defence services. Theodora Benson, a volunteer driver for the Chelsea ARP, noted that her colleagues were, like her, rich enough to own their own cars; the officers were mostly 'tradesmen' and the stretcher-bearers 'all sorts'. 'We had all of course met and liked people like each other before [the war], but had never mingled our lives so intimately, and it widened all our horizons,' she wrote.[21]

Ambulance Station 22 was tucked away in the yard behind No. 18 Danvers Street. The stables next door to the station were rented to George Roberts, a greengrocer, who kept his horse and cart there. The main thoroughfare was a mix of residential properties and businesses. There were heating engineers at No. 20, a hostel for day servants across the road. In 1910 the medieval mansion Crosby Hall had been dismantled in Bishopsgate in the City and reassembled at the southern end of the street. The rest of Danvers Street was made up of nineteenth-century terraced houses, mostly converted to flats and occupied by a social soup typical of London: bus conductors, engineers, journalists, pharmacists and their families.

Like many other auxiliary ambulance stations in London, AS22 had been requisitioned from its proprietors. The premises had been shared by Thomas Alfred Blanch, motor engineers, and Woodall & Napier, dairy farmers. In many ways, the site was ideal for its new purpose, consisting of two double-height brick-built sheds, one of which was used to house the vehicles and the

20. Michael Molyneux Hope Lumley (1917–1943), of the RAF Volunteer Reserve 106 Squadron, died with six other crew over the Netherlands; Tom Laurie James Burroughes (1902–1993).
21. Eleanor Theodora Roby Benson (1906–1968); her book *Sweethearts and Wives* was published in 1942.

other the crews. It had a petrol pump and an office. Although the main drawback was the glass roof, which was potentially lethal if shattered by a bomb, it was by no means the most problematic of the London auxiliary stations. At AS103 (Cannon Street Road in Shadwell in the East End), which had previously been a petrol station, the fire risk was so great that crews had to vacate the premises during air raids. Other stations were converted warehouses or school buildings, many of which had become obsolete after the evacuation of children from London. Some stations shared facilities with other ARP services. At Berkeley Square House in Mayfair the LAAS crews, demolition, rescue and stretcher squads as well as the Red Cross were housed together in a huge underground garage. There was another subterranean station in the warren of storerooms at the Adelphi behind the Savoy Hotel on the Strand.

At AS22 the office in the accommodation shed was a wooden structure built into the corner and equipped with a desk and phone; on the wall outside there was a pinboard where maps of the local streets and order sheets were posted. There was also a cloakroom area, where the crews hung their overcoats and tin hats, and a relaxation area, with armchairs and tables donated by members of the public and, later, furniture reclaimed from bomb sites. Here the crews would read, play cards, knit or listen to the radio. Some stations had ping-pong tables, an attempt to mitigate the long hours spent waiting around with nothing much to do. Left-wing artist Marjory Nicol-Smith, who served in Chelsea, took down-time as an opportunity to carve wooden chess pieces. 'The kings were always Falstaffian figures. The knights, morris dancers on hobby horses. The pawns were workers carrying hammers and sickles,' she told *The Mirror* thirty years later.[22] Clashes between crew members were inevitable—in a letter to her sister, Rose Macaulay mentioned her feelings of annoyance when the former taxi drivers at her West End station talked over the BBC news.[23]

At some stations, the night shift slept or rested in bunks or on

22. 28 April 1970, 11B.
23. Macaulay, *Letters to a Sister*, p.96.

The ambulance crews at AS22: once duties had been completed the challenge was to fend off boredom.

camp beds and stretchers on the concrete floor. At AS22, after the Blitz began, they squeezed lilos (inflatable mattresses) into the dugout, which was a concrete-topped shelter built into a corner of the shed and lined with sandbags. It was roughly segregated, with women at one end and men at the other, at least to begin with—June wrote of gossipy late-night sessions with everyone mixed in together drinking coffee made on a primus stove.

Although June's duties were not especially onerous, at this stage of the war there was plenty to occupy her. She was trained in basic mechanics and in driving through the blackout—probably in Battersea Park just across the bridge—and taught how to behave at incidents and how to recognise different types of bombs. Ambulance crews also regularly took part in dummy-run first aid exercises with the fire auxiliary crews, heavy rescue, stretcher-bearers and demolition men, and attended lectures on gas attacks and other hazards. They cleaned the ambulance stations and practised drills. Sometimes, when there were no war-related call-outs, they took over routine accident and illness calls. Recruitment was always a problem. Soon after joining, June was put on 'picket' duty, which involved walking around Hyde Park with a loudspeaker, appealing for volunteers.

After the first few days, June was on duty for real. What did her

*Outside Lindsey House: June Spencer in her
'flit coat' with her gas mask and 'tin hat'.*

shift entail? She and her fellow crew members had a set routine. First, she checked the contents of her first aid box and replaced any missing items. Then she made sure the ambulance had the correct number of hospital blankets in the back, all folded lengthways on the stretchers, and that gas suits and fire extinguishers were on board. Afterwards, the crews were informed who they would partner with for that shift.

The crew members were responsible for every aspect of their vehicle. Tyres had to be pumped, wheels cleaned, batteries and wheelnuts inspected and the toolset checked; exteriors were mopped and polished weekly and interiors were scrubbed out daily. June and her colleagues washed the mess floor, prepared simple meals (the station had a cook), tidied food cupboards, swept out the garages and cleaned the windows. There were also routine housekeeping tasks: blankets and sheets had to be taken to the laundry and a new supply collected.

The London Ambulance Auxiliary Service had six divisions and a hundred and twenty stations, each with about thirty to fifty personnel, seven ambulances and five cars, but there were variations within that. At the beginning, many of the vehicles were donated saloon cars, lorries, tradesman's vans and obsolete buses, or even privately-owned cars, but as the summer of 1940 went on some of these were judged to be unsuitable and replaced with repurposed saloons. American Ford Pilots and V8s, Buicks and Hudsons, as well as British cars such as Vauxhall, Morris and Rolls-Royce, were preferred. The bodywork behind the front seats was removed and replaced with a van-back kitted out with basic wooden bunks, blankets and stretchers, and the exterior painted grey (although AS22 did not get around to this until December). For speed of access the back doors were removed and a cloth curtain strung across. White lines were painted on bumpers and sides, and headlights were dipped and masked, the nearside with a cut-out 'A' to make them easier to identify as they approached incidents. Apart from this, in the blackout, once painted grey, the ambulances were more or less invisible.

> *Monday 17 June* We had a yellow warning practice after lunch in a pub by the river. We went out on a first aid exercise and I heard the ghastly news that the French had surrendered.

After the Fall of France London seemed to empty rapidly. Those who could, headed for the countryside. Mollie Panter-Downes,[24] a British journalist writing for *The New Yorker*, described a city that was 'quiet as a village'. 'You could have heard a pin drop in the curious, watchful hush. At places where normally there is a noisy bustle of comings and goings, such as the big railway stations, there was the same extraordinary preoccupied silence. People stood about reading the papers; when a man finished one, he would hand it over to anybody who hadn't been lucky enough to

24. Mary Patricia (Mollie) Panter-Downes (1906–1997). Quotations are from her *London War Notes* 1939–1945, pp.69, 73.

get a copy, and walk soberly away.' Londoners did not particularly want to discuss what had happened. To speak about it somehow made the danger more real.

Measures taken by the government only ratcheted up the tension. On 15 June, fifteen million copies of the government leaflet 'If the Invader Comes: What To Do—And How To Do It'[25] were delivered to households. It exhorted the public to 'Be clever. Be brave' and glibly advised people to stay at home unless told by the proper authorities to leave, 'because, if you run away, you will be machine-gunned from the air, as were civilians in Holland and Belgium.' They were warned not to supply the enemy with food, petrol or maps and to report suspicious matters to the police.

Although there had been as yet no great aerial assault on the capital, on 18 June there were serious air raids targeting strategic sites in Essex, and occasionally enemy bombers dumped their loads randomly in suburbs and in central London. The public now assumed it was a matter of when, rather than if, attacks would begin. They were under no illusions about how bad they would be. Many people were in the habit of going to the cinema every week where the newsreels showed them the aftermath of bombardments on Barcelona, Guernica and Shanghai, so they knew what to expect.

On Tuesday 25 June Londoners experienced their first real taste of what was to come. Three waves of German bombers crossed the coastline and headed inland. June noted it in passing in her diary:

> The first red warning[26] in London last night. Susan MC and
> I sewed for French Red Cross all the afternoon in 25 Belgrave
> Square... Back to Curzon Street. Dinner at Carlotta's.

Mollie Panter-Downes also heard the sirens: 'The ARP services went into action smoothly and efficiently, and people who were

---

25. Available to read at the Imperial War Museum website: iwm.org.uk/collections/item/object/1502003592
26. A red warning meant that an attack was in progress or imminent.

walking home after visiting friends found themselves politely but implacably headed off into public shelters and kept there until the all-clear sounded, which it didn't until four hours later. An unidentified plane droned high overhead and searchlights were in action, but nothing happened, and the only unusual sign next day was the universal snappishness of the public temper.' Lack of sleep was taking its toll.

> *Monday 8 July* Scrubbed my ambulance! 3.30 bathed and changed. Borrowed a bicycle from Ann Channer.[27] John and Pen [Gough] had a small drinking party in P's room. Lance Wright[28] came. JP [John Perfect][29] and I and another girl dined at Jo's, then Lombard.

Ann Channer, the daughter of a retired lieutenant-colonel in the Royal Marines, was to become one of June's closest friends. They had much in common: both were born in 1916 into similarly upper middle-class families. Ann, brought up in Bideford, Devon, was educated at a boarding school in Bath for the daughters of officers and at a finishing school in Belgium. When she met June, Ann was working as a secretary at the Foreign Office and also at an organisation called Political and Economic Planning (PEP) at Queen Anne's Gate, which came to play an important part in June's life later in the war.

The Battle of Britain, fought in the skies, began on 10 July with attacks by the Luftwaffe on shipping convoys in the Channel and on coastal ports and radar stations. Hitler planned to defeat the RAF and disrupt Britain's supply of food by destroying ports, shipping and warehouses. Four days later he ordered that Operation Sealion, the invasion of southern England, take place in the autumn.

The mood in London was tense but not without hope—there

27. Ann Georgette Mary Channer (1916–1984), later Kempe.
28. Lance Armitage Wright (1915–2003), June's first cousin, son of her uncle Edmund, who died in 1916 at the Somme.
29. Arthur John Strode Perfect (1917–2002), a medical student.

was a feeling that the German pilots were not as skilled as their British counterparts and some clung to the 'miracle' of Dunkirk as proof that 'plucky little England' would win out over the odds. Visiting Americans discerned a 'new vitality' in the city, born of the acute peril the country faced. The revival of the West End meant that theatres and restaurants were packed once more and the city was filling up with new arrivals—troops from the Empire and the Dominions, Canada, Australia and New Zealand—but there were also business people, refugees from the south coast of England, and scores of elderly expats who had lived in the Riviera for decades and had been forced to flee.

Among those newly arrived in London was Betty Stucley.[30] Tall, blonde, commanding, straight-talking and warm-hearted, Betty, who was a friend of Ric Stewart-Jones, had been working in France as a volunteer driver for the Mechanised Transport Corps. As the Germans advanced across France, she found herself stranded near Bordeaux in charge of five badly wounded British soldiers. She had the good sense to pay a French ferryman to take them half a mile out to sea to a British passenger ship. It was her own mini-Dunkirk and earned her a mention in despatches.[31] Much later in the war, the resourceful and compassionate Betty was to prove a rock when June was tossed about on the stormy seas of life.

30. Elizabeth Florence Stucley (1906–1974), later Northmore.
31. *Western Morning News*, 14 Feb 1942, p.2C; *London Gazette*, No. 35458, p.708; No. 35469, p.954.

Summertime

Friday 26 July 1940 Packed all the morning, and left
Lowndes Street and arrived at Cheyne Walk in time to
be at the ambulance station.

IN LATE JULY 1940 Ric Stewart-Jones offered June a room in
No. 97 Cheyne Walk. Her new home was a stone's throw from
the oozy, muddy reaches of Cheyne Wharf, just by Battersea
Bridge. There was an almost coastal feeling at that wide sweeping
bend of the Thames, with seagulls cawing, the ebb and flow of
the tides and the dank marine smell of the water. The mansion
and surrounding Georgian terraces have been compared to ocean
liners standing proud of the cottages around them, a world of
their own with little in common with the rest of the metropolis.

Lindsey House, Nos. 95 to 100 Cheyne Walk, was built in
1674 by Robert Bertie, the third Earl of Lindsey, and incorporated
within it an earlier house built on the site of Sir Thomas More's[1]
farm. It is thought to be the oldest house in Chelsea. In the mid-
eighteenth century it was reconstructed by Count Zinzendorf as
the London headquarters of the Protestant Moravian Brethren,[2]
and later subdivided into separate residential properties. Over
the centuries, behind its grand façade, Lindsey House became
a warren of extensions and additions. In the nineteenth century
No. 98 was home to father-and-son engineers Marc and Isambard
Kingdom Brunel and for twelve years from 1866 the artist

---

1. Thomas More (1478–1535) famously fell out with Henry VIII over his divorce
from Catherine of Aragon and the split from Rome, and was beheaded.
2. The Moravian Brethren is a Protestant denomination originating in the
fifteenth century with the Hussite movement. Zinzendorf was a bishop of
the church.

*Lindsey House, the 17th-century mansion in Cheyne Walk where
June had a room on the fourth floor overlooking the river.*

James McNeill Whistler lived at No. 96 and painted the famous
portrait of his mother there. The building is, even now, sometimes
referred to as Whistler's House.

Lying to the southwest of the centre of London, bordered
by Fulham, Kensington and Westminster, Chelsea was, and still
is, something of an enclave, retaining the pastoral qualities of
centuries past. To the east, past Battersea Bridge is the brick-
built All Saints, known to everyone as Chelsea Old Church. It
was established around the twelfth century, and had two private
chapels, one dating from the fourteenth century and the other,
from the sixteenth, named after Sir Thomas More, its founder.
A railed-off memorial to Sir Hans Sloane, the physician and
plant collector who gave his name to Sloane Square, stands just
outside. Further to the east, on the far side of Albert Bridge is the
Chelsea Physic Garden, established in 1673, casting a glance back
to Chelsea's past as a place of market gardens.

Chelsea is also home to the Royal Hospital, where red-coated
old soldiers live out their final years, and to Hans Town with its
handsome nineteenth-century redbrick mansions. The main

shopping thoroughfare is the King's Road, in 1940 densely packed with retail businesses: bakers, drapers, grocers, pawnbrokers, shoe repairers, tobacconists, restaurants, with independent services such as foot clinics, photographers and dressmakers in the upstairs premises. At the upper end, at Sloane Square, is the department store Peter Jones, an icon of 1930s architecture, with its clean lines and glass curtain wall, a fraternal twin to John Lewis on Oxford Street. This was one of June's favourite places to shop.

At the start of the war when children were evacuated from London, some of the remaining adults opted to move to the suburbs, or even the countryside, and commute into the city to work rather than take their chances as sitting targets in bombing raids. Although many children returned to their families during the Phoney War, the population of London remained depleted. In Chelsea, the number of residents fell from about fifty-eight thousand to sixteen thousand,[3] their places taken, to some extent, by refugees from Belgium and the Netherlands, France, Czechoslovakia, Germany and Austria.

The light, the river with its mists and mysteries and the green spaces of Chelsea have long attracted artists. In the 1940s, it was like any other London village favoured by the wealthy and well connected: it embraced a range of people. The rich lived alongside 'ordinary' people—plumbers and mechanics, nurses and cleaners, and their families. There were also plenty of people who were short of money but well-endowed with creative talent.

For a very reasonable £1 a week Ric gave June one of the best rooms in the house, a large attic on the fourth floor furnished with a couple of beds, a chair and a gas ring. This she called her 'studio'. Like the rest of the house, it was cold and dilapidated, with peeling paint and crumbling plaster. There was an open fireplace but rarely any coal available. June hardly noticed. She

3. Melanie Backe-Hansen, 'Chelsea in the War'. *Chelsea Society Annual Report* (2015), p.68. The lower figure is an estimate of population during the worst of the air raids.

*View from 94 Cheyne Walk with Lots Road power
station to the right and the boatyard below.*

could open the french windows on to the balcony overlooking the
water and lean on the iron railings to take in the view—to her
right the massive Lots Road power station with its chimneys
belching out smoke, and its mirror at Battersea on the south side
of the river, down below in the water the Chelsea Yacht & Boat
Company, to the south-east the railway hub of Nine Elms, and in
the distance the City and the far-off East End.

In 1935 Ric bought No. 94 Cheyne Walk, which sits to the
eastern side of but is not part of Lindsey House, using a legacy
from his father, Captain Thorold Stewart-Jones, a barrister
and businessman in civilian life, who was killed in action in
1915.[4] He then set about purchasing the individual residences
of Zinzendorf's mansion with the aim of reuniting them in
their original configuration as one mansion. While he worked

4. Thorold Arthur Stewart-Jones (1873–1915).

on making that happen, he rented out the many rooms at his disposal.[5] His properties could accommodate at least forty people comfortably.

Ric, an extrovert chain-smoking infectiously energetic, patrician eccentric, was happy to take 'lame ducks' under his wing and to encourage anyone who interested and amused him. It helped if they were as obsessed with music, art and architecture as he was and he was especially keen on those who could play an instrument; they would be able to participate in the musical evenings held in his sitting room at No. 96. His particular passion was the eighteenth century and he combined this with a personal mission to preserve the buildings of Chelsea.

On the first floor of No. 96 an impressive ballroom stretched from front to back. To raise money for its restoration Ric hired it out for parties, weddings and concerts and he and his friend, and secret lover, James (or Jim) Lees-Milne used it for dances and exhibitions to benefit charitable causes.[6] After war was declared, and while Ric awaited his army call-up, the two of them curated an exhibition in aid of the Finland Fund.[7] Ric described it as 'desultory works of art associated with Chelsea' and, in his *faux* modest memoir *Another Self*, Jim said the items were 'almost anything that could be gathered together at that time'[8]; while that may have been true, the exhibits told another story. They included pieces lent by the King and Queen, as well as works by contemporary Chelsea artists—Augustus John, Philip Wilson Steer and Ethel Walker among them[9]—and artefacts such as a bishop's cope purported to have been embroidered by Catherine of Aragon and relics from Scott of the Antarctic's expeditions.

5. Kroyer, pp.117-9. Stewart-Jones did not acquire No. 98.
6. Eton-educated James Lees-Milne (1908–1997) was a writer, wit, conservationist, historian, novelist and dedicated diarist.
7. *The Times*, 27 June 1940, 9C. The British public donated £300,000 for the support of Finland after the Soviet Russians invaded in November 1939. The Winter War ended in March 1940 with Finland making territorial concessions.
8. Lees-Milne, *Another Self*, p.155.
9. Welsh artist Augustus Edwin John (1878–1961), who had a studio at 153 Old Church Street, was a leading portrait painter; Philip Wilson Steer (1860–1942) was based in Chelsea; Ethel Walker (1861–1951) was a Scottish artist.

*Jean Woodard ('Mrs Joe') ran the kitchen
catering for boarders at Lindsey House.*

From time to time Ric's mother Eva,[10] a noted suffragist as a
young woman, his sisters Diona (known as Di) and Elizabeth, and
nanny Christiana Sams joined him in his apartment on the second
floor of No. 96. Joe and Jean Woodard (known as Mr and Mrs
Joe or The Joes),[11] caretaker and cook, plus Charlie Parsons, a
handyman who had served with Ric in the merchant navy, and his
wife Jane,[12] as well as a commissionaire and a handful of female
domestic staff, also lived at Lindsey House. The Royal Historical
Society rented the ground floor, except for the dining-room at
the back where the boarders took breakfast and supper, prepared
by Mrs Joe. They were for the most part personal friends of the
Stewart-Joneses, and lived at Nos. 97 and 94, with the top floor of
No. 96 reserved for young men and designated 'Cads' Alley'.

The house was a hub of never-ending arrivals and departures

---

10. Eva Joan Holland (1883–1942), later Stewart-Jones.
11. Joseph Powell Woodard (1882–1943); Jean Taylor Woodard (1892–1969).
12. Charles George Parsons (1891–1963); Jane Roe-Ely, later Parsons (1901–?).
In the Thirties, Charles was employed to 'mind' Michael Stewart-Jones, Ric's
youngest brother, who was born with disabilities.

as people joined up or were assigned jobs in the military or civil defence or left London for work elsewhere. At the beginning of the war the crew of the Emergency River Police, whose vessel was moored in the water below, used the facilities at Lindsey House for washing and sometimes sleeping, and were counted as living there in the 1939 census, which also listed a Church of England priest working for Dr Barnardo's children's homes, a couple of middle-aged doctors, a diplomat, an editor, an actress, a handful of company directors and several women of private means, as well as three drapery saleswomen, and Jim Lees-Milne, then working as a British Red Cross stretcher-bearer. Ric himself appeared at the house intermittently; sometimes he was away serving with the mercantile marine (he had been rejected by the army because of heart problems), at other times he was at the family home in Lewes, Sussex.

For June, the move to Lindsey House meant that her life was now her own. She had a new privacy, not available while she perched in friends' flats, and she also had a ready-made social circle to add to her network of friends and acquaintances. In wartime, circumstances could change in an instant—everything was short notice—but for now she was with a group of people, many from a similar social background, who were fun and, at this stage at least, fired up by the changes brought by the war.

June's friend Esther Darlington, one of Ric's earliest tenants, looked back on her time at Lindsey House as 'a mixture of drama, humour and warmth... irresistible'. Fred Oppé,[13] a scion of a British-German-Jewish family (his uncle was the art historian and collector Paul Oppé) and an occupant of Cads' Alley, remembered the atmosphere at Lindsey House as a permanent house party of dozens of lodgers, at the centre of which was Ric's 'unquenchable energy'. Some rooms in adjoining houses were connected by internal doors, enabling the residents to slip between them, but the Stewart-Joneses did not encourage residents to indulge in illicit sexual activities. One remembered No. 97 as 'full of young

13. Armine Frederick Oppé (1913–1995).

and up-and-at-it people, including several very attractive girls, whose whereabouts in the house never succeeded in eluding Nanny's eye.'[14]

Christiana Sams, Nanny, had spent her entire adulthood in service. Starting life in Little Bardfield, Essex as one nine of surviving children of a farm labourer and his wife, by 1911 she had joined the Stewart-Jones household as a nurse to baby Di and her sister Elizabeth. Three more children followed: Edward, Ric and finally Michael, who was born with special needs.[15] Now aged 65 and dressed in an old-fashioned long black dress and white cap, possibly unconsciously evoking the spirit of Whistler's Mother, Nanny swept around the premises on the hunt for boarders' misdoings. The Stewart-Joneses appreciated the fierce loyalty that lay beneath her hawk-eyed demeanour, but the boarders were wary and crossed her at their peril. Even so, they knew that her presence was invaluable to them.

She would wake them in the morning for their shifts. June complained many times that Nanny forgot and, given the animosity between them, assumed this was intentional. More importantly, she ensured that the unconventional living arrangement at Lindsey House remained respectable, and acceptable to the boarders' families. Lax morals were all well and good for the bohemian artists of Chelsea but the parents of the younger women tended to be conservative in outlook. 'When the idea was first mooted that I should come and join my brother John [at Lindsey House] my mother, when she heard it was a mixed establishment, doubted if it would be very suitable! But, on hearing that Ric had his mother and sisters living with him, not to mention a Nanny, she was completely reassured!' wrote June's friend Penelope Gough.[16] June's parents were more tolerant than most but without Miss Sams at Lindsey House even they might have drawn the line. It is likely that Nanny and the boarders'

14. Pulford, p.52.
15. Elizabeth Eva (1910–1975), later Pulford; Edward Thorold (1912–1972); Thorold Stephen Michael Stewart-Jones (1915–1949).
16. Pulford, p.48.

Richard Stewart-Jones (left) and his friend and lover James Lees-Milne met in 1938 and shared a passion for architectural conservation work.

parents were unaware of the illicit sexual relationship between Ric and Jim but just as likely that some of the boarders suspected it. Ric and Jim met one evening in March 1938 when Jim, then Secretary of the National Trust, was visiting an empty property overlooking St James's Park and awaiting the attendance of a committee member from the Society for the Protection of Ancient Buildings. He was more than a little surprised when 24-year-old Ric, looking like his idea of the poet Shelley, pitched up and proceeded to flirt overtly with him. Jim wrote later that their friendship 'exploded like a rocket, instantly'. It was more than friendship: a passionate love affair ensued. For eighteen months, until Ric rejoined the merchant marine and Jim joined the Irish Guards, they were inseparable.[17] Their relationship had to be kept secret. Homosexual acts between consenting adults, even those over the age of 21, were illegal.

17. Lees-Milne described their relationship, minus the sexual element, in Pulford, p.29.

June had already found common ground with Ann Channer, and the two of them also became friendly with Patience Clifford,[18] whose room at 94 Cheyne Walk had a balcony, from which she could shout over to June on hers. Patience was another of the cohort of professional women coming through: she had recently qualified as an architect and had a job designing camouflage for buildings and military installations, to protect them from air attack. June, Ann and Patience, all born in 1916, spent as much time together going to cinemas and nightclubs, sharing confidences, discussing clothes as their timetables allowed. Patience, like June, loved dressmaking.

June was also friendly with Honour Sayer,[19] another dress designer, and with Charlotte Waterlow, who had graduated from Cambridge University with a first in history and for whom she made clothes suitable for her job at the Ministry of War and Transport. There was also Janet Perfect, a secretary for an employment bureau, who was a friend of the Stewart-Joneses from Lewes; Katharine Scott, an architecture student and part-time auxiliary ambulance driver; and Elizabeth Lindsell, who June knew from Hitchin and who was working as a private secretary.

Amid the carousel of friends, acquaintances and visitors, June, Ann and Patience held the centre. The three of them sewed and made tea and toast on the gas rings in their rooms, lay out in the sun on the balconies or in the garden, huddled under the bedclothes in winter, went to church together and listened to each other's woes. It was only when they parted that they expressed what they felt about each other and even then, as befit the times, they were reticent.

18. Patience Lisa Clifford (1916–2008), later Bayne-Powell. No relation to the author of this book.
19. Honour Magdalene H. Sayer (1915–1997), later Stern, later Hammond; Charlotte Waterlow (1915–2011); Katharine Scott (see footnote page 39); Elizabeth Mary Barber Lindsell (1909–1998), later Corbett. The relationship of Janet Mary Perfect (1912–1946) to John Perfect is unclear.

Saturday 3 August Nanny [Sams] forgot to wake me and I
was an hour late at the station. PT [Physical Training] and gym!
Very hot. Sunbathed in the square and wrote letters. Edward
Warner[20] called on us. There was a wedding reception here.
Bed early... Richard Shuttleworth was killed flying.[21]

Sunday 4 August Very warm day. Gym in the garage. Sunbathed
in the garden. Cool breeze up the river in the evening. Wrote
letters. Talked to John [Perfect]. Ended the evening singing in
the dark in the Scotts' flat.

There was a strong rumour that the invasion would start on
4 August, the anniversary of the outbreak of the First World
War, and although that did not come to pass, people knew that
Germany wanted to invade before the winter and before Britain
could take delivery of US planes. Tension was cranked up not
just by the Germans dropping propaganda leaflets entitled
'A Last Appeal to Reason' over Britain and giving the text of
Hitler's 19 July speech to the Reichstag but also by the British
government's own leaflet campaign. 'Stay Where You Are'[22] again
instructed the population not to join the fight but to 'stay put' and
protect themselves, their families and their homes but, like the
previous leaflet, failed to offer clear guidance on how this was to
be achieved.

Wednesday 14 August Breakfast late with Penelope [Gough]
and wasted most of the morning after lunch. Slept until 5.30 and
did some [sewing] work for Esther [Darlington]. Supper at the

20. Edward Redston Warner (1911–2002), later knighted, worked in the
Middle East section of the Foreign Officer and was a member of the Executive
Committee of PEP. See page 138.
21. June's friend Richard Ormonde Shuttleworth (1909–1940), a racing driver
and aviator, a member of the Royal Air Force Volunteer Reserve, was killed
in a cross-country training exercise when his Fairey Battle aircraft crashed
into a hill.
22. Ministry of Home Security, 'Stay where you are,' Monash Collections
Online, repository.monash.edu/items/show/33606.

Lombard[23] and a long walk in the wind down the river and over
into Battersea Park. Back in time for the news and wrote letters.
Tremendous air fighting at the coast. It still seems like a dream...
Tomorrow was Hitler's chosen day to arrive in London!

The previous day the Luftwaffe had started to attack airfields
and radar stations, focusing on those in the south-east. RAF raids
on Germany raised public morale and most people, in any case,
took pains to appear unconcerned. Any display of fear or dread
would be interpreted as letting the side down. Despite this, in the
absence of air raids, Londoners became increasingly annoyed and
bored with the endless warnings. It made them feel foolish to run
off to shelters and wait—for nothing. It was now a badge of honour
to ignore them. Inez Holden, a writer and broadcaster, noted that
'Some of the people who go to shelters walk more slowly after the
siren sounds. They look like people going to church.'[24]

On Thursday 15 August, after the sirens went at 7pm, June
and a crowd of friends, unperturbed, were at a party at the
Foreign Office. Two days on, when some of the fiercest fighting
of the Battle of Britain was taking place, she spent an afternoon
playing tennis at Roehampton in west London. 'There was an air
raid,' she wrote, 'but no one took the slightest notice.'

Saturday 24 August On duty at 8.30. We were drilled and
we were complimented on our Guardsman corners!! Pen
and I went off to swim... We drank at Scott's [restaurant].
An air raid! A large fire in the City and we drove down to watch
the [barrage] balloons where the flames were reflected in the sky.

German pilots missed their intended target—the oil deposits
at the docks—and instead hit residential areas in the East End.

23. The Lombard restaurant, which also operated as an exhibition space, was
at 65 Cheyne Walk.
24. Holden, p.148. Beatrice Inez Lisette Paget Holden (1903–1974) was a
writer, Red Cross volunteer and munitions worker.

June and her friends on the balcony at
94 Cheyne Walk, adjacent to Lindsey House.

Over twelve thousand houses were destroyed or damaged. In retaliation, Churchill ordered an immediate attack on Berlin, during which RAF pilots also mistakenly bombed civilian rather than their intended military targets. After this, Hitler discarded any previous decision not to bomb the residents of London.

On the ground in London, some people felt a sense of relief that the long-anticipated blitzkrieg seemed to have started at last. Raids and the expectation of them began to form part of the day-to-day routine. If you were on the street, you could shelter in pubs, which remained open while 'Wailing Willie' sounded. After the war, Kitty Parker, a concert pianist and composer attached to the King's Road ambulance station, remembered passers-by taking refuge in her block of flats, Chelsea Cloisters, in Sloane Avenue: 'When there was a raid, people would come in off the streets to the lower floors for safety. The noise outside would be deafening. You just can't describe it.'[25] At the Queen's Hall in Langham Place in the West End, soloists entertained the audience while a raid

25. Katherine ('Kitty') Parker (1886–1971) quoted in *The Examiner* [Australia], 4 Apr 1950, 9A.

raged outside. The best place to be when caught in a raid while shopping became a common subject of conversation: Harrod's was the winner—it provided chairs and first aid workers.

Tales of fortitude were tempered by the appearance of obituaries in newspapers. Cause of death was not published—too demoralising—but everyone understood the euphemism 'very suddenly'. The government strictly controlled reports on bombing incidents. Locations and casualty figures could only be reported twenty-eight days after they occurred.

> *Sunday 25 August* On duty in the AM. Came back to find Pen and John Gough sleeping. So had tea with Ric, Jim Lees-Milne and Di. David [June's brother] came from Odsey in time for supper and I went to see him off at the bus in a purple warning.[26] Came back in a bus with Janet Perfect as the warning went and we all retired for a short time to the cellar.

> *Monday 26 August* Slightly jaded having been lugged twice out of bed to the cellar. Very hot. Back to bed early and the sirens went again. But we slept on.

Although the cellar was Lindsey House's designated shelter in the early days of the Blitz and was used often, the residents also bedded down in the spacious hall at No. 96. June wrote of 'stumbling over bodies' when she returned in the dark early hours from her ambulance shifts. Women slept in the wide entrance with the men in the dining room at the back, a division strictly policed by Nanny Sams.

Penelope Gough remembered a 'particularly noisy' night later in the war, when everyone was exhausted from extinguishing incendiary bombs on the roof. Di Stewart-Jones was just getting into her sleeping bag in the hall when there was 'another awful crash'. 'Then suddenly down the beautiful staircase walked Nanny in her dressing gown, carrying a candle, with her hair in a pigtail,

26. A purple warning was issued to premises with lighting exemptions as an order to extinguish their lights.

Esther Darlington, a fellow boarder at Lindsey
House, who became a close friend.

and a quiet "Nanny voice" said, "It's quite all right Miss Diona, it was another incendiary; I've put it out and it's time you all got to sleep." Whereupon she blew out the candle, and left us with the night light and we all said "Goodnight Nanny," and settled down, I at least feeling quite safe again, and way back in the night nursery of long ago.'[27]

The conditions in public shelters were very different to this. Across London, the shelter situation was dire. Anderson shelters, built of corrugated aluminium, required the use of a garden. Millions of Londoners lived in flats. There were some deep-level shelters under large warehouses but these were always overflowing. People queued to get in or had to show a ticket. Conditions inside were horrible—flooded, freezing or insanitary.

Chelsea was dense with private apartments and social housing blocks. There was extensive Peabody Trust housing[28] to the west of Cheyne Walk near World's End and just around the corner from Danvers Street in Beaufort Street, a series of six-storey red brick mansion buildings, their residents a mix of

27. Pulford, p.48.
28. A housing association founded in 1862 by American banker George Peabody providing model dwellings for the poor.

tradespeople and professionals. During an air raid, these people could not take themselves off to a hall or safe cellar, or even to the Underground. There were no stations nearby and the nearest Tube lines were essentially large trenches cut into the ground and topped with Tarmac, offering none of the protection of the deep-level tunnels to be found elsewhere in London. In any case, the stations were out of bounds in the early days of the Blitz. Fearful of encouraging a 'bunker mentality' that might allow defeatism to spread, the government ordered the police to lock the doors or put barbed wire across the entrances.

In Beaufort Street, residents were forced to use brick-built and flat-roofed street-level shelters, a type common across London. They had been designed with the understanding that raids would occur during the day, and not as overnight refuges in use for twelve or fourteen hours at a stretch, day after day. They were overcrowded, dank and smelly with only the most basic toilet facilities and, like any location where large numbers of people gathered, if they were hit by a bomb, the result was usually massive loss of life.

'Tried to sleep. Too hot,' wrote June on Thursday 4 September. For days the weather had been stifling, with clear blue skies and daytime temperatures reaching nearly thirty-two degrees (90°F) and it did not cool down much at night. The next morning June and Esther sunbathed in the garden and afterwards drove down to Roehampton to relax by the pool with their friends Betty Arrowsmith and Gill Gambier-Parry and her brother Richard.[29]

> Extremely hot. The pool was a mass of brown bodies. A lot of
> French film stars and other fugitives. We drove out in Richmond

29. Betty Margaret Arrowsmith (1919–2006), later Roderick, daughter of the Rector of Chelsea; Gillian Gambier-Parry (1921–2017), later Lady Williams, in September 1945 one of the first British servicewomen to enter Berlin (she was a subaltern attached to General Eisenhower's HQ); Richard Gambier-Parry (b.1926).

Park for a picnic tea among the bracken and little deer. Back to a picnic supper with Honour Sayer and others in her room.

At 11.30pm on 5 September June started her shift at Danvers Street. She spent most of it sitting in the dugout and chatting to her ambulance colleagues, including John Crocker,[30] a Sandhurst-educated former army major. She discovered that he was related to her friend Piers Edgcumbe, who had died at Dunkirk.

Despite the sirens and a long raid somewhere else in London, it was a quiet night in Chelsea and only one ambulance went out.

---

30. John Delamain Crocker (1907–1989) later left the ambulance service to enlist as a marine gunner in the Maritime Artillery on the dangerous route across the Atlantic, defending the British ships from German submarines.

Without Turning a Hair

Saturday 7 September 1940 To the hairdresser. Met Ann
Channer and we went to the West End. Drink at the Berkeley with
Derrick Seebohm.[1] Went there again an hour later for lunch with
a man from the Ministry of Economic Warfare. It was very hot.

ON THE SULTRY afternoon of 7 September, at about 4pm, at
Bentley Priory on the northern edge of London, RAF Fighter
Command spotted a mass of about three hundred and fifty German
bombers and sent twelve fighters to intercept it. The British pilots
were appalled to see that behind that first wave came another, of
over six hundred fighter planes. The controllers assumed these
were headed for airfields. They were wrong. It was a trick. The
enemy planes turned towards London.

June, like other Londoners, had no inkling of what was to
come next.

After lunch I returned to the garden to sleep but an air raid
began and for the first time I saw hundreds of planes in the
sky, not bigger than pinpricks.

The loud, low growl of planes brought people out onto the
streets, some of them becoming so transfixed by the swarm of
bombers hemmed in with fighters, like queens surrounded by
worker bees, that they stood watching the skies rather than head
for the shelters. It was obvious to most that the target of these
'black birds', the 'pinpricks' that June saw, was the Port of London
and the East End docks, the hub of supply chains to the rest of

---

1. Derrick Seebohm (1907–1981), a friend from Hertfordshire.

the country. If the Germans managed to destroy railway lines, power stations and warehouses, Britain's war production would be seriously hampered.[2] But they hoped to destroy morale as well as infrastructure. The area surrounding the docks was densely populated, with many people living in crowded tenements close by the wharves and factories.

It was the beginning of a long night, often referred to as the First Night of the Blitz. June continued:

> No bombs fell and the warning was over soon and I went back
> to my bed in the garden—but the noise of the engines was too
> much to sleep so I bicycled with a young boy in the direction
> of the fire, for exercise partly. The fire was tremendous, far away
> by the docks. One half of the sky was black smoke.

By 5.30 the docks—Woolwich Arsenal, Victoria and Albert Docks, West India Docks and Surrey Commercial Docks—was an inferno and the sky had turned into a mad canvas of blazing colour, with anti-aircraft guns going, bombs exploding, and dogfights between the RAF and the Luftwaffe. Burning oil storage tanks sent black clouds upwards and, in the streets below, the smoke created a thick choking fog of glowing cinders and floating ash. By six o'clock forty fires were burning out of control, and warehouses on both sides of the river were in flames. Firefighters were overwhelmed. Crews from as far away as Birmingham and Bristol were called in to assist.

Across London, at least in the areas not affected by the attack, people felt a curious emotional detachment from the action, and a

---

2. It was not merely Hitler's fury about the RAF's raid on Berlin that triggered the attack but an active decision made by Goering and General Field Marshal Albert Kesselring. They believed that the RAF had been fatally weakened and that luring it into battle, with a major blitzkrieg on London, would destroy morale, break Britain's industrial capacity and end the war. Adolf Galland, 'Bombs on England' in *The First and the Last* (2018), Reading Essentials (Kindle edition); Douglas C. Dildy (2016); 'The Air Battle for England: The Truth Behind the Failure of the Luftwaffe's Counter-Air Campaign in 1940.' *Air Power History* (2016), Vol. 63, No. 2, pp.27–40.

kind of guilty relief that the Germans had chosen specific targets. It meant that they themselves were spared. William Sansom,[1] a volunteer with the Auxiliary Fire Service (AFS) in Westminster, saw the red glow in the east with the black London roofscape silhouetted against it, yet to him, and evidently to June, it felt anticlimactic and separate. She was not the only one compelled to go out and see what was happening. South of the river in Lewisham, ambulance driver Nita Marcus noted that 'All the hill-tops here (which give a fine view of the Thames and dockside and half of London) were covered with sightseers.'[2]

Only four miles from the conflagration, Barbara Nixon, an ARP warden in Finsbury, north of the City of London, saw a white cloud growing steadily like a 'huge evening cumulus' and heard fire engines rushing by, their klaxons clanging. She felt detached. 'From our vantage-point, it was remote and, from a spectacular point of view, beautiful. One had to force oneself to imagine the misery and havoc down below in the most overcrowded area of London; the panic and the horror when suddenly bombs had fallen in the busy, narrow streets and bazaars, and on the rickety houses,' she wrote.[3] Cambridge student Eileen Alexander[4] watched from a top-floor window in high-up Hampstead, and the following day described the scene in a letter to her boyfriend: 'The houses were chocolate-coloured, darling against a translucent sky, the colour of *vin rosé*, and there were bulges of smoke welling up, feathered at the edges—and occasionally the dazzling comet-fall of a flare and the light of an anti-aircraft shell—as though an electric switch had flashed on and off.' She was entranced by the elegaic action. 'It was beautiful, darling.'

1. William Sansom (1912–1976) was a writer, journalist and actor. The AFS, part of the Civil Defence Service, used part- and full-time volunteers to supplement the work of local brigades. It was replaced in 1941 by the National Fire Service.
2. Quoted in Peter Chrisp, *The Blitz*, a 1987 booklet on Mass Observation published by the University of Sussex Library.
massobs.org.uk/images/booklets/Blitz.pdf
3. Nixon, p.14.
4. Eileen Alexander (1917–1986). The quotations are from *Love in the Blitz*, pp.103–4.

Chelsea resident Aymer Maxwell-Hyslop[5] was visiting friends in Richmond, west of London, when he saw an enormous mushroom of smoke. 'It was so big, and towered up in the sky so high, that one couldn't believe it was smoke at all, and for a long time we didn't know what it could be. We'd heard the guns going and we'd heard the sirens going but we never dreamt of anything like this. And then we got up to the top of this rise in Richmond Park... and we said—My goodness, that must be somewhere near Hammersmith. And then we bicycled on, and we said—Well, it must be Chelsea. And finally when we got home, it was only then that we realised it was ten or twelve miles away from us still. And then we went up on the roof of our flat and saw this great horizon plainly, this red column of smoke towering up into the sky, a terrifying sight.'

Among the accounts of life in Chelsea during the war that have come down to us, there is one that provides detailed daily information on attacks on the area. Jo Oakman,[6] an artist, worked as an ARP warden and was based at Cook's Ground School[7] in Old Church Street, a five-minute walk from June's ambulance station in Danvers Street. Her many duties, tirelessly carried out, were to patrol the streets, put out small fires, rescue residents where she could, administer first aid, direct the homeless to rest centres and investigate reports of unexploded bombs, but she also managed to keep her own private log of air raid incidents and to illustrate it with sketches.

At 5pm she saw three planes come down and two barrage balloons go up in smoke but within an hour everything stopped and at 6.30 the solid tone of the all-clear sounded. Like June, she got on her bike to view the fire in the east.

In Chelsea, people began coming out on to the streets from

5. Aymer Robert Maxwell-Hyslop (1912–1993), a civil servant working for the Board of Education, quoted in Constantine Fitzgibbon, p.44.
6. Josephine Oakman (1900–1970), born in Battersea. Her journal, which included sketches of incidents she witnessed, is in the archives of the Imperial War Museum archives. See an example on page 119. A typewritten transcript of the log is kept at Kensington & Chelsea Library.
7. Later renamed Kingsley School, then Jamahiriya School (now closed).

their shelters. Theodora Fitzgibbon had spent the afternoon in the Eight Bells pub on Chelsea Embankment with Donald Maclean, until recently a diplomat at the British embassy in Paris, and the poet Dylan Thomas, the three of them 'glued together with dread'. After the all-clear sounded, they emerged to see the sky 'the colour of a blood orange, a seething, flaming mass'.[8] It was terrible but at least it was over, and far away.

Barbara Nixon left her flat in Finsbury and headed to Soho for dinner. Like most people, she had failed to understand that the aim of the first wave of bombing was to set the ground alight and provide a beacon for the next. At 8.35pm the sirens wailed again, just as June was returning to Cheyne Walk:

It was dark when we got back and the sirens were going again. But the sky was bright scarlet and remained so all night. The windows of the houses were brilliant sparks of reflected light.

Three hundred more enemy planes had arrived over London, this time using the fires already raging on the ground to illuminate the streets and guide them to drop more high explosives, parachute mines, time bombs and oil bombs. Theodora Fitzgibbon saw them sweep down the Thames 'which was lit up like a horrifying pantomime, past London Bridge, Victoria, Chelsea, dropping their deadly cargo indiscriminately'.

From across the river in Battersea Park came the roar of the AA guns. Windows rattled and shrapnel ricocheted outside. The sky throbbed. June was due on duty:

I went to the ambulance station at 11.30 and sat in the little cells all night listening to the air activities and the screaming of bombs in the distance that for some reason never seemed to explode. It got very cold in the dawn and every two hours we went up to the

8. The quotation is from Theodora Fitzgibbon, p.72 ; Fitzgibbon (1916–1991) née Rosling, later Morrison, wrote a memoir, *With Love,* covering her time in Chelsea during the Blitz; Donald Maclean (1913–1983) was exposed in 1951 as a spy for the Soviet Union; Dylan Thomas (1914–1953).

office for cups of tea. There were no calls for the ambulances but no doubt the danger must have been immense elsewhere.

June was closer to the danger than she knew. Jo Oakman reported seeing two screamer bombs[9] and seven others drop over towards Kensington. She had felt a bomb fall nearby and ducked into a street trench. At nine o'clock teenager Joan Wyndham, who was living just over half a mile from Danvers Street in Evelyn Gardens, was looking out through her top-floor window. 'We saw four bombs fall on Kensington High Street—flash, boom!—and sparks and debris shot into the air four times in quick succession,' she wrote in her diary. She went to a shelter and heard 'screaming bombs, falling right and left.' Each moment she thought would be her last. Finally, at 5am, the all-clear sounded.[10]

Victoria station, a mile and a half from Cheyne Walk, had taken four bombs and three people were dead. Bombs had fallen in Battersea, directly across the Thames from Chelsea, where a hit on a shelter in Rawson Street killed eight people, and there were bombs on Albert Bridge Road and Chelsea Polytechnic. Two high explosives landed in the Thames near Flood Street.

Altogether, across London there were 843 incidents. Over eight hundred and fifty people were killed, including a hundred and thirty children; many more were seriously injured and thousands made homeless, mostly in the East End where whole streets were wiped off the map. In the docks, massive fires raged out of control, many of them tackled by the AFS, which was staffed, like the Auxiliary Ambulance Service, with amateurs with no real experience, twenty of whom were killed. East Enders began referring to 7 September as Black Saturday.

Despite the loss of over forty German aircraft, Goering was pleased with the night's work. He was under a time restraint. The

9. Some bombs were fitted with tailfins which gave them a distinctive 'screamer' sound.
10. After the war Joan Olivia Wyndham (1921–2007) stashed her diaries and forgot about them until her daughter encouraged her to seek publication. They appeared in print as *Love Lessons* (1985) and *Love Is Blue* (1986). Wyndham, *Love Lessons*, pp.143–4.

seaborne invasion had to take place before 21 September. After that date weather conditions would not permit it.

London had gone from terror at the prospect of instant annihilation when war was declared to disbelief that bombs would ever fall and that money spent on ARP services had been wasted, and now, abruptly, to a state of emergency. 'That day London changed,' wrote Barbara Nixon, likening the city to a drunk man suddenly sobering up when he receives tragic news.[11] Phyllis Pearsall, creator of the *London A to Z* and an accomplished artist, also noted this alteration. While sketching scenes at AS104, the underground auxiliary ambulance station at the Adelphi, one of the older women, a veteran of the Spanish Civil War, told her: 'For most of them [the younger crew] that first night... must have been like a torero's first bull fight when, in place of the chair he had been train to fight against, a real bull charges him.'[12]

While the emergency response was organised and efficient, there were gaping holes in provision for the thousands of displaced people who streamed away from the ruins of their homes to look for shelter. Some had bundled salvaged possessions into battered prams, but most had lost everything. They had nothing: no food, no clothes, no money and no jobs. East Enders faced the greatest hardship, not only because their homes were among the prime targets of the enemy but also because their housing was comparatively flimsy and collapsed easily. Shelters in their areas were both in short supply and inadequate, and there were few alternatives. Some East Enders trekked to other parts of the city, others to its outskirts—Epping Forest, Hampstead Heath, the caves at Chislehurst in Kent—perhaps feeling that a lack of buildings would make them safer. Some slept in the woods and walked back to jobs and their bombed-out homes during the

11. Nixon, p.18.
12. Pearsall, p.63. Phyllis Gross, later Pearsall (1906—1996), map maker, businesswoman, artist and writer. Already the publisher of the *London A to Z*, Pearsall was commissioned in July 1940 by the novelist Graham Greene in his role at the Ministry of Information to visit civil defence and military posts and produce a sixpenny book, *Women at War*. It never saw the light of day, but was reconstructed and published by Ashgate Editions in 1990.

War artist Robert Fuller's sketch of the underground ARP station based in the Adelphi shows ambulances fitted with curtains rather than doors.

day; some took over abandoned buildings and lived as squatters; others broke the locks on deep-level Tube stations such as Warren Street, Goodge Street and Highgate, or simply ignored the police guards and barged in.

❖

Sunday 8 September It was quite cool and dull after breakfast. I slept all the afternoon. Went over to the ambulance station and we had tea. Wrote letters and went to church at Chelsea Old Church. Coming back there was a lovely sky and against it coming over the bridge a line of great guns on carriers and lorries, which seemed a sudden reminder and broke into a peaceful interlude.

The 8th had been designated a National Day of Prayer some time earlier, but the day now took on a special meaning. June was not the only one to feel the weird contrast between what felt like all-out war at night and the calm of a new day. Theodora Fitzgibbon, like June, found it difficult to reconcile 'the peace of the morning with the noisy, fire-drenched hell of the night before.'

June may have drawn some comfort from the fact that Chelsea had escaped relatively unscathed—but this was not to last. The area was firmly in the firing line, the hundred-degree turn in the river a marker for German pilots. The Thames was a map, guiding them towards London's East End docks, riverside railheads and power plants but also showing them where to break off to left or right to target specific areas. West London, with both Lots Road power station and, across the river, Battersea power station, as well as the open spaces of the easily identifiable and iconic Royal Hospital, was a prime target in itself.

> Honour [Sayer] and I had supper in at 97 with everybody. Went over to Belgrave Square to sew [for the Red Cross] and the sirens went. Ann [Channer] arrived with a girl she had found with no shelter. We drank coffee and talked until I went off [to the ambulance station] at 11 o'clock. The guns were hard at it by then and bombs could be heard in the distance.

> I was in the office all night with [Irene] Briggs and [Margaret] Roberts. The bombs continued until we were almost used to it. We would say to each other 'here it comes' and would listen to the whining whizz which sounded [like] it was for us every time. Until one which was even nearer and we clung to the walls as everything shook and heaved... It seemed several moments, that time of the whistling rush growing to a deafening rush before the crash.

When bombs fell, the civil defence routines set up and practised for months kicked into gear. The Report or Control Centre, where information about bombing raids and the deployment of teams for emergency rescue and repair work was coordinated, was at the heart of ARP operations. There was one in each borough of London. After a bomb fell, the police or an ARP warden called the 'telephone girls' in the control room, who wrote details of the address and the response required on a slip of paper. Fire service and heavy rescue crews would go out first to cut off

*Danvers Street (AS22 was in a yard on the right), painted in
1941 by ambulance driver and artist Sybil Gilliat-Smith.*

the gas and water supplies. Stretcher parties, ambulances and
mobile units (a car with three nurses and a doctor) were ordered
up as required.

When the call came in to the ambulance station, the station
officer would sound a whistle and issue instructions; drivers and
attendants would collect their coats, waders and first aid kits and
run to the ambulances. Engines would start, creating a roar; a
cloud of fumes would fill the garage.[13] The ambulance crews were
sent out from the station in rotation, with some staff remaining
at base to attend further incidents or to make hot drinks for other
crews. On 8 September June was told to stay behind but she could
not resist the temptation to find out what was happening.

I hopped out of the garage door (expecting to see nothing but
ruin) and saw flames and smoke rising from Paultons Square at

13. Pearsall, p.65; *Illustrated* magazine, 1 Feb 1941, quoted in Raby, p.65.

the end of the street. Two ambulances went out, one to Beaufort Street and two cars. The planes continued to drone. Two people disobeyed an order and were dismissed on the spot. A gas main had been hit in the square and the flames were very high, making a wonderful splash of colours. Nobody was hurt.

The flames reached the height of the houses. Many years later, John Jesse, then a child small enough to sleep in a chest of drawers, remembered the scene. 'My mother Betty lifts me out of the tallboy and quickly dresses me. We run out into the dark and head towards the corner of the King's Road where I see a tall and ferocious pillar of flame bursting from a hole in the middle of the street. Surrounding it is a phalanx of fire engines and firemen dousing the flames with great arcs of white water. Already, a large crowd has gathered, their faces flickering and glistening from the spray.'[14]

It was a different story in nearby Beaufort Street, which runs parallel to Danvers Street. A bomb had hit one of the apartment buildings, glanced off the pavement and landed on a flat-roofed street-level shelter.

Between 70 and 80 were killed but 35 were alive. Daphne Catt and Irene Briggs took them to hospital. In the office I made quite 80 cups of tea I should think during the night. There was no gas or water and many homeless were undressing in the streets.

Jo Oakman, her ARP colleagues and people who had been taking shelter nearby rushed to help evacuate people from flats that were now uninhabitable, while men from the heavy rescue squad worked on stabilising collapsing walls, shutting off the water and electricity and extracting the living, and later the dead, from the ruins.

At each bomb scene the relief effort was coordinated from a hastily established incident post, which was marked out with two

14. Jesse, p.10. Shortly after this incident four-year-old Jesse was sent to boarding school.

Ambulance drivers John Crocker (with pipe) and Bernard Crowley (forefront) in Paultons Square. The other two men are unidentified.

blue lamps placed one on top of the other. The walking wounded, wandering about with faces blackened with soot and dirt, pieces of brick and shards of glass embedded in their skin, their clothes torn and bloody, might be screaming or eerily quiet, unable to answer simple questions. In shock, they might insist on returning to their flats or houses to continue cooking or whatever they were doing when the bomb dropped, or refuse to leave the scene if their children or pets were missing.

In the dark, with only feeble hand torches, hurricane lamps or the dimmed headlights of ambulances and the heavy rescue squad's vans, ARP teams would try to locate victims, some of whom might be unconscious or buried in the rubble. The best way to find them was to listen: every so often, the call would go out for silence so that the location of a faint cry might be identified.

In a letter to her sister, Rose Macaulay described a bombing she attended in Camden Town: 'Two fallen houses, a great pile of ruins, with all the inhabitants buried deep. The demolition men worked & hacked away very skilfully and patiently, and we all encouraged people inside, telling them they would be out in a short time, but of course they weren't. There was a mother and a crying baby, who were rescued at 10.0 next morning after I had gone. I drove to hospital another mother, who had left two small children under the ruins. I told her they would be out very soon—but they never were, they were killed. The demolition men were splendid—we passed milk down to the baby, and water for the others, and the men kept saying to them "It'll be all right, dear. Don't you worry." They were very nice and matey.'[15]

Every incident had huge potential for misunderstanding, muddle and conflict. Although civil defence workers appeared calm, under stress emotions ran high. Jurisdictions were inadvertently or deliberately infringed and arguments would break out. One branch of the Civil Defence Service would complain about another.

The dark and now alien landscape of broken bricks and masonry, of unseen stairs and gaps, of falling beams and escaping gas was a minefield of hazards. The surrounding cacophony was impossible to ignore: bombers still droning heavily, AA guns firing, high explosives shrieking down, while walls fell, rescue workers sawed and drilled and shouted instructions to each other, and the trapped and wounded hacked out the dust in their lungs or cried for help.

Irene Haslewood,[16] a driver for the Chelsea ARP stretcher-bearers, was at the Beaufort Street incident. 'Huge slabs of concrete trapped poor, mangled bodies beneath their jagged weight,' she wrote. 'Poor twisted bodies—blackened and begrimed from the blast and dust. Bits of bodies lay in puddles of water, blood and filth. Dear God! That first glimpse of Hitler's work! I felt my stomach heave for a paralysing second and I thought I was going to vomit, thereby disgracing myself and my squad for ever.'

Light and heavy rescue crews brought out the injured to the stretcher parties, whose job was to assess whether the casualties

15. Macaulay, *Letters to Sister*, pp.114-15.
16. Irene Sylvia Haslewood (1902–1971), who lived at 9a Cresswell Place, Chelsea, gave her account in a diary now held in the Imperial War Museum (Documents.12994).

should be taken to a first aid post or hospital and to prepare them for transportation (they tied parcel labels to them—X for internal, T for tourniquet and M for morphine) so that by the time the ambulances got to the site at least some of the casualties would be ready to depart with a treatment plan in place.

It was the job of the ambulance driver to manoeuvre her vehicle as far as she could up to the centre of the bombed area without becoming stuck in the rubble or ripping the tires, and then to wait for casualties to be brought to her and her assistant. The concept of the 'golden hour' of emergency medicine, during which rapid intervention can prevent death, was not yet widely known, although the most seriously injured were stabilised by a nurse or doctor on site before they were deemed ready to be taken away. In reality, the ambulance crews often dived in to help the minute they arrived. They would splint broken limbs, cover gaping wounds loosely with bandages, strap in the patients and, once the ambulance was full, having first cleared the windscreen of dust from pulverised buildings, set off for the hospital or first aid post, at a maximum speed of 15mph. The driver had to navigate bumps and holes in road surfaces possibly now slick with brick dust wettened by the firemen's hoses; in the darkness, sometimes in peasouper fogs, the vehicle was guided off the scene by the torch of a white-helmeted ARP warden, while the attendant did her best to prevent the bewildered injured from trying to get out of the vehicle through the back curtains, and watched for signs of deterioration or shock. As soon as the patients were decanted, the ambulance crew returned to the scene to collect more casualties. There was little time for niceties, either in manners or driving style. Occasionally, years after the war, sweet-natured Chelsea ambulance driver Pauline Nagle would astonish her relatives by redeploying her wartime parking method: nudging vehicles in front and behind to make space for her car.[17]

Jeanette Marx, known as Frenchy, a young Jewish refugee from Germany working as an ambulance attendant in the East

17. Felicee Mary Pauline Nagle (1898–1980), private information from Nagle's family.

End, recalled, 'We were so busy we had to come back right away to pick up more people. It gave us no chance to talk to them, the few seconds we had it was just, "You'll go to the hospital and they're gonna do everything for you..." If they weren't dead they thanked us for helping them.'[18]

In the dark it was sometimes impossible for rescuers to tell the dead from the living. Ambulance crews were not supposed to take corpses, which would be collected later. Peggy Crowther,[19] an ambulance driver in the West End, remembered attending the bombing of the Dominion Theatre in Tottenham Court Road and finding the dead laid out under rugs in a back street.

At Beaufort Street the crews worked all night and got seven people out 'more or less alive'. The last was a young boy who was extricated with no visible injuries but who died of shock later. Harvey Klemmer, an attaché at the US embassy, observed one man standing mutely at the barriers for hours. His wife and children had been in the Beaufort Street shelter. All were killed.[20]

At the first aid station, Frances Faviell,[21] an artist, writer and Red Cross volunteer nurse, observed the quiet demeanour of the survivors. 'None of them wanted to say much—I think the dirt and mess with which they were covered and their anxiety for missing relatives or friends were uppermost,' she wrote in *Chelsea Concerto*, her memoir of the Blitz. Three days later, Jo Oakman noted in her diary that the dead of Beaufort Street included her ARP colleague 34-year-old Jean Darling,[22] the shelter warden.

18. Jeanette Marx Grunfeld (1921–2013), quoted in Shaler, p.92.
19. Marguerite ('Peggy') Hodgson (1911–c.2014), later Crowther, quoted in Stephen Moss, 'Remembering the Blitz: "I took my ambulance out when others wouldn't"', *The Guardian*, 7 Sep 2010.
20. Harvey Klemmer, 'They'll Never Quit: Newborn Baby Killed in That Chelsea Blitz.' *Daily Boston Globe*, 29 Apr 1941, p.16.
21. Faviell, p.96. Frances Faviell was the pen name of Olivia Faviell Lucas (1905–1959), later Fabri, later Parker. She was on the Committee of Women who worked with refugees, mainly Belgian and Italian; they held some of their meetings at Lindsey House.
22. Jean Darling (1906–1939) was a housing estate manager. Jean Darling House, a low-rise sheltered housing block near the site of the shelter where she died, commemorates her.

As dawn broke June had her first proper view of Beaufort Street, where ARP crews continued to work.

> They were being wonderful, especially the demolition party who were working like mad without turning a hair, pulling out bits of bodies, taking them in bunches in the blankets and leading the ambulances to go to the mortuary.

'They were loaded wrapped in blankets in the back—I went back and forth till the mortuary filled and I had to find another one,' June said years later. Klemmer, observing the 'horrifying shambles' at Beaufort Street, was told that a dead baby had been found but there had been no way to identify the mother, so the rescue workers had placed the body in the arms of a dead woman they had found. Looking through the lists of civilian casualties published after the war, I tentatively identified the child as two-month-old Maureen Gurney who was killed with her mother and three-year-old sister. She was the youngest of the fifty-seven victims, the oldest being 99-year-old Lavinia Dowsey. A third of the victims were elderly and over two-thirds female. Thirteen children died. Fourteen families lost two or more members.

Everyone in the rescue and emergency services had a different response to a bomb scene. Angela Raby, whose biography of her aunt May Greenup, an ambulance driver in the West End, noted the dry humour of the civil defence workers who were given to remarks such as, 'People would not believe how heavy a severed leg was to lift.'[23] Stanley Rothwell, a stretcher-bearer in Lambeth, south London, wrote of scooping up pieces of bodies using a stiff yard broom and shovel and washing the blood away with buckets, while trying to keep hungry dogs at bay—thousands had been abandoned to fend for themselves when their owners left London. He described his team weeping as they worked or dropping to their knees and praying. He would vomit discreetly.[24]

Some casualties showed little sign of damage. William

23. Raby, p.xii.
24. Rothwell, p.17.

Sansom, the volunteer fireman, described an incident at Marble Arch on 17 September when a bomb pierced the roadway and detonated in a well-reinforced underground subway. The blast ripped the tiles from the walls and the clothes from the victims. Twenty died, their bodies found naked with 'hardly a scratch' on them. In a confined space the airless vacuum created by the explosion would fill with expanding gas, stopping hearts and collapsing lungs.[25]

On her way back to the station after a run to the hospital, June took a quick detour past Lindsey House, where she 'found no windows and the roof looking rather bald!'

> [There] was a line of workers all in good spirits picking out remaining bits of glass and sucking up water which had filled the cellar and ground floor. The dinghy in the front lawn was very nearly launched! The sun was rising. There was a huge crater at the gate of 100 Cheyne Walk. I went back to continue making tea in the office.

The crews returning to AS22 at the end of the incident made out a report and sat down with a cup of tea, but had to be ready to go out again at a moment's notice.

> More people came to relieve us and I came off duty. Breakfast as usual in the dining room which was very damp and cold. Then I went off to see Irene Briggs as she was alone in her flat after the night's ordeal. There I had a bath and looked at her pictures and paintings. Lovely photographs of her grandmother's home in Austria.

> At 12 I came back to 97 and went up to the roof of 94 [where Patience Clifford lived] where there was no broken glass and it was quiet. I woke at five to hear the all-clear going. The windows in my room in 97 were the only ones intact. Queer little things

25. Sansom, p.43.

had happened: my suitcase had come open, a china plate had whizzed into it and it shut again, some pictures were down and of course thick dust everywhere.

After attending a bomb incident the crews were filthy. Dirt and grit encrusted their scalps, gathered under their fingernails and found its way into every fold and crevice; their eyelids were inflamed with dust. Sometimes they went to the decontamination unit at the ARP Centre to use the overhead showers. Bathing and washing her hair after incidents were important enough to June that she routinely included them in her diary.

June never described in detail her feelings on seeing dead bodies or parts of them, so we don't know what her reaction was, but she did tell her family of returning to the peace of Lindsey House when she was released from her shift and the surreal experience of dining with all the other paying guests conversing politely about their jobs: '"Did you have a nice day?" they would ask. All you could say was "Yes, thank you," because ambulance workers were under strict instruction not to give away anything about incidents.' Soaking in the tub at Irene Briggs' flat, away from the platitudes of her fellow boarders, was perhaps a better way to recover.

It is easy to see why June felt so safe in Irene's company. Nearly twenty years June's senior, she had already seen much of the world, both geographically and emotionally. After a conventional childhood in Yorkshire as the middle of three daughters of William Hale Savile, the aristocratic rector of Beverley, and Mabel von Bothmer, who was from an equally aristocratic German family, she had been married and divorced by her mid-twenties. Now aged 40 and ten years into a second marriage, to William Francis Eggington Briggs, who was serving with the Royal Engineers, she had previously suffered the loss of a days-old baby son and remained childless. The 1939 Register recorded her occupation as 'unpaid domestic duties' but June described her as an artist.

June was off-duty the next day. As the thick smell of plaster dust and burning buildings hovered in the air, she and Ann

Channer went out to lunch, but they were back at Lindsey House at five o'clock when the sirens went. They went down to the cellar armed with a bottle of wine. On the surface, eight people were killed when a high explosive bomb demolished three houses in nearby Bramerton Street.

The casualties included the family of Dr Richard Castillo, a local GP. Four days after the bomb fell, 12-year-old Mildred Castillo was found alive and conscious but pinned by the neck, arms and legs by timbers which were supporting tonnes of debris above. She was given biscuits and tea through a tube; she asked for her rosary. For seven and a half hours, while bombers circled above, George Woodward, Wally Capon and George Pitman from the heavy rescue squad worked to pull her out. The bodies of her mother Gertrude and her 11-year-old brother Anthony were later found in the rubble.[26]

26. On 19 September 1940 George VI and Queen Elizabeth visited Bramerton Street where they talked to the men who had rescued Mildred. George Samuel Alfred Woodward (1905–1981), a general foreman, Walter Capon (1884–1963), cabinet maker, George William Pitman (c.1897–?), a labourer, were awarded the British Empire Medal in 1941 (Capon and Woodward also received the George Medal in 1944 for another rescue). See Faviell, p.100; *The Times*, 19 Sep 1940, p.10B; *London Gazette*, 35143, 22 Apr 1941, p.2342; 36696, 8 Sep 1944, p.4214.

A Battleship on High Seas

Tuesday 10 September 1940 Breakfast was late after a long
night of raids. I spent the morning washing up. Everyone was
still working at the windows. There was no water or gas as the
main was hit at the gate. On duty again in the garage at 3.30.
They were still retrieving the bodies in Beaufort Street. The
buses were still going merrily on, pushing their way down all the
little side streets. The warning sounded that night for the third
time as we finished our supper in the canteen.

SOMETIMES IT IS the juxtapositions in June's spare prose that
spark the imagination: London buses going politely about their
business while a few metres away bones and flesh are being
excavated from collapsed buildings. Ordinary life did not stop or
go away; it just took place in extraordinary circumstances.

One of June's rare long passages described the journey she
and Irene Briggs made on 10 September to collect a 'lunatic' from
a hostel in Victoria and deliver her to Fulham Hospital,[1] one of the
last remaining psychiatric facilities in London, most of the beds
for mental cases having been requisitioned by the government for
military and domestic casualties. If it had not taken place in the
middle of a huge aerial bombardment the job might have been too
routine to mention. The freshness, the vividness of June's words
indicate that she wrote them within minutes of returning to AS22,
perhaps while ensconced in the concrete dugout, waiting for the
dawn and her shift to end.

1. The identity of the institution from which June collected the patient has been
difficult to pin down. The best candidate is the Girls' Friendly Society at
29 Francis Street, perhaps repurposed in the war. Fulham Hospital was at
St Dunstan's Road, Hammersmith. Charing Cross Hospital now occupies the site.

It was 10 o'clock at night—the worst possible time to be out on the streets—when the call came through.

> It was my very first time out during raids at night. We sped
> through the garage under the glass roof... It was a queer
> sensation driving through the red lights.

Above them was the incessant drone of enemy planes in a sky crisscrossed with tracer bullets; in front, the hazards of the blackout. While starlight or moonlight and glimmers of residual light might help a bit, the darkness was intense, illuminated, if the driver were lucky, by the flash of gunfire or the phosphorescent glow of incendiaries. Their first stop was at the Public Assistance Office on the King's Road to pick up the Relieving Officer for the borough[2]—part of this man's remit, a leftover from the days of the workhouse, was to authorise the transfer of mental patients to hospital—and once he was aboard they set off to the hostel.

> Briggs went in [to collect the patient] with the Relieving Officer,
> leaving me outside by the ambulance. There always seemed to be
> a plane just overhead. At that second I heard the shriek of a bomb
> and a voice said 'Flat—quick!' and I was under the ambulance
> on my face, my tin hat crashing into another underneath, which
> was a policeman. I clung to him as the increasing shriek was
> a deafening crash and it had burst 15 yards [14 metres] away.
> Briggs came out to see if all was well.

> I went in with her, leaving the policeman by my ambulance.
> In the home all seemed to be chaos. Poor feeble-minded women
> were wandering from their rooms to the cellars with stupid
> enquiring expressions on their faces. An odious ghastly-looking
> creature was shouting out orders and I realised he was our
> Relieving Officer. Our patient was produced and he took hold
> of her roughly, asking the poor girl her history. Had she been to

2. A tentative identification of the Relieving Officer is Philip Need (1895–?) listed in the 1939 census at the Public Assistance Office, 250 King's Road.

prison etc? Where was the last asylum she was in and why was she there? The girl was too terrified by the air raid to answer these questions and we went out again into the night with the odious officer who persisted in badgering the poor simple-minded girl in the ambulance until we stopped. By then she was on the verge of another attack of hysteria. He then went in front of the ambulance... to help direct the way.

That drive seemed the longest I so far remember. I lay on top of the girl to keep her from falling and screeching, and talked to her. She quieted and then proceeded in telling me her past history, clutching my hand till her fingers nearly went through my bones. I turned the light off in the ambulance and through the crack I could see the slashes of searchlights and every now and then hear the scream of bombs. Some in the distance, others close by. The ambulance lurched and faltered and all the time that steady droning noise of planes overhead. The ambulance came to a sudden standstill.

We were in walking distance of the Fulham Hospital which was out of bounds that day. It was surrounded by time bombs and half of it had been completely wiped out.

I got out and followed the Relieving Officer, leaving Briggs with the ambulance, climbing through the wire which surrounded the Hospital. In the darkness I clutched the petrified patient with all the strength of my two arms. We crept along a wall for 200 yards, passing time bombs and crouching low every time we heard the sickening scream of a bomb in the neighbourhood. We came to some iron gates. They were locked.

After feeling the gate posts for five minutes the man found a bell. By this time, they had a plane in the searchlights directly above the hospital. We heard an officer [on] the other side of the gates. They opened and we dashed in. Frightened nurses came flying in all directions. Then came the crash. A few minutes after, a few very odd-looking students or young doctors emerged in pyjamas and coats. They said it must be the other end of the hospital, which had gone... I tried to get out to see if Briggs was all right but they wouldn't let me out. I went with their men and my patient to the mental department. It was the only one left in London. That was why we had had to come there. I found a nice nurse who I was able to tell about my views of the Relieving Officer and my experiences outside the Francis Street home.

I went back to the main part of the hospital where, to my joy, I found Briggs. The bomb had missed the ambulance and she had been rescued by a policeman just in time. The battle was still raging overhead and it was obvious that we couldn't leave for some time. We talked about it with some students and nurses. The ghastly Relieving Officer from whom we tried to escape was a horrid sight, spitting and coughing over everything. He had heavy bags under his yellow eyes and filthy face with a deep scar across his nose. We made off down a long dark passage to get away... We came to a door marked Women Only, went in and shut the door. Here it was warm. The rest of the hospital was very cold as there were no windows left. We wrapped ourselves in blankets. We giggled at each other, feeling rather secure and safe. The all-clear went at 6am.

I drove back to the station, over sheets of glass in places, dropping the Relieving Officer off on the way. On arriving at the office we found the others in a state of exhaustion. They told us the garage had been surrounded by incendiary bombs. They had to evacuate all the ambulances. The Fire Service had been marvellous and everyone, by working like mad all night, had got it all out. The stable next door was hit and three horses were burnt.[3]

3. One of the horses belonged to George Roberts, the greengrocer who rented space in the stables next to the ambulance station. The impact of the loss on Roberts was devastating. He was forced to buy another horse, which went lame and had to be put down, leaving him with no means to sell his stock, which

We were all talking in the tiny wooden office at the corner of the garage. A voice said behind me 'What is this?' I turned and saw an old man showing me in his hands a long shining silver bomb about 18 inches. He was shaking it. I shoved him out of the garage and sent him hurtling down to the river!

The 'long shining silver bomb' was an incendiary. Thousands of them showered down during the air raids, their dual purpose being to light the way for the next wave of bombers and to intimidate and wear down the population. They weighed only about a kilo (2.2lb) but were capable of penetrating a tiled roof, and exploded with a bright white flash and a string of loud staccato reports. Sometimes batches were dropped in wire frames, nicknamed Molotov breadbaskets, which burst on impact, scattering bombs over a small area, their clatter sounding like iron bedsteads dropped from the sky. Householders were reluctant to call the firemen out to deal with them because that would result in the complete drenching of their home and possessions, so they usually extinguished them themselves using a stirrup pump (a hose, nozzle and bucket of water) or by smothering them with earth or sand. In Pall Mall, volunteer fireman William Sansom witnessed a young woman who had earlier kicked an incendiary into the gutter return to put it out with soil, presumably lifted from a flower bed, which she had wrapped up in her evening cloak and slung over her shoulder coal-man style.[4] After December 1940 the Germans included an explosive charge in incendiaries and those tackling them had to be considerably more wary.

Wednesday 11 September I wandered back to 97 where I heard that an incendiary had fallen on the roof. Di had leapt out of my

then started to rot. 'That broke me,' he told the police court when he was charged with selling vegetables unfit for human consumption. He gave up his business and 'went on war work as a porter'. The magistrate showed sympathy for his plight and dismissed the summonses against him. *Chelsea News*, 25 Jul 1941, p.1D.
4. Sansom, p.59.

bedroom window and put it out with sand. I saw the remains
of it on the ledge outside the window and a large piece of shell
fragment in the bicycle basket just outside the front door.

Slept until after lunch. On duty again at 3pm. Lee[5] and I were
first out. The warning went for the third time that day at 8. It was
the first night of the most tremendous gunfire. Everywhere shook,
even the little concrete shelter we were in. The guns sounded all
round us. They were naval guns on lorries patrolling the streets.
The din was most comforting. Eleven o'clock came at last and
there was a single call and I went home to 97.

The sky was brilliant with flashes from the guns and shell
fragments were falling everywhere. But they were pennies from
heaven after the bombs. All night they continued and 97 felt
like a battleship on high seas.

The RAF found that it was not possible, and a waste of resources,
to engage with the enemy during bombing raids, especially at
night, and stopped doing so. Many Londoners interpreted this
as an overall failure to respond to the raiders overhead. During
the nights of the 7th, 8th and 9th September, people had only
occasionally heard AA guns above the din of the enemy planes.
East Enders in particular felt that more could have been done to
protect them. General Pile,[6] who was in charge of the anti-aircraft
defences, ordered that extra guns be brought in and positioned
around London. They were to fire everything they had.

The journalist Mollie Panter-Downes wrote that ARP
wardens had been warning people that 'something special and
noisy' would be happening. In Chelsea, people in the shelters sang
and cheered to the sound of the barrage, thinking that it would
deter the Luftwaffe and that they would now be able to sleep at
night. But those who had not been tipped off assumed that the

5. Lee is unidentified.
6. Sir Frederick Alfred Pile (1884–1976), General Officer Commanding
Anti-Aircraft Command.

*June's LAAS colleagues Daphne Mulholland and Irene Briggs in
Paultons Square, which shows signs of bomb damage.*

attack was coming from the enemy.[7] Vere Hodgson, a charity
worker in Notting Hill, found the cracking gunfire and whining
shells terrifying. 'It lasted all through the night. I believe a shell a
minute. Scarcely slept until after 5 a.m. when All Clear went. Saw
all these people returning from the shelters. But everyone said:
"The noise was ours!"'[8]

When Churchill broadcast to the nation on Wednesday 11
September he compared the threat of invasion to the Spanish
Armada and the Battle of Trafalgar and urged everyone to be
prepared to do their duty, 'whatever it may be'. The next day June
met her father for lunch at the Carlton Club in St James's.[9] She
thought people now wore 'a gay look on their faces', brightened by
the amplified barrage General Pile had ordered. The noise boosted
morale but while the guns helped to drown out the drone of the
bombers, they rarely reached their targets.[10] They also created a

7. Panter-Downes, p.101.
8. Hodgson, p.43.
9. 69 St James's Street.
10. According to Luftwaffe pilot Galland (see footnote page 77), the AA

new hazard: the public were warned not to exit shelters too soon after the all-clear for fear of shrapnel dropping on them.[11]

June went on shift that evening but did not write her diary. In all probability she assisted at Chelsea Manor Buildings, a complex of social housing where five high-explosive bombs landed on the shelter; three exploded, bursting a water main, and four people drowned. The ARP warden Jo Oakman estimated that eighty-one trapped people were rescued.

Although the East End bore the brunt of the attacks during these first few weeks of the onslaught, Londoners understood that nowhere was safe. On Friday 13 September Buckingham Palace was deliberately targeted, for the third time, in broad daylight. A single German raider flew low along the Mall and dropped a stick of five high-explosive bombs eighty yards (75m) from the King and Queen who were standing in a small drawing room near open windows. Four people were injured and one died later.

Saturday 14 September Breakfast early. Caught bus to Hitchin which was extremely crowded and full of evacuees. Met by Mummy. To see Grandmama. Slightly dazed at seeing everyone exactly the same and very peaceful, everyone quite oblivious of the hell which was only 40 miles behind me. Tried to wire [telegram] to London and found all communications cut off, so no wonder. It was lovely to get to the top of Gallows Hill again. Everywhere was looking fresh and lovely... It was too wonderful to step into a real bed again and sleep.

Despite visits to London, June's family was unaware of the extent of the widespread destruction of the city, partly because government censorship ensured it was played down by newspapers and the BBC but also because they had not experienced nights under more or less constant attack from the air. It was a perception that

response had the effect of forcing the bomber formations to fly higher, reducing their accuracy.
11. *Chelsea News*, 13 Sep 1940, p.1E.

*June on the roof of Lindsey House looking over at the wharves
and mills of Battersea across the river.*

also struck the memoirist Inez Holden. An army officer of her
acquaintance told her that he 'had very little news of London, and
had always supposed the bombardment to be much exaggerated.
It was clear from his conversation that he was rather in the dark
about events in the capital, although he was stationed only forty
miles away from it.'[12]

Although June did not say so, writing her diary in these first
few nights of the Blitz had acted as a form of relief. It was cathartic
to put down, at speed, the events of the day. June never again
wrote as expansively as she had about the journey with Briggs
to Fulham. She may have been too busy, too exhausted or too
upset to describe events in detail, or she simply may have felt that
putting her experiences on the page was a process that brought
diminishing returns. In the main and with some exceptions, she

12. Holden, p.160.

recorded where she dined and with whom, which nightclubs she went to, the timings of her shifts, the films she saw, along the way dropping small hints on her mood. Her diary is quite different to the log compiled by the ARP warden Jo Oakman, which lists the exact times sirens and all-clears were sounded, as well as the strength of the AA response. Despite her dispassionate tone, there were times when Oakman's emotions emerged. 'One must have a heart somehow and somewhere—and mine I think broke,' she wrote after she succeeded in reuniting a lost and injured young boy with his distraught parents.

For June, this strange new world could not be improved by its forensic documentation—quite the opposite. After the initial shock of the onslaught, describing horrendous events, or even just listing them, forced her to relive them, when what she most wanted was to fold them quietly away. Talking would not necessarily help. She could not coolly tell her family about dismembered and drowned bodies without seeming callous; and if she broke down she might be seen as weak. It was better to note the incidents, almost in passing, amongst the lunches, trips to the cinema, parties and evenings out. Inez Holden identified the reasons for this: those in the line of fire had to actively suppress their imagination so that 'they are not really able to react any more'. 'The night-shifts work on in their factories, Civil Defence men, nurses, roof-spotters, and so on take up their posts automatically. They say at the sound of the siren: "Oh, here's old Adolf and his Loofterwaffer again!" or else they don't even refer to it at all.'[13] Some people coped by affecting nonchalance or exaggerated cheerfulness, relying on catchphrases such as 'London can take it' to mask their feelings. June's reticence was not simply an effort to stiffen her upper lip. It was a way to administer enough self-care to be able to get up and start each day.

Stoicism was admired amongst civil defence workers but this did not mean that they did not feel. Nina Clement, a volunteer ambulance driver in Liverpool, wept as she delivered the bodies

13. Holden, p.170.

of four babies to a makeshift morgue. She was reported and reprimanded.[14] 'People react, of course, according to their nature,' wrote William Sansom, the auxiliary firefighter in Westminster. 'Coldly in some, warmly in others. One girl ambulance driver, for instance, was physically sick back at the Depot after her night's work was done; she was able to hold on during the moments of needed action, but on relaxing afterwards was overcome with a delayed physical nausea.'[15] Phyllis Pearsall, an observer commissioned by the Ministry of Information, quoted one young woman working at an ambulance station in the West End: 'We were so busy, we could not stop to think. I think I went out five times with the ambulance that night. I didn't realise I had never seen hurt or dead people before, but the next morning I was sick and nothing has worried me since.' One quiet night Pearsall saw the 'ambulance girls' sleeping on stretchers in the duty room. 'It shows at least that the horror of their work does not leave much of a mark,' she wrote.[16] She may have been looking for stories that confirmed her expectations.

How could you process feelings you barely acknowledged were there? My own father-in-law, Paul Rowntree Clifford, a Baptist minister and academic who was an ARP warden in West Ham, one of the worst-hit areas of London, retreated on his leave days to the Reform Club in Pall Mall where he was able to refresh his spirits with prayer, a good supper and a comfortable bed. June went home to Hertfordshire for sleep, home-cooking and the healing balm of parental affection.

On 14 September, while June was with her family at Odsey Corner, a drama, artfully stage-managed, was playing out at one of her favourite West End venues. Led by Phil Piratin, a hat designer

14. Reminiscence of Nina Clement for BBC project WW2 People's War (2004). bbc.co.uk/history/ww2peopleswar/stories/48/a2169948.shtml
15. Sansom, p.28.
16. Quoted in *Women at War: Women War Artists 1939-45* (catalogue of the 7th Annual War Art Exhibition), published by Sim Fine Art, pp.6-8.

and Communist Party councillor in Stepney (and later an MP), a group of about seventy people walked from Hackney in the East End to the Savoy Hotel on the Strand, the epitome of high-end luxury and self-indulgence, patronised, in Piratin's opinion, by 'parasites'. Carrying babies, bottles of milk and blankets, and with banners calling for better shelters hidden under their coats, they demanded to be let in to the hotel's famous basement shelter.

'There was some effort to stop us, but it was only a matter of seconds before we were downstairs, and the women and children came streaming in afterwards,' wrote Piratin later. The staff were 'filled with consternation' while the East Enders looked around in amazement. '"Shelters," they said, "why we'd love to live in such places!" Structurally, the lower ground floor of the Savoy had been strengthened with steel girders and by other means. But the appearance of the place! There were three sections. In each section there were cubicles. Each section was decorated in a different colour, pink, blue and green. All the bedding, all the linen, was of course the same uniform colour. Armchairs and deck chairs were strewn around. There were several "nurses"—you could easily recognise them. One happened to be standing around and she was wearing the usual nurse's white outfit, with a big red cross on the bosom. We were not quite sure what she was supposed to be nursing, but she was very attractive.'[17]

Keen to get ahead of the competition, some West End night-clubs and restaurants were offering a 'get you home' shared taxi service, but others, such as Hatchett's and the Hungaria,[18] the Lansdowne, Grosvenor House and The May Fair, and of course the Savoy, went a step further and installed camp beds in the basement, with the facilities open to customers using their bars and restaurants, who arrived in evening attire, carrying their gasmask, nightwear and toothbrush.[19]

Once Piratin's party was inside the hotel, the police were called but the invaders refused to budge. Then the sirens sounded,

17. Piratin, pp.73–4.
18. The Hungaria was at 16 Regent Street.
19. Woon, p.176.

at which point, understanding that sending women and children out into an active raid would not look good, the management wisely gave in.

It was a relatively minor incident but it was reported around the world, and it helped persuade the authorities to think again about the provision of shelters and the use of Underground stations. A week later June, travelling on the Tube from King's Cross after a respite break at Odsey Corner, saw 'platforms packed with families spending the night there as they always do now'—their presence was still illicit, although tolerated. Londoners simply bought Tube tickets and then bedded down on the platforms. By 25 September Home Secretary Herbert Morrison was forced into a U-turn and conceded that Londoners could use the deep-level stations. About eighty stations were designated official shelters and equipped with bunks and toilets. They began accommodating 177,000 people a night.

While Piratin was at the Savoy, the Luftwaffe was targeting Chelsea, particularly Lots Road, the huge cathedral-like coke-fired power station sitting to the west of that easily identifiable bend in the river by Lindsey House. The German pilots missed the power station but a high-explosive bomb fell through the roof into the crypt of the Catholic Church of the Most Holy Redeemer in Upper Cheyne Row, killing nineteen people sheltering there, mostly women and small children. Amongst the bricks, dust, severed limbs and bloody children's shoes, Jo Oakman found the body of her ARP colleague Bert Thorpe.[20] 'I rolled him over and saw his face,' she wrote in her journal. 'He had none... [I] recognised him by his hair, uniform and ring on his hand.'

The ARP workers, bereaved by another death of one of their own, felt overwhelmed. 'The injured seemed endless,' wrote Oakman that night. 'I thought the fire brigade would never come—stirrup pumps seemed so little effective. There was a shortage of ambulances (the wounded were lying in Upper Cheyne Row in stretchers) [and] first aid stuff at the Post and no iodine,

20. Albert George Thorpe (1893–1940).

only dry dressings and they were not big enough.' Later, aware that another wave of bombers was coming, she and her colleagues hauled a dozen mangled bodies into the church garden to await the morning when they were removed, in requisitioned Harrod's vans, to the mortuary.

A few metres away, in Glebe Place, a bomb fell on an apartment house killing, Oakman thought, seven people. Among them was Eleanor Foxall, a 38-year-old ambulance driver from Liverpool who was working with the LAAS. Her sorrowing parents buried her ten days later at their parish church in Heswall.

Oakman was on duty again in the morning and reported that the barrage was 'heavier' and there were fewer enemy bombs coming down on them. At 10pm she went off duty to find that her own home in the King's Road had been hit and the back of her house demolished. She retrieved a few of her possessions and went to spend the night with a colleague.

On Monday June was back in London and on duty at AS22.

> It was pouring with rain... On duty at 3. There was a raid on
> and had been for the last four hours. Consequently I found
> the others all very hungry. I went down the King's Road in
> search of food and stepped through the windows of the nearest
> cake shop (there seems to be no glass left anywhere) and looted
> the shop. Off duty 8 o'clock and so was able to choose my pitch
> on the floor in the hall with everybody.

> *Tuesday 17 September* Supper at 97. Bed at 9 o'clock. Slightly
> less night air activity. Terrific gun barrage at times. A spy
> had been shot for signalling from the top of the Lots Road
> power station.

If June's story about the spy on the roof was true, I have found no corroborating record of it. There was an epidemic of spy stories, especially after Churchill referred to the 'malignancy in our midst' in a Commons speech following the retreat from Dunkirk and the launch of a Ministry of Information campaign against gossip and rumour with messages such as 'Careless talk costs lives', 'Keep it under your hat' and 'Keep mum she's not so dumb'. Far-fetched theories about how spies might be communicating with the enemy proliferated. There was a groundless but widespread urban myth that enemy pilots—who flew at a height of 7.5km (4.7 miles)—could be directed towards targets by the lighted tip of a cigarette in the street or a flashing ARP torch.

That nervy edge, twitchiness about who was letting the side down or who was not entirely loyal, affected everyone. It even extended to AS22 where it had been discovered that cash had been disappearing from the 'kitty', the pool of money set aside for buying tea and biscuits. Who was the thief? There was a prime suspect, whose identity was spoken of in whispers, but it took months to catch the guilty party red-handed.

Wednesday 18 September Very good night's sleep. Off early to shop on bicycle between raids... Up to Oxford Street, which was in a mess. John Lewis had been completely gutted and was still burning. Bicycled for two hours round Bloomsbury in order to get to Regent's Street. All roads blocked by fallen houses and every road was covered with broken glass. The BBC [in nearby Portland Place] was still standing, being the obvious objective.

Back to tea with Esther Darlington. It was her birthday and drinks with her taken in her room. On duty at 8. Night in the office with Daphne Catt and Sgt Roberts. Very many incendiary bombs dropped all around garage in streets, which we dealt with as the wardens seemed to leave it to us. One man was badly burnt. He said, 'I was at Dunkirk and this is much worse.'

The West End was not bombed in the way the East End was—it had no industrial base—but it was a target because it was the site of numerous government offices and of Broadcasting House.

Oxford Street had 'caught it' in the early hours of Wednesday; five department stores were severely damaged. John Lewis got the worst of it. An oil bomb had scattered burning oil and petrol, and although the two hundred people sheltering in the basement survived, three firemen died when another high-explosive bomb fell. Thirty fire crews battled the flames, which were whipped up by winds and took a week to fully extinguish.

Some people resented the publicity given to damage in the West End. Barbara Nixon, the Finsbury ARP warden, viewed the gossip about it as tactless—'Have you seen Lewis's? Isn't it terrible?'—as few had died and it implied the suffering of ordinary people in residential areas was less important. For most, however, John Lewis became another symbol of London's fortitude. The editors of the store's in-house magazine expressed their tenacity with a burst of declamatory mock-heroics: 'We shall defend our partnership with the utmost energy. What matter if we are bombed out of John Lewis? We shall fight on at Peter Jones!'[21] The staff set up trestle tables on the pavement and sold off smoke-damaged goods, the naked girders of the building and piles of debris standing forlornly behind them.

The first phase of the Battle of London lasted for fifty-seven consecutive nights. The relentless bombing, from October almost exclusively after dark, took its toll on spirits, but the numbers of dead and injured were not on the scale originally predicted. One report by psychiatrists forecast that millions of people would be affected on some level by neurosis and panic, that hospitals would be overrun with patients suffering a version of shellshock, that populations would flee cities in fear. That psychological holocaust did not come to pass. This is not to say that people were not terrified. A friend has told me that his mother's abiding childhood memory of taking cover in the family Anderson shelter was the smell of urine from her mother wetting herself. For most,

21. Quoted in Bell, *London Was Ours*, p.42.

however, the strain of being under attack manifested itself more quietly, in symptoms of anxiety and depression: eating disorders, short temper, sleeplessness, trembling, tics and weeping.

Fatalism ('I thought the bomb had my name on it') and superstition ('Bombs don't strike the same place twice') were pervasive and, while Londoners continued to appear cheerful, their volubility sometimes took on a heightened intensity. Many on the home front line felt a physical need to shed their anxieties, and it was this that drove June and her friends and thousands like them into the West End for nights of manic dancing and drinking.

Like Wolves

Monday 23 September 1940 On duty at 7am. One or two raids but we did not go to the shelters. Lovely sunny autumn day. Came off duty at 2. I met Margarita[1] and boyfriend Frank who squashed me into their car and took me for a drink. Back to 97. John Perfect [June's medical student friend] arrived and after tea we went up to the West End to have drinks at the Ritz which was fairly full, mostly French. A few debs.

We went over to the Berkeley which was quite empty and then down to The May Fair to book a table... We dined and danced in the raid shelter below until 1.30. Then we came up to the ground and found the gunfire very heavy outside. So we stayed there [at The May Fair] with an amazing collection of people who looked as though they spent most of the night on the sofas there... The gunfire was still too heavy to venture out without tin hats.

FOR YOUNG PEOPLE particularly, parties, dancing, laughter, food and drinking with friends and strangers were an affirmation that they were alive and had a future. As Chelsea teenager Joan Wyndham put it: 'I can't help feeling that each moment may be my last, and as the opposite of death is life, I think I shall get seduced by Rupert tomorrow.' Frances Faviell, the Chelsea Red Cross worker, said the Blitz made her 'long for a party—for a bit of fun. "Let's go out!" we would suddenly decide.'[2]

June found that intensity of experience in the hotels and clubs of the West End, where she rubbed shoulders with military

---

1. Margarita Lucy Whidborne (1895–1951), later Wharton, a fellow resident of Lindsey House.
2. Wyndham, pp.143-44; Faviell, p.194.

attachés, diplomats, bombed-out aristos, journalists, prostitutes and politicians. The luxuriously appointed May Fair Hotel, tucked behind Berkeley Street, had been the site of many a debutante ball. She and John Perfect would have eaten well in the restaurant—*The Bystander* magazine praised the food as 'very good indeed'[3]—and the nightclub in the lower ballroom doubled as a deep-level shelter. Here, protected from the destruction above, they danced to peroxide blonde New Yorker Evelyn Dall[4] singing with Ambrose and his Orchestra.

The band music of Bert Ambrose,[5] who was born Benjamin Baruch Ambrose, a Jew, in the East End, had a broad appeal and was loved as much by working-class families gathered around the wireless as by the wealthy clientele at The May Fair. Not all Jews were so well-regarded. Two years after the first wave of refugees fleeing Nazism in Austria, Czechoslovakia and Poland landed in London, anti-Jewish feeling was running high. While it was generally accepted that Jews would be anxious about their future, given that little but the British home front now stood between them and the Nazis, they were the victims of both overt and underhand antisemitism. There were tensions in the public shelters of the East End, with Jews being accused of grabbing places early in the day. George Orwell wrote of a 'fearful Jewish woman, a regular comic-paper cartoon of a Jewess' in the Underground at Oxford Circus, who fought her way off the train during a raid and 'landed blows on anyone who stood in her way'. 'What is bad about Jews is that they are not only conspicuous, but go out of their way to make themselves so,' he complained.[6] Antisemitism spanned a seam from the bottom to the very top of society and politically from left to right.

Orwell's was an attitude shared by one of June's admirers, 'Buzz' Lloyd, an army engineer who had proposed marriage to her

3. *The Bystander*, 18 Sep 1940, 32B.
4. Evelyn Dall, born Evelyn Mildred Fuss (1918–2010).
5. Benjamin Baruch Ambrose (1896—1971).
6. *Orwell Diaries 1938–1942*, 25 Oct 1940:
orwelldiaries.wordpress.com/2010/10/25/25-10-40/

in 1938. 'The boat coming back [from Italy to Shimla in India] was packed with German Jewish refugees—900 of them,' he wrote to her in the summer of 1939. 'They are allowed their passage money and a credit of 500 lira each on the boat which must be spent on board... My German journalist [an acquaintance] thought it all a great joke, so it is of course if you have a sense of humour. I must say I cannot blame the Germans for wanting to get rid of them.'

How did June feel about this? She mentioned Jews sporadically in her wartime diaries but was never hostile and did not express the routine antisemitism that many considered socially acceptable at the time. She certainly knew people of Jewish heritage, including Lisel Raikes (possibly) from Hertfordshire and Fred Oppé, who lodged at Lindsey House, and his family, and regarded them as friends. She also dropped an intriguing sentence into her diary for 8 October 1940: 'Off to work at Bloomsbury House.' This building in Great Russell Street was home to a number of Jewish aid organisations working under the umbrella of the Central Office for Refugees. We can only guess at what she was doing there—fundraising or applying for a job perhaps—but whatever it was, it might indicate that she would have objected strongly to Lloyd's sentiments. It could be significant that in her diary for 14 May 1940 she merely minuted that Buzz had phoned her and never wrote of him again.

Tuesday 24 September Bathed and breakfasted at The May Fair after air raid. Then out to the bank and back to Cheyne Walk before lunch. Ric [Stewart-Jones] was there on leave for the night. We had coffee at the café before going on duty at 2. John Perfect called and we had a drink in the local with Pen [Gough]... Off duty at 7 to dinner at 75 Onslow Square with the Ames family.[7] Walked back from the station with Daphne Catt... Gunfire was terrific by 9.30 and the bombing was bad. Red glow over

7. Violet May Wallis (1894–1966), later Ames, and Blanche M. Ames (b. 1881) lived at 75 Onslow Square with Hazel H. Ames (1922–1999), later Van Overstraeten.

Chelsea. Rang 97 and found all was well so stayed the night in the basement on comfortable beds fitted out by various members of the household.

The cause of the 'red glow' was an intense shower of incendiary bombs. That night twenty-eight incidents were reported in Chelsea, including a fire at Peabody Buildings in Lawrence Street, where the whole top floor was set alight, and there were blazes at Harrod's Depository, Chelsea Polytechnic, Beaufort Mansions and Chelsea Library, where fifteen bombs fell. The ARP warden Jo Oakman watched as the back of the reference library caved in. It was a bad night, but there was worse to come.

Wednesday 25 September Very good night's sleep. But no one else seemed to have slept at all owing to the noise... I bid good morning to Pam and Mrs Ames and Hazel, who had just come off night duty at a hospital, and went home to 97. Got on a bus and the conductor refused to allow me to pay for my seat. 'It's an honour, Miss,' he said looking at my frightful uniform I still had on. Pretty flattering I thought.

Pen and John Perfect were still having breakfast. It was a glorious morning and there was still a lovely mist on the river. We climbed onto some boats in the moorings opposite and talked to some old subalterns. There was a raid and we watched the tiny puffs of smoke in the morning sunlight. We talked to a man whose boat had been gutted by an incendiary bomb. John Perfect and I went to the Antelope to drink Pimm's and lunch. Walked back to the ambulance station, on duty at 2. Lecture on childbirth. Off duty at 7pm. Lovely sunset. Found roses in my room. Supper and bed early in the hall.

Thursday 26 September Very good night's sleep. All-clear at 6am. As usual slept two hours in bedroom. After breakfast very busy in the house, doing odd little jobs and making skirt for Diona. Out on bicycle to shop. Two raids during morning. Up to

West Kensington... On duty at 7pm. Raid began little later than usual at 9. We were all in the sandbags again in the garage.

Friday 27 September Off duty at 7am. Unusually quiet night. No one went out. Came down to breakfast to find Tony Waterfield[8] still asleep in the dining room. News of 45 more survivors of the sunk liner on her way to Canada with children. They had been picked up in a lifeboat after 8 days at sea. To bed to try and sleep without success... and of course the sirens, 3 times ringing out like wolves and echoing in the houses down the river. I got up at 4... and walked down the King's Road to Sainsbury to get my rations for the weekend in the country. On duty 7.

The 'sunk liner' was the SS *City of Benares* which had been evacuating children to Canada and was torpedoed by a German U-boat at night amidst a terrible storm. The crew later claimed, plausibly, that they had not known that children were on board. The ship went down within half an hour, with many lives lost when the lifeboats were lowered jerkily, tipping their contents into the swirling seas. Among them was the artist and former Chelsea auxiliary ambulance driver Sybil Gilliat-Smith.[9] In all, fifty-one adult passengers and a hundred and twenty-two crew died. Of the ninety children aboard, seventy-seven died in the sinking.

June would eventually have been aware of Sybil's death, but did not mention it in her diaries. Perhaps, given that she had herself tried to volunteer to take children to Canada, it was a case of 'There but for the grace of God...'—too close. Sometimes the things a diarist leaves out are as significant as those she puts in.

June frequently wrote of sleep, whether she had a good night, when she took naps, where she slept. It was not an obsession but for her, as for many in London, it became a concern. Depriving

8. Anthony Henry Vanhurst Waterfield (1909–1983), in 1939 a civil servant in the Air Ministry.
9. Sybil Gilliat-Smith (1915–1940). See pages 43 and 85.

Time away from civil defence duties was treasured.
June (left) and friends relax at the back of Lindsey house.

Britain of rest was part of the Nazis' strategy. After the first intense daylight blitzes, the Luftwaffe shifted their energies to nighttime raids lasting ten or twelve hours. Londoners acclimatised quickly to their new routine—they knew when an attack was likely to start and how much to expect from the RAF and ground defences—but after the first two weeks most were suffering a paralysing tiredness. They began to ignore the daytime raids, as June often did, unless they knew the threat was on their doorstep.

Londoners learned how to catnap on buses, in armchairs, standing up or sitting on benches in dank shelters. Inez Holden noticed that extremes of tiredness could 'make an individual into another person, a half-conscious creature removed a little way from the things that were happening'.[10] Workers became robotic, too exhausted to feel either fear or empathy. Wherever they were, in their beds, hunkered down in shelters or under tables, they collapsed into sleep.

10. Holden, p.81.

This is not to say that people were not frightened. If they woke in the dark small hours, when enemy planes were close or overhead, their feelings of dread were magnified. As another London diarist, Olivia Cockett, put it, in August 1940, 'Because of my fear, sweat is extra stinking, needs much more cleaning up.' Cockett also noted her own jumpiness: 'My heart misses a beat whenever a car changes gear-up [sic], or when someone runs, or walks very quickly, or says "Sshh!" or whistles blow, or a door bangs in the wind or a mosquito buzzes in the room... Skin feels all puckered round bomb-crater eye sockets.'[11]

'Woke still in my own bed between sheets for the first time for a month,' June wrote on 7 October. It had been a relatively quiet night in Chelsea, but the coming day brought fresh drama. A huge unexploded bomb had dropped into the small green in front of 24 Cheyne Row, just by the statue of Thomas Carlyle, the nineteenth-century Scottish writer and polymath who had once lived there. According to Jo Oakman, who went to see the bomb in the afternoon, the pit it made was so clean 'it looked as if it has been cut out with an apple corer'. A team of Scottish Royal Engineers was working on it. They had constructed a pulley above the hole, started to excavate the space around the bomb and given it a nickname—Ernestine. She was now less a fearful conglomeration of metal and explosives and more an inconvenient interloper, female at that, needing simply to be deconstructed and taken away.

With the services making light of unexploded bombs, civilians could do nothing else than follow suit. It was a patriotic duty not to exhibit panic, distress and anger; only steadiness, forbearance and a willingness to pitch in were acceptable. Wry humour was fine. A photograph published in *The Sphere* showed the managing director of a engineering company calmly reading his correspondence seated in the front of a car while two female secretaries in the back bash at typewriters balanced on their knees. A handwritten sign announces that this is now 'Head

11. Cockett, pp.160-61.

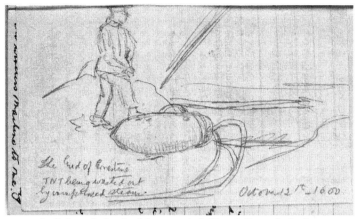

*Jo Oakman's sketch of the unexploded bomb 'Ernestine', after
its extraction by Scottish Royal Engineers from a hole in Cheyne Row.*

Office'. 'The London blitz produced a brand of humour of its own,'
wrote a correspondent in American *Vogue*, citing a sign outside
a sagging-roofed barber shop: 'Close shave, eh?' and a bombed-
out department store's hastily scribbled poster, 'You ought to see
our Berlin branch'.[12]

On the evening of 7 October June and Ann Channer were invited
to supper at 16 Montpelier Place in Knightsbridge with Geoffrey
Turner, a wine merchant, and his wife Jane. Ann had lodged
with them before she moved to Lindsey House. The Turners also
invited Paul Ziegler, a part-Jewish German-speaking refugee
from Prague who had arrived in England in 1938 with his older
brother Heinz.[13] The Zieglers were witty and intellectual—June
referred to Paul as The Philosopher—and both brothers had

12. 'After the Bomb Raids: The Spirit of the People—and Their Humour—
Is Unbroken'. *Sphere*, 3 May 1941, p.157A; Virginia Cowles, 'Humour—the
Bomb-Proof Kind', *Vogue* (US), Jan 1942, p.54A.
13. In 1939 Paul Gerhard Ziegler (1908–1986) and Heinz Otto Ziegler
(1903–1944) lived at 29 Montpelier Place, Knightsbridge, having left
Czechoslovakia the previous year.

reputations as determined 'ladies' men'. Heinz did not let the fact that he had a wife in Czechoslovakia impinge on his romantic pursuits in Britain; Paul was single, and this evening may have been the start of his affair with Ann. She was probably not aware that she was entering a complicated web of relationships and could not have predicted that these would be immortalised in a series of novels epitomising the wartime experience of the young upper-classes.

June ate well at the Turners'. Food and rations were on her mind and, for the first time in her diary, she listed exactly what she had been served: potatoes stuffed with liver sausage, beef mince with beans, tomato sauce and cheese, baked apples with raisins and sultanas, and thick black coffee and cream. She had forgotten to bring her steel helmet and, as the barrage was severe, she and Ann felt it would be safer to spend the night on the Turners' kitchen floor.

The next night in Chelsea was dreadful: incendiaries and high-explosives, one of which hit a paper mill and a timber yard, which burned on and off into the next day. The trees across the water in Battersea Park were ablaze and the sky glowed red with shooting flames. The river looked as if it were on fire.

Meanwhile, the sappers were still at work on Ernestine. Jo Oakman went to see how things were progressing and took them tea on a tray. June turned up in the afternoon.

Friday 11 October On duty 7. Stumbled out in the darkness over the chaotic figures in the hall... Off [at] 2. Walked along the embankment under barriers to look at time bomb under [Thomas] Carlyle's statue. Royal Engineers were working on it. They pulled me over the fence to have a look. It was 20 feet down, 600 pounds [272kg]—a soldier was sitting on it and another was swinging over the hole on a rope.

The team washed out the TNT with compressed steam, dismantled the cone and shell and handed out shards of the outerwork to spectators like favours at the end of a party, before loading the remains onto a lorry and hauling them away. It had taken four days to dig Ernestine out.

> Back to 97. Changed. Met Philip James[14] in the West End.
> Dinner at Ritz. Rather empty. Piccadilly out of action. Bad Blitz.
> On to Mayfair... We wandered out at 2am [and] I managed to
> get a taxi. We drove in the blitz through red lights...

❖

On the night of the 15th a full moon, so beloved of pilots, shone over London. In a clear sky, the cityscape was pointed up even before the Luftwaffe dropped their incendiaries. To June, who was not on duty, it seemed a good time to spend the night away from London. As the attacks from the air intensified, she increasingly felt the need for respite and diversion. Ric Stewart-Jones's sister Di had offered her the use of her car for an overnight visit to Hertfordshire—driving would be easier than navigating the packed trains and buses. All June had to do was fill it with petrol; she had no choice but to acquire that on the black market.

> Very bad night. Time bomb on bridge. Bad damage on Milner
> Street. Down to the garage at 7.30 to get petrol. Mac gave me a
> note which I took to a friend of his in a mews. The friend, looking
> very nervous, beckoned me to a nearby garage, then gave me a
> dirty bit of paper. He appeared again at the filling station and
> came out to give me petrol. I handed back the dirty bit of paper
> and was filled up. Guns were firing hard so I hurried back.

The sale of petrol was restricted in the days after war was declared and only registered owners were entitled to buy it. All private motor owners were issued a basic monthly ration and, although they were allowed to apply for extra if they could prove their need was essential, they could not roll over unused coupons. Branded petrol disappeared, replaced by 'pool', which was

14. Possibly Philip S. James (1914–2001), a barrister living in Pembroke Road, Kensington.

dyed red. Illegal hoarding was rife, with people keeping petrol in containers in sheds and workshops and even in the boots of cars. Car sharing and hitchhiking were encouraged—June herself 'lorry-hopped' from Hertfordshire to Cambridge and London several times. As the war went on, petrol rationing became more severe. In March 1942 it was announced that the basic civilian ration would be withdrawn for all vehicles and that fuel would only be available to those on official business.

While June was away at Odsey, the blitz in Chelsea was particularly bad. A few streets away from Cheyne Walk, Joan Wyndham made no bones about it: 'This is certainly hell and no mistake. Hardly a minute's pause between each load of bombs and each one sounding as if it's going to hit our house. Gosh, it's awful; this is the heaviest bombing we've had since the war began, the absolute poetry of destruction.'[15] There were fifty reported incidents in Chelsea including a big fire in the Carlyle Laundry on Cheyne Walk, an oil bomb at Sloane Gardens, two high-explosives in Riley Street, and an incendiary fire at June's ambulance station. In Westminster bombs hit St James's Church in Piccadilly, the Carlton Club in Pall Mall and the garden at the Treasury. At 12 Lowndes Street, five doors down from the flat where June had stayed before moving to Lindsey House, while bombers circled above and a flaming gas main lit the scene, two ARP wardens scaled a lead waterpipe and, using knotted-together sheets they had found in wrecked rooms, rescued a woman trapped on the second floor.[16]

There was no let-up. Three days later, now back in London, June wrote: 'We went to go out [to the West End] but the raiding was fierce. We had supper—and all to bed in hall.' It was one of the few times that the blitz completely ruined her plans. It was also having an impact on her health. Always slender, she was now thin. 'To Chelsea Old Church with Esther. Service interrupted twice by raids. My knickers came down. Esther whisked me behind organ and took them off,' she wrote on 20 October.

15. Wyndham, p.171.
16. Sansom, p.59.

In late October June took a bus to Tewkesbury to try to recapture the peace she found there the previous winter. She found Canon Gough playing with his model boats. 'So amazingly peaceful. No warnings ever,' she wrote after reaching this refuge. 'One can't believe the windows have real glass in them.' While she was away, four high-explosive bombs fell on the area around Shawfield Street, a fifteen-minute walk from Lindsey House. The ARP stretcher party driver Irene Haslewood[17] was among the first to arrive and found half the street demolished. Fourteen people died, according to Haslewood, one of them because air raid wardens were quarrelling at the control post and were late in calling out the ambulances.

Chelsea had been quiet on the night of 2–3 November, the first time London had not been raided since 7 September, and the following night too. Of course, it was not to last.

17. See footnote page 88.

Searching for Escape

Sunday 10 November 1940 Neville Chamberlain died in the night. Great earthquake in Romania. Walked in the sun in Kensington and Holland House Gardens with Esther Darlington. Very few English people about... Ambulance station at 2... We all went to sherry at Montpelier Place [to see the Ziegler brothers]. Out to dinner in the blitz. While we were sheltering and dining in The Piccadilly,[1] a bomb landed in Piccadilly. We walked around the Circus climbing over enormous boulders until we found two craters. Back in the moonlight.

Monday 11 November On duty eight. Very wet. Off duty 2. Worked in my room. Tea with Nanny and Jim [Lees-Milne] and shopping in the rain, cold. Supper. All-clear at 9.30, in bed, in the real bed.

Tuesday 12 November On duty 8. Filthy. Off at 2. With effort changed and out to shops. Tea with Honor Waterfield[2] in Cheyne Row. Tony [Waterfield] came and we walked back to supper at 97... [John] Crocker came in from the ambulance station.

12 NOVEMBER WAS another bad night for Chelsea. A high-explosive bomb weighing over 900kg (2,000 lbs) fell on the rear carriage of a train as it was leaving Sloane Square Tube station. The blast from the bomb was sent along the underground tunnel rather than up to the surface, propelling the rest of the train almost to the next station. In her memoirs, the Red Cross nurse

1. A luxury hotel spanning Regent's Street and Piccadilly.
2. Honor Mary Waterfield (1911–1989), née Northen, married to Tony Waterfield. See footnote page 116.

Frances Faviell recalled the scene that greeted her: the ground strewn with glass, flaming jets from a gas main that had cracked in the explosion, and the 'ultra-modern newly designed Peter Jones building [standing] proudly without a pane of its acres of glass broken.'[3] Body parts were being put on stretchers and taken to nearby houses, to be assembled later. Of the thirty-seven people who died, at least sixteen were London Transport staff; seventy-nine people were injured.

From 14 November the Luftwaffe started directing their attentions outside the capital. They demolished Coventry city centre first, and although they returned to London on the 15th, the blitz in Chelsea eased enough for June and Ann to feel it was safe to sleep in June's room on the fourth floor rather than downstairs in the hall with Nanny Sams. However, in that 'winter of bombs' a respite, perceived or real, could not be relied upon. How could you know what would suddenly come your way? June and Ann's interlude upstairs was delicious but after only two nights they returned to the throng.

During the day, respite or not, Lindsey House buzzed with preparations for Diona Stewart-Jones's wedding to Patrick Granville Murray, a major in the Royal Artillery.[4] Di's mother Eva was up from Lewes and her brother Edward, who was working as a metallurgist, a protected profession, had also arrived. Ric was home on leave from the merchant navy. Jim Lees-Milne, still recovering from an encounter with a bomb in Hyde Park Square a few weeks previously, was there too. The blast had flung him into some iron railings and although he managed to recover enough to get back to his platoon in Brighton the next day, he subsequently collapsed and was in and out of hospital for the next ten months.[5] Eventually he was diagnosed with a form of epilepsy and discharged from the army.

3. Faviell, pp.161-2.
4. Patrick Granville Murray (1910–1990), the son of a tea broker. In the 1939 Register he was listed as the Secretary of the Anglo French Art and Travel Society and later was appointed head of the British Council in Scotland.
5. Lees-Milne, *Another Self*, p.164.

Saturday 23 November Nice service. The choir consisted of
mainly Cheyne Walk past and present. Pen [Gough] arrived in
the middle in uniform from Coventry where she had been with
her mobile canteen. On to reception in the ballroom... Diona
looking lovely. Saw Di and Patrick away and then all to tea with
the Waterfields. Very cosy party. More arrived for drinks and
Tony Waterfield and I went to Daphne Catt's 21st birthday party
at Cranmere Court. On to Le Suivi with an odd collection, where
we danced until 4.

Only family and 'Cheyne people' were invited to the wedding,
which was held at the Old Church, but there were so many guests
that it was full to bursting. June thought Di looked 'ecstatically
happy' but Ric wrote later that he was worried that his sister
was so elated as she walked up the aisle on Edward's arm that
she would break into 'unseemly laughter'.[6] What most did not
realise was that behind Di's hyper-happiness lay real anxieties,
for her new husband's fate, of course, but also for her new
responsibilities. While Ric was away, she was to take over the
running of Lindsey House. At times it was a heavy load, even with
the support of Nanny Sams. Her duties included scheduling the
ceaseless arrival and departure of boarders whose lives revolved
around the demands of wartime service of one kind or another,
managing the Joes and the other domestic staff, and dealing with
the endless bomb damage to Lindsey House, which was in a poor
state to start with.

June had her own preoccupations. Romantically unattached,
bored by shifts at the ambulance station, which were, in that fatal
combination, both tedious and important, she was yearning for
something to change. While she cast about for a new direction, she
and her friend Gill Gambier-Parry started to plan a fundraising
dance in the ballroom at No. 96, with the proceeds going to the
FAU (Friends Ambulance Unit), for which her friend Pen Gough's
brother John was a supervisor in a 'model' air-raid shelter under

6. Pulford, p.50.

the Lloyds building in the City.[7] 'Broadcast by John G[ough] from his part of the shelter under Lloyds. Very amusing,' wrote June on 8 December after listening to a BBC radio report on it. Ric also heard it. 'Johnny Gough has sprung to fame for running the most efficient shelter in London. It is remarkable the way the "Quakers" have once again stepped in at the most crucial time and are in terrific demand having gone through a hellish time of tribunals and mud-slinging as conscientious objectors,' he wrote to his sister Elizabeth.[8]

On Saturday 30 November, on returning to Lindsey House from the ambulance station, June found a large hole in her bedroom ceiling, 'with daylight and fog streaming through', and other windows in the house blown out. While Nanny Sams and Di organised repairs, June took herself off to Sloane Square to shop, but that proved no less perilous. Although the Luftwaffe preferred to bomb at night, they were still sometimes raiding during the daytime.

Bomb missed bus by yards coming down Sloane Street. Got to Peter Jones and was whisked to cellar... At last was able to complete shopping and home by 11am. Worked hard in my room with workmen and Nanny working inside and out on the hole and cleaning up the mess. Finished black dress by teatime. Thick fog outside and no taxis owing to blitz. Jim [Lees-Milne] and I braved the fog together and eventually got taxi. Arriving late to dine at the Lansdowne... Tim Clayton band very good. Then on to Le Suivi. Very full... No possible chance of a taxi back as fog too thick. Lady Caroline Howard[9] offered her car but found more convenient to go back to The Dorchester... After one more attempt got a taxi to accept Cheyne Walk. Back by 1am. Very cold.

7. The FAU, first set up during the First World War, was re-established in 1940 and staffed by young people who were either Quakers or shared their pacifist views on war service. See 'From Coventry to the Burma Road', *The Manchester Guardian*, 15 Jan 1942, 3D.
8. Pulford, p.51.
9. Ankaret Cecilia Caroline, Lady Howard (1900–1945), later Jackson, a barrister.

Sunday 1 December Ann and I up just in time for breakfast at 10. Out for long walk at 12. Very cold so we lunched in Brompton Road. Walked through Hyde Park... Bought cakes for tea which we ate before we got home. Gill and Ann Gambier-Parry arrived for tea in our room and we all discussed [the] dance. They were very sweet. On duty at 6. A strange shift. Marcelle Ferguson, a newcomer, drank Burgundy in the office where Ackroyd... told my fortune in cards.[10] Very funny... I must beware on Thursdays... Very tired, bed. The men tucked me up in their end of the shelter and then forgot about me.

June reached for the reassurance of a fortune-teller several times during the war. In August 1941 she went as far as to pay £10, five times her weekly wage, for a card-reading by a Mrs Wright ('wild Norfolk... stinking to high heaven'). Just as in the First World War, when no one could be sure in which direction the world would go or even whether they would survive, many people craved certainty and hoped that someone with 'the gift' could provide it. Astrology, looking to the stars for help navigating through a thick wolf-infested wood, gained a huge following.

Although nothing came of the plans for an FAU ball, June later became the driving force behind other fundraising parties at Lindsey House. These were opportunities to use her social nous to create something she could take pride in to benefit others, but they were big, intrusive events and contained a tripwire—the feelings of Diona, jealously guarded by Nanny Sams.

Saturday 7 December Up late. Worked all the afternoon in the studio. On duty 6. In the office all evening. No warning at all. Though quiet, was too sinister and strange. Bed in dugout.

Sunday 8 December Off duty at 8. Back in the dusk to a late-sleeping house. Laid a fire in my room. Bathed. Down

10. Ferguson and Ackroyd are unidentified.

to breakfast to find Ric [Stewart-Jones] had come back. Worked in my room, with Esther, Ric and Di inspecting the holes in the roof. On duty 6. In the office, extremely noisy night. Slept to make up for previous night. Many planes over all the time, many large fires started. The sky scarlet. Many telephone enquiries but no ambulances out.

The attack on London on the night on 8 December, which was delivered by some three to four hundred bombers, was particularly severe. The Luftwaffe dropped over three hundred and eighty tons of high-explosive bombs and at least three thousand incendiaries, eight times more than on 7 September, the day the Blitz 'started'. Chelsea escaped relatively lightly, with six high-explosive bombs falling in the borough and only one fatality, but across London about two hundred people were killed and six hundred seriously injured. A parachute mine fell on BBC HQ in Portland Place, killing a policeman and injuring passers-by. In Bermondsey scores died when a shelter in the foot tunnels of a railway arch took a direct hit. Eight firemen, seven of them auxiliaries, perished when their substation at Gainsborough Road School in West Ham was hit.

One might assume that people lost hope after such an exceptionally ferocious raid. In that long, dark December there were also massive bombing raids on Liverpool, Southampton, Bristol and Birmingham. Hungary, Romania and the Slovak Republic had joined the Tripartite Pact with Germany, Italy and Japan, so for those on the home front it felt that, even with the power and might of the British Empire behind them, they were facing the struggle isolated and alone. Although individuals may have felt new levels of fear and despair, outwardly most managed to go on as normal. The government was keen for everyday life to continue, as far as possible. Society events, and the brave faces that attended them, were seen as part of that effort.

June planned to go to the Blitz Ball at the Grosvenor on Park Lane on Saturday 14th, which was held to raise money for Queen Charlotte's Hospital's maternity care of servicemen's wives. It was the first big evening charity event for months, and, unusually for

*June regarded Ann Channer (left) as her greatest friend and support,
and was devastated when she was posted abroad.*

June, she had no partner—'frantically searching,' she wrote. As luck would have it, her brother David, on leave from his Officer Training, turned up unexpectedly at Lindsey House.

> On duty 8. Off at 2. Ann [Channer] to Cheshire... Drinks back at 97. Bathed. Supper... We changed and off to Grosvenor House for the Queen Charlotte's Blitz Ball. Amazing crowd of mixed foreigners and long-forgotten people, almost unrecognisable. Back to bed at 1... No warning!

June must have given some thought to her coming out three years earlier and the night in that grand underground ballroom when, dressed in their court gowns, crowds of young women curtseyed to a cake. The Blitz Ball was much more fun, with nurses in uniform taking part in a hobby-horse race, scads of Canadian officers and an atmosphere of jolly informality.

As 1940 neared its end, June's diary entries became very brief. She noted that the ambulances at AS22 were at last being painted grey and listed some of the other social events she attended: a dinner given by the 2nd Battalion of the Irish Guards and carol singing with the ARP wardens. Her plans to go to Odsey Corner on Christmas Day after a night shift were scuppered when she missed the only train. There was nothing for it but to return to Lindsey House, where she joined Di and her mother for the service at Chelsea Old Church. It was a dismal evening.

❖

Sunday 29 December On duty 8am. Very cold. Off at 2.
Tea with the Gambier-Parrys. The Blitz began at 6, and I
stayed to supper. Very heavy firing and signs of bad fires,
so down to the basement...

While June was sheltering with her friends, a hundred and thirty-six German attackers dropped thousands of incendiaries on the City, the ancient symbol of London's strength and prestige, and fire was spreading from rooftop to rooftop. A second wave of bombers arrived, bringing a conflagration beyond anything London had ever seen. The wind picked up and fanned the flames, whipping up a firestorm. The Germans had timed the raid to coincide with low tide in the Thames, knowing that this would make it difficult for firefighters to bring up water; then a bomb struck the principal water main, further hampering their efforts. The inferno came to be known as the Second Great Fire of London. A third wave of bombing by the Germans was cancelled only because the weather had deteriorated.

From her roof in Notting Hill, Vere Hodgson watched the fire in the east: 'At Shepherd's Bush [in the west] flames were leaping and towards the City they were gigantic. A great red glow filled the sky—I had no need of a torch—I could see every step I took and could have read a book if I had wished.'[11] In nearby Chelsea, where no bombs fell that night, Joan Wyndham was awestruck but energised by the sight she took in from the steps of her house. 'The aeroplanes never stopped and the sound of their engines

11. Hodgson, p.100.

dive-bombing was deafening,' she wrote. 'The sky was already red as blood—it looked as if half London was on fire. Flares lit up the street like daylight and the stars were all put out.'[12] June, by contrast, was weary and unable to take in the enormity of what was happening. She could not get home that night and stayed with the Gambier-Parrys.

The next morning, the dawn glowed with shades of scarlet, the fires visible for miles. City workers picked their way through alleyways and cut-throughs, stepping over fire hoses, broken glass and rubble, while firemen, filthy from their toil, tried to extinguish the flames. A hundred thousand bombs had fallen, the majority of them incendiaries igniting unoccupied buildings, where they burned freely.

Five hours of bombing had destroyed the historic heart of the City, which was more vulnerable than other parts of London because it had few residents to firewatch. Entire streets were obliterated. Thirty-one guild halls and nineteen churches, including St Lawrence Jewry and St Andrew by the Wardrobe, were razed. Twenty-eight bombs fell on St Paul's or in the vicinity, and the vulnerability of the cathedral prompted Churchill to hand down the order that it was to be saved 'at all costs'. Paternoster Row and Ave Maria Lane, the centre of the publishing and book trade, were destroyed, as was Stationers Hall. A hundred and sixty civilians died during the raid, and many more succumbed later. The dead included fourteen firefighters. Once again, many people feared that the inferno was the prelude to an invasion.

The Home Secretary, Herbert Morrison, blaming the damage on 'slackers' who could not be trusted to protect their own premises, ordered men aged 16 to 60 to firewatch for forty-eight hours a month; this was later extended to women. Businesses were to be guarded and have firefighting equipment available. There were new arrangements for water supplies: static water tanks were built into basements. The ATS was strengthened with a draft of women, among them June's friend Ann Channer, then working

12. Wyndham, p.212.

at the Foreign Office, whose task was to pinpoint enemy planes, although as a woman she was not allowed to fire the guns herself.

> *Tuesday 31 December* On duty 6. New Year's Eve. Cherry brandy in the Black Lion.[13] Spent the evening in the office with Millie and Daphne [Mulholland][14]... Two wardens came to visit me and Daphne at the wardens' post at 12. Daph feeling ill so I went with Gabriel the Egyptian [a fellow auxiliary] to the warden post in Cook's Ground school, drank hot rum and saw the New Year in with 30 wardens, all very merry. Gabriel filled my pockets with nuts and raisins and stole a bottle or two and we passed back to the station office to celebrate there. Roly Poly Dudley[15] and a gang of wardens arrived to wish us a happy year. I went to sleep in the dugout. There were no raids all night.

Ten days of relative peace in London followed, interrupted on 4 January 1941 by the sound of distant explosions—engineers were demolishing damaged buildings in the City. Other British cities were now bearing the brunt of the bombing but on the 11th the lull in London was over. Fifty-one people died when a high-explosive bomb destroyed Bank Underground station, blowing people on to the live rails and creating a crater so wide that in the following days Royal Engineers had to build a temporary bridge across it to allow traffic through. In Chelsea, a mass of incendiaries fell in a swathe through the centre of the borough, including on the ambulance station in the King's Road.

In the ensuing days, Chelsea ARP warden Jo Oakman noted the sporadic bursts of gunfire from the AA guns and the bright flash of incendiaries dropping. It was nothing like the attacks of the autumn but there was no guarantee that the relative respite would last.

13. The Black Lion, on the corner of Old Church Street and Paultons Square.
14. Probably Mary Wynne Jacob, later Balfour, later Bell (1908–1996). Daphne Norah Mulholland (1915–1983), later Ward. See also page 101.
15. Gabriel the Egyptian and Roly-Poly Dudley are unidentified.

June's frenetic social life—she was taking every opportunity to dance, dine and drink—was taking a toll. Her diary entries indicate the hectic pace of her life. A typical diary entry: an oyster and Champagne party in West Byfleet in Surrey attended by a 'vast crowd' of people, followed by a dash back to London for dancing at The 400 club, reaching her bed at 4am, to be woken by Nanny Sams for her 7.30am shift, after which it was up to Grosvenor House, where she 'danced once or twice', then headed back to No. 97 for dinner. When an ambulance service friend, called to take her to the ballet, 'he looked at me once and said I don't mind if you don't come.' She spent a quiet, if busy, evening writing letters, visiting friends for tea, sewing and listening to the news on the radio. This gave her a surge of hope: British and Australian forces had captured Bardia in Italy and taken thirty thousand prisoners. There was good news from the Libyan front too, but the continued refusal of the Americans to join the war was disappointing.

A break in the bombing meant there were fewer incidents to attend. Maintenance of the vehicles and equipment always had the highest priority no matter how busy the crews were but now there was time for long overdue jobs such as sourcing spare parts for the ambulances and recruiting new members. These tasks may have kept the crews occupied but they disguised a serious problem when bombs were not dropping: boredom. With all the work completed, there was nothing much to do. For June, who liked to fill her days with activity, the idleness was torture.

The restlessness she was feeling before she volunteered for the ambulance service resurfaced. Then she and Daphne Catt had a brainwave. They had seen an advertisement appealing for candidates to join a contingent of women drivers to be sent to Albania with ambulances donated by Americans. On 20 January they arranged to see Alison Tennant,[16] of the Motor Transport Corps, who was organising the expedition. It was worth a shot, but after June and Daphne ran through the rain and arrived wet and bedraggled for the interview they failed to hit it off with Tennant.

16 Alison Tennant (1903–1986), later Reece.

'Nearly resulted in bad giggles,' wrote June. And, in any case, 'the whole affair seemed a social ramp.' This was probably an accurate assessment and was borne out by a photograph later published in the society pages of *The Sketch* showing a male commanding officer and the eleven posh women who were eventually chosen, only one of whom could speak Greek. A few weeks later Ann Channer gave June 'rather an amusing bit of news'. She had learned at the Foreign Office that the ambulance unit had not been allowed to go as 'it would be too tough out there by then'.[17]

The rest of January and most of February was quiet in Chelsea—nothing more than a few incendiaries fell—but that changed on 19 February. German pilots started aiming more obviously at nearby bridges as well as at Lots Road power station and at Battersea power station across the river. Although they all missed their targets, St Stephen's Hospital in Fulham Road was hit. Twenty people died and fifty-four were injured, and there were also bombs in Limerston Street, Cheyne Hospital and the King's Road. June noted that the AA guns were very noisy and that, when she got back to No. 97 from a cocktail party, a few bombs had landed quite close, but she was not yet aware that Paultons Square had taken a high-explosive bomb, as had Danvers Street.

> *Thursday 20 February 1941* Breakfast 9.30. Very cold.
> Jo [Ainsworth] came in and said a bomb had hit my ambulance station. We went round by the garage to see. Found bomb crater only in the street. Two houses on the other side demolished and part of the King's Road cut off. I shopped with... Janet [her sister] went off to lunch with Daddy and interview. Walked back to Cheyne, stopping for lunch on the way. Got down to some sewing.

'All the windows had been blown out in Danvers Street,' wrote June the next day. 'They had already been replaced by a thick

17. *Daily Boston Globe*, 14 Feb 1941, p.17E; *The Times*, 14 Feb 1941, p.5F; *The Sketch*, 26 Feb 1941, p.271.

kind of cellophane. The house next to the ambulance station was badly damaged.' The bomb had had another effect. It confirmed the identity of the ambulance station thief. 'While the bombs were falling, Morris... who somehow never had been caught red-handed, had surpassed himself by yelling "Gas!",' she wrote.[18] 'While the other men who had been playing cards with him put their masks on, Morris grabbed the kitty and everything else he thought worthwhile.' It was a minor diversion—Morris was doubtless sacked from the service—and June thought nothing much of it. Months later she was surprised to learn that Morris had not been the only one in the frame for the spate of thefts.

The pace of the war on the home front was changing but it was impossible to predict what would come next. Despite the closeness of the bombs and the camaraderie of the shifts, June remained unsettled. Her application to join the Albania expedition showed, if nothing else, that she needed something new in her life. Little did she know that her world was about to expand in two contrasting directions.

18. Morris has not been identified.

Beautiful Dolls

Friday 28 February 1941 Met Daphne [Catt] at Fortnum's at 11... We went off to *Vogue* feeling very brave, hoping to be used as models. Called my condolences to Harry... Walked across the park to lunch with Ann [Channer] at Queen Anne's Gate at PEP. A lovely house, lunch in the club at the amusing large family luncheon table, with Edward Warner and Charlotte [Waterlow], Kenneth Lindsay MP, Ann's boss. Looking rather rough. Ann rather pink due to my tactless enquiries I am afraid. Met Mike Streatfeild.[1] Tea with Honor [Waterfield] in Cheyne Row. Back to Cheyne Walk. Bed early. Patience and Ann had coffee chez moi...

STEPPING INTO THE offices of *Vogue* magazine in Old Bond Street took some courage. June was well aware that she was good-looking and she was accustomed to the attention that came with that, but volunteering yourself for inspection by Britain's foremost fashion magazine with the possibility of being found wanting was brave. She and Daphne Catt passed the first hurdle and a few days later they were called back to be photographed in the studios. The interlude provided a much-needed lift to her spirits. 'Rather thrilled with the afternoon,' she wrote.

Like other women's magazines of the time, *Vogue* encouraged its female readers to retain their obligation to glamour, to combine what was seen as their innate vanity with their new, more masculine roles in the services, civil defence and manufacturing. As influential women they had a duty, to themselves and to public morale, to be properly coiffed and manicured whether they were

1. Kenneth Martin Lindsay (1897–1991), MP for Kilmarnock between 1933 and 1945; Eric Michael Streatfeild (1903–1988), a banker and part-time volunteer with the Auxiliary Fire Service, a friend of June's from Hertfordshire.

in an air raid shelter, working a shift in a bomb factory or hosting a drinks party. If they were not actively serving the country, their consumption of beauty products was a valuable contribution to the economy—although that thinking was to change later in the war, when women were encouraged to 'Make Do and Mend'.

Vogue published tips on growing your own vegetables and cooking meals, more essential now that servants had left to join the services or work in essential industries. It also looked seriously at the world. In 1940, with its American editor stranded on the other side of the Atlantic, the British edition had a new woman at the top. Audrey Withers[2] was an Oxford graduate and Labour voter, who took *Vogue* in new, progressive directions, commissioning pieces on subjects she thought would interest intelligent, sophisticated women. She famously hired Lee Miller, US *Vogue*'s fashion-model-turned-photographer, to supply reportage on the war in Europe.

Vogue's political stance was probably not what propelled June and Daphne into its offices, which is not to say that June was uninterested in the world and its future. Almost as if to prove this point, when her test was over, June went on to an informal 'club' lunch at Political and Economic Planning (PEP), which was based in an eighteenth-century terrace house near St James's Park. The invitation did not arrive out of the blue—Ann Channer, in addition to working at the Foreign Office, acted as secretary.

PEP, which later became the Policy Studies Institute, was established in 1930 and aimed to formulate policy on the future of social services, health, the press and housing in Britain. The outbreak of war was seen by many as an opportunity to build something better, a Christian democracy with regard for human rights and the control of profits, with safeguards for the welfare of all parts of society. The group's founding members included the biologist and internationalist (and eugenicist) Julian Huxley and Dorothy and Leonard Elmhirst, who had set up the progressive school Dartington Hall at Totnes in Devon in 1926, and PEP's

2. Audrey Withers (1905–2001), editor of *Vogue* between 1940 and 1960.

events were attended by Israel Sieff, Max Nicholson and Ann's boss at the Foreign Office, the National Labour MP for Kilmarnock Kenneth Lindsay, and other journalists, civil servants, economists, businessmen and academics. Charlotte Waterlow, June's fellow lodger at 97 Cheyne Walk, who now worked at the Foreign Office, became a full member in 1942.[3]

Why did June start attending these lunches? She had not previously expressed interest in PEP's sphere of work, at least not in her diaries. Even so, she was probably swept up in a tide of feeling that 'things' had to be 'better' after the war was over, that a national health service should be brought in, for instance, and that the new less formal relationship between the classes could be used to build a kinder, fairer society. June was certainly encouraged by Ann and Charlotte's presence at PEP, and she may also have been curious about Ann's relationship with handsome unmarried 45-year-old Kenneth Lindsay—was he the subject of her 'tactless enquiries'?—but I think there was more than that. As Audrey Withers understood so well, women like June craved recognition as well as information about the world.

On their part, why did PEP members value June's presence? It is difficult not to conclude she was invited for mixed reasons. The lunches were opportunities to tap into what the generation below Lindsay and his colleagues was thinking—a sort of small-scale Mass Observation exercise—but they were also arenas where attractive young women could be befriended and possibly seduced by the predominantly male participants.

On 28 February, after that first lunch meeting, June arrived back at Cheyne Walk glowing with warm feelings induced by PEP's food, wine and cigars. These evaporated abruptly when she read in the newspaper the 'horrible news' that her friend Yvonne Vereker's husband Sandy, a second lieutenant in the Grenadier

3. Julian Huxley (1887–1975); Leonard Elmhirst (1893–1974) and Dorothy Payne Whitney (1887–1968), later Elmhirst; Israel Moses, Baron Sieff (1889–1972) was a businessman; Edward Max Nicholson (1904–2003), was a pioneering environmentalist, ornithologist and internationalist, and a founder of the World Wildlife Fund.

*Alec MacTavish joined the heavy rescue service
when he was rejected by the army.*

Guards and one of the last officers evacuated from Dunkirk, had picked up his service revolver and shot himself two days after suffering concussion in a motorcycle crash. He was the eldest son of John Vereker, 6th Viscount Gort, a distinguished British army officer, but had himself been a reluctant soldier.[4]

It was a shattering event, marked in the diary with little more than a passing note and a resolution to write to Yvonne. This was not an unusual response, either for June or for any of her contemporaries. The accepted antidote to awful loss was simply to go on as if nothing disruptive had happened. Whatever the scale or circumstances—whether you yourself had narrowly missed death, witnessed people in terrible suffering or had lost

4. Charles Standish Surtees Prendergast Vereker (1912–1941) married Yvonne Frances Barnett (1913–1993) in 1938. An inquest at Wimbourne, Dorset concluded that Vereker had killed himself 'while the balance of his mind was disturbed'. *Western Morning News*, 1 Mar 1941, p.6F.

someone near and dear—a muted reaction was the appropriate one. Anything else was pointless and undignified, for one could not alter the past.

❖

> *Saturday 1 March* Up late. A few small jobs. Walked to the hairdressers. Letters from Mum arrived with weaving she had done for me... On duty 2. Feeling miserable. Met Jim [Lees-Milne]... Ann out. Out to dinner with the runaway couple: Jackie and Alec MacTavish. Patience came too. They were in a flat in King's Cross above J. Beresford Fowler's house.[5] Delicious meal cooked by Jackie. A basket of onions an amazing sight... A warning, very short. Walk back in brilliant moonlight. Warm spring air. Bed.

June probably met Alec MacTavish[6] while on duty at a bomb incident. A doctor's son from Penrith, he was nursing disappointment at his rejection by the army—his lungs had been damaged by childhood disease—and was now assigned to the ARP heavy rescue squad in Chelsea, arguably a role that required more than adequate lung capacity. The job of these men, who in the main worked as carpenters, bricklayers, civil engineers and plumbers in the construction trade or for the local council, was to make ruined buildings safe enough to begin a rescue, and to bring out any survivors to safety or to retrieve the remains of those who had perished. Alec, a handsome 21-year-old art student, clicked with June from the start and she was soon friendly with his new wife Jacqueline Ffrench. They couple had just returned from a dash up to Edinburgh to marry.

In the first two years of the war, there was a sharp increase in the rate of marriage. The number of men marrying aged under 20

5. John Beresford Fowler (1906–1977) was an interior designer and co-founder of the firm Colefax & Fowler.
6. Alexander Stuart MacTavish (1919–1985) and Jacqueline Frances Mary Ffrench (1919–1999) married in January 1940. MacTavish left the heavy rescue service to join ENSA (Entertainments National Service Association), stage-managing shows for the troops in Egypt, North Africa, Sicily and Italy.

rose by 77 per cent and between 20 to 24 by 48 per cent.[7] Divorces spiked in the late 1940s, following the end of the Second World War. This was partly because of women's increased participation in the workforce—couples were no longer as financially dependent on each other—but also because many of those wartime unions were created in haste by people looking for hope and joy in a world filled with death and uncertainty.

By the early part of 1941 June was making increasingly frequent references to food in her diaries. At Agnew's restaurant in Sloane Square she had a 'lovely dinner' of jugged hare, vegetables, coffee and chocolates. Dining at the Mirabelle with her latest admirer, Captain Peter Vaughan,[8] she ate 'masses of food', specifically Morecambe shrimps, veal, three green vegetables, potatoes, pudding with cream, and coffee. Now that people were more used to life in the shelters, food was a favoured topic of conversation: ways to make rations stretch, clever substitutes, how trimmings and sauces could transform unappetising meals.

Sugar, meat, fats, bacon and cheese were already rationed. Later in 1941 rationing was extended to tinned meat, fish and vegetables, followed in early 1942 by dried fruit, rice, sago, tapioca and pulses, tinned fruit, tomatoes and peas; condensed milk and breakfast cereal, syrup, treacle, biscuits, oats, soap, chocolate and sweets were added in mid 1942. Bread, beer and cigarettes were not rationed, nor were fish and chips and meat pies from the chip shop although, rather than beef, the latter were more likely to contain Spam, salty fat-laden pig-meat.[9] The government encouraged people to grow their own vegetables in their gardens and allotments in a scheme known as 'Dig For Victory'. Ministry of Agriculture public service films urged people to plant 'beetroots

7. Office for National Statistics, Marriages in England and Wales (Provisional): 2012, ons.gov.uk
8. Charles Peter Vaughan (1911–1975), in 1941 a Captain in the Welsh Guards. In 1944 he was wounded in Burma and awarded the DSO. The Mirabelle was at 56 Curzon Street.
9. Utterly disgusting but somehow delicious.

rather than begonias' and gave tips on growing potatoes and how to hoe between rows. Some vegetables were in short supply, notably onions—before the war they were imported from France and now British crops were affected by blight. As June wrote on 1 March, a basket of onions was indeed an amazing sight.

Despite the food shortages, June never worried about where the next meal was coming from. Like the other residents at Lindsey House, she would have handed over her ration card to Mrs Joe, who would purchase food for the kitchen; she also ate out regularly—in pubs near Cheyne Walk such as the Eight Bells on Chelsea Embankment and the Antelope in Sloane Square and in modest establishments—Carlotta's, Roma's café, the Old Lombard, the Blue Cockatoo Café, the Good Intent and Au Cordon Bleu.[10] June dined at private members' clubs—the Lansdowne and the Junior Carlton feature often —and in expensive West End restaurants like the Mirabelle and Hatchett's,[11] as well as in hotels such as The Dorchester and The Savoy. She had the money to do this but she was also part of a trend. During the war more people were consuming more meals away from home, in canteens, cafés and restaurants, than ever before.

Diners were still able to book restaurant tables and order anything they liked, limited solely by the size of their purse. The only government restriction, imposed in July 1940, was that they could have only one course of meat. It was not until May 1942 that restaurant meals were limited to three courses, coffee and alcohol excluded, for a maximum price of five shillings, although luxury hotels were allowed to add on costs for service, dancing and cabarets.

At a time of shortage, substitutes and make-do, after ration books had been introduced to make the availability of food seem

10. The Antelope, 22 Eaton Terrace; Eight Bells, Chelsea Embankment; Blue Cockatoo Café, 35 Cheyne Walk; Roma's café, near Cook's Ground School; Old Lombard Café, Cheyne Walk. The Good Intent at 316-8 King's Road was a society haunt, known for its striking murals of historical figures. Au Cordon Bleu was at Jubilee Place, Chelsea.
11. The Lansdowne, 9 Fitzmaurice Place; Junior Carlton (see footnote page 33); Mirabelle (see footnote page 142); Hatchett's, 67a Piccadilly.

fair for everyone no matter their annual income, how were these grand hotels and restaurants still able to offer luxury menus? In part this was because they were agile. The Savoy, for example, set up a poultry farm supplying the kitchen with chicken and fresh eggs—so they could avoid offering their clientele the powdered variety. Beef was rationed but game was not, so June's jugged hare at Agnew's was typical fare, along with rabbit, pigeon, rook, woodcock, kid and even horse meat. Although lobster, oysters and caviar might have been discreetly removed from the menu, as at the Ritz, they were still available if you whispered the right words in the *maître d*'s ear.

Grumbles about food unfairness reached the national press when William Connor, writing as 'Cassandra' in the *Daily Mirror*, and Labour MP Tom Driberg, writing as 'William Hickey' in the *Daily Express*, both objected to the ease with which the rich circumvented rationing. Increasingly aware that obvious inequity was causing resentment, the new Minister of Food, Lord Woolton[12] chose to launch on 18 March 1941 the pie recipe that came to bear his name at a lunch at The Savoy for the Pilgrims Society, whose aim was to promote goodwill between the UK and the US. The message was that if Woolton pie was good enough for the guests, among whom were Churchill, John Winant, the new US ambassador, most of the Cabinet and the elite of the business world, who were dining in the epitome of West End indulgence, it was good enough for everyone else.

Woolton pie, the creation of François Latry,[13] *maître chef des cuisines* at The Savoy, was a *mélange* of carrot, swede, turnip, cauliflower or whatever vegetable was at hand or left over, topped with pastry or mashed potato. Whether Woolton's careful positioning of his austerity dish had the desired effect of assuaging public scepticism about food fairness is difficult to know. The recipe was not regarded with much affection, although it continued to be served up well into the 1960s, usually on

12. Frederick Marquis, 1st Earl of Woolton (1883–1964), Minister of Food 1940–1943; Sweet, p.123.
13. François Latry (1889–1966).

Fridays, by school cooks keen to see the week's leftover vegetables put to good use.[14] June never mentioned eating it.

The launch of the pie coincided with Woolton's announcement that there were to be new communal feeding centres in over a hundred towns and cities. Here the public would be able to consume cheap nourishing meals off-ration. British Restaurants evolved from the LCC's free meal service, funded largely by American donations, for people who had been bombed out of their homes. The driving force behind the scheme was Flora Solomon,[15] who had been in charge of Marks & Spencer's staff canteens at the beginning of the war. The first was set up in Kensington staffed by M&S employees and another was established in Coventry after it was blitzed in November 1940.

At British Restaurants, for ninepence, you could get a rib-sticking three-course lunch—perhaps of skilly (an unappealing but nutritious soup of grated carrots and oatmeal), cottage pie, swede, and apple crumble—with no dent in the ration book. This was not dining out as June knew it, of course, but eventually over half a million people a day ate in these not-for-profit establishments. For workers without access to a canteen, exhausted housewives and the lonely elderly, who were given a discount, they were a godsend.[16] The struggle to find, make or serve filling food on the ration was reduced. Later in the war, as we shall see, June herself came to be involved in the British Restaurants project.

Even with the relative abundance available to her, June continued to lose weight. While she was dancing at a party at the Foreign Office with Ann, her knickers 'came down in the middle of the floor'. It was the second time her underwear had failed her. Her male companions gallantly averted their eyes while she

14. I know this from bitter experience.
15. Andrew Wilson, 'The woman from Marks who gave Kim Philby away,' *Observer*, 14 Jun 1981, p.3A. In 1962, Flora Solomon (1895–1984), née Benenson, played a part in exposing Kim Philby as a Soviet spy.
16. 'Communal Restaurants', *BMJ* (1943), Vol. 2, No. 4328, p.790. See also P.J. Atkins, 'Communal feeding in war time: British restaurants, 1940-1947'. In: *Food and War in Twentieth Century Europe* (2011). Farnham, England: Ashgate, pp.139-53.

picked them up and 'ran for it'. 'It certainly brightened the party,' she wrote.

Most nights, when not eating out or at Odsey, June had supper at Lindsey House in the dining room run by Mr and Mrs Joe. It was at that time, before a pall hung over it, a convivial and friendly place. June's friends Tony and Honor Waterfield, who lived around the corner at 25 Cheyne Row, often took their meals there. 'An atmosphere of intelligent insouciance prevailed over those suppers whether there was a raid or not,' they wrote years later. 'This atmosphere was Richard [Stewart-Jones]'s particular gift to his friends. Otherwise those meals were rather dim, both as to food, of the spaghetti variety, and lighting, which was subject to the Germans' vagaries. But they were entertaining and delightful evenings and we never thought of going anywhere else.'[17]

June often invited her friends to eat in her room. The prospect of tea and toast made on the gas ring or shop-bought buns with peanut butter, the stunning 180-degree views of the river, beds to sprawl on, an open fire if she could get coal, interesting people popping in and most of all June's sparky company was irresistible. June had discovered that one way to mitigate the gloom of wartime was to make her room into a hive of flirting and friendship.

> *Saturday 8 March* A sunny spring morning. Drove with Ann to shop... To hairdresser's until lunchtime... Walked back down King's Road, running into Dickie the fireman who insisted on a drink at the Lord Nelson.[18] Back to Cheyne. Ann and Pat sat in my room. I finished the tweed while Ann pulled out the white hairs in my head before Queen Charlotte tonight... We all had tea at the Good Intent. Back to change for dinner. Warning at 8.

Later that evening June and Peter Vaughan, in full evening wear, set out in his little Alfa Romeo for Grosvenor House in Park

17. Pulford, p.52.
18. The Lord Nelson, at 200 King's Road, is more recently known as The Trafalgar.

Lane for Queen Charlotte's Ball, the only big function for the debutantes who would have been presented at court if the country had not been at war. At first June thought little of the warning siren. Two and a half miles away in Notting Hill Vere Hodgson recorded that 'fearful raids' were going on, with 'planes roaring overhead, guns thundering out, glass breaking, bombs screaming through the air.'[19] It was to be the worst night of the London Blitz since December. June and Peter's journey was eventful:

> There seemed to be many planes above and a heavy barrage as we drove up the King's Road. The barracks were lit up by incendiaries. There was a fire on the other side where a bomb had just fallen. A stick of incendiaries fell in the road as we passed. The Alfa Romeo seemed to be moving so terribly slowly...

> In Brook Street I felt a sickening fear I had forgotten about. Longed for a tin hat as another stick came down, but far off. Glad to arrive at Grosvenor House ARP. Ballroom was an enormous throng—about a thousand. A wonderful display of cream brocade and slipper satin. No trace of a war except a rather anaemic cake and a row of beds around the balcony. Very heavy blitz... Rather a good lot of debs. How elderly I feel. Not very many familiar faces.

While travelling on the road at times of extreme peril, the slightest of protections could take on talismanic qualities. Barbara Emary, who worked at Elstree Studios and was a part-time ambulance driver in Kensington, recalled how she convinced herself that the canvas hood of her little Morris Minor convertible would keep the incendiaries at bay while she drove into London. 'I felt absolutely all right driving as long as I had the hood up and it was only canvas, and there was shrapnel and all sorts of bombs falling but you felt quite different if you had the hood up,' she said years later.[20] Similarly, June felt that she should have been

19. Hodgson, p.137.
20. Interviewed in 1988 by Bob Allen, Bob Dunbar for The History Project: historyproject.org.uk/interview/barbara-k-emary

wearing her ARP helmet, even though it would not have saved her had she and Peter been caught by a high-explosive bomb.

At 9.45pm, while June was in the underground ballroom at the Grosvenor, a mile away in Coventry Street, near Leicester Square, a fifty kilogram (110lb) bomb came through the Rialto cinema, down a ventilation shaft and into the half-filled Café de Paris, where it exploded. A second bomb hit the dance floor but failed to detonate.

At least thirty-four people were killed, some literally blasted to pieces, others unmarked, the air sucked out of their lungs. Dozens were seriously injured, but scores escaped practically unscathed. The next day, Joan Wyndham, who was at home that night, wrote in her diary: 'They were dancing to "Oh Johnny" when the bomb fell. The couples on the floor, killed by the blast, stood for some seconds as if they were still dancing, just leaning a little—then fell, heaped on top of one another.' The dead included the much-loved 26-year-old West Indian bandleader. Wyndham lamented his death: 'Gentle, magnetic Snakehips Johnson with his thin elegant face and his joyous rhythm—the best swing band in London gone.'[21] The intact bodies were brought up to pavement level and laid out on the street. One survivor described them: 'They lay quite still in their beautiful dresses, beautiful colours, covered in sawdust—sawdust must have fallen on them when the bomb had exploded down below, and this dust gave them a kind of unreal sheen, they looked like beautiful dolls that had been broken and the sawdust come out.'[22]

Not everyone was transfixed by their ethereal beauty. 'One hears a lot about the bravery during the war, but there were also some very nasty people... these people slipped in pretty quickly and it was full of people—firemen, wardens, police—so it was very easy to cut off a finger here [to get a ring] or steal a necklace, and it did happen,' remembered a voluntary police constable on duty that night.[23]

21. Wyndham, p.227. See also footnote page 34.
22. Anthony Jacobs, quoted in Constantine Fitzgibbon, p.264.
23. The policeman was Ballard Berkeley (1904–1988), born Blascheck, who

The uninjured emerged onto the street and pushed through the gathering crowd in a state of shock. With the blitz still going on, Ulric Huggins and his wife walked towards Piccadilly Circus station and caught the Tube. It wasn't until they reached home that they looked at each other: 'She'd been in a nice dress and the dress was indescribably filthy, her hands and arms up to about her elbow were bloodstained, her hair was all over the place and she was cheerful but somewhat exhausted, and then she looked at me. My naval uniform was in much the same sort of state—grey—but the sleeves of my reefer, my monkey jacket, were completely soaked in blood and I had to throw that uniform away in the end.'[24] Others wandered in a daze over to Le Perroquet. Joe Gilmore, who was serving behind the bar, recalled they asked for 'something with a sting in it'. 'So there and then I invented the Berkeley Stinger. That was one night I shall never forget.'[25]

News of the Café de Paris bomb reached June at Grosvenor House, but like many Londoners she showed, at least to us, a surprising level of composure:

> All Clear given at about 12 [midnight]. On to The 400 by the Café de Paris. There were a few people standing outside, but no signs of the destruction visible. 400 packed out. Everyone talking of the Café tragedy, some say 50, some 74 dead. Someone had come out alive and come in to dance at 400. It made very little visible impression on anyone.

> On the way home we stopped outside the Café where the car ran out of petrol. Went to the entrance to find the poor policeman on guard feeling ill. Everyone had been taken away hours ago. Only heaps of debris to be seen down the stairway. 40 had been killed and many injured. Back to bed in the early hours.

in later life played the Major in the TV comedy series *Fawlty Towers*, quoted in Mortimer, *The Longest Night: Voices From the London Blitz*, p.53.
24. Ulric Huggins (1913—2001). His words are quoted in Constantine Fitzgibbon, p.263.
25. Joe Gilmore (1922—2016), quoted in *The Daily Telegraph*, 15 Jan 2016. Le Perroquet was at 31 Leicester Square.

Sunday 9 March Breakfast 10.30. Walked with Ann and Patience
before lunch. On duty 2 until 6. Everyone still talking about the
Café de Paris. Honour Sayer arrived for night. Terribly tired.
Bed very early. Kept awake by heavy bombing and barrage. They
seemed to be coming more in waves at intervals of ten minutes.

However cool June seemed on the outside, inside was another
story. Cracks had already begun to show. Her life was full of near-
misses and could-have-beens and although none of her friends
were directly caught up in the Café de Paris bomb most of the
victims were people very like herself and her set. She had danced
at the nightclub often. Her feelings were becoming uncontainable.
'Shall burst if I don't get away to the country very soon,' she wrote.

The next day she rushed off to King's Cross station the minute
her shift finished and when she reached Odsey Corner tried hard
to forget about London. She played with some newborn chicks,
took tea with her grandmother and walked with her mother to the
beautiful village of Therfield. To be near nature was comforting:
'So sweet in the village. Glorious walk back. Huge view. Deep
shadows. Faint evening mist.' She did not write her diary for the
next five days, so we cannot know whether she stayed at Odsey
or returned to the city. When she did bring herself to pick up her
pencil, she described herself as 'flat as flat' and her handwriting
was more scrawly than ever. Feelings of helplessness and
hopelessness had accrued from months of suppressed anxiety and
fear and lack of sleep, and would not leave.

There was another ferocious attack on London on 19 March,
the biggest since 29 December, but it was followed by a relative
lull lasting several weeks. At the end of March her life, consisting
of largely uneventful shifts at the ambulance station and routine
activities such as shopping for material to make her belts and
dresses, dancing (The 400 was 'packed tight, rather so myself')
and cinema trips, and dinners out with Peter Vaughan and
friends, had acquired a new rhythm. Underneath, however, she
was distracted and preoccupied. When she and fellow Lindsey

House resident David Lidderdale[26] ('a genuine nice plain person') dined at the Berkeley on 25th, she wondered if he could tell she was miles away, 'talking, although really thinking of something else'. As ever, the only real cheer, for her, was provided by the colour and warmth of the spring: the blossom on the chestnut tree in front of No. 97 and the 'mass of flowers' in the parks and squares.

26. David William Shuckburgh Lidderdale (1910–1998), House of Commons clerk, knighted in 1975.

Disaster

Wednesday 16 April 1941 On duty 8–4pm. Very warm spring
day. The square gardens are a mass of flowers. In the evening
out to dine with Sydney Cuthbert[1] (on leave, Scots Guards).
We dined at the Spanish restaurant [The Barcelona], Soho,
in the ARP wine cellar.

ON 9 APRIL RAF bombers carried out a major raid on Berlin.
Among the casualties was the Opera House on the Unter den
Linden, which was gutted. Hitler ordered its restoration, as well
as swift and devastating retaliation. Seven days after the Berlin
raid, while June was dining with Sydney Cuthbert, whom she had
not seen since they skied together in Austria in 1937, the first of
seven hundred German bombers arrived over London. This raid
and those that followed were to be not preludes to the much-
feared invasion but an effort intended to punish the British and
divert attention from Hitler's eastern campaign.

In London a weary populace headed for the shelters or opted
to stay in their homes. Vere Hodgson in Notting Hill wrote in her
diary: 'The air above me, as I write, is thrumming with Germans.
They have come over in dozens tonight. Have heard one big
packet drop. It is our night for a Big Raid—guns are biffing away
for all they are worth.'[2] In Chelsea air raid wardens equipped
with their respirators, lamps, tool belts, torches and first aid
packs gathered at the ARP post in Cook's Ground School. Reports
started to come in: parachute flares, bombs in Battersea, fires.
The Post Warden decided to cycle around to see for himself what
was happening—not much, it turned out, but on his return to the

1. Sydney John Cuthbert (1914–1944), a major in the Scots Guards, was killed
in action at Calvados, France. The Barcelona was in Beak Street.
2. Hodgson, p.154.

roof of the school he could see a large fire near Victoria. June and Sydney were still tucked away in the basement of The Barcelona.

> Heavy bombing shaking everything by 9.30. Came out to find
> Piccadilly blazing—to The 400 to dance for 2 hours. Bad news
> of Chelsea.

The moon was not full but it was a light night and visibility was good. At Cook's Ground School the wardens reported that bombs were falling near the power station at Lots Road. ARP warden Jo Oakman described the bombers coming over London in swarms of fifty, and in layers, diving incessantly. The barrage was 'terrific and continuous'. At 11.30pm an aerial mine hit Chelsea Royal Hospital infirmary, destroying the east wing. All the crews from AS22 were called out to attend. Forty people were trapped and the rest of the building was so badly damaged that it was later demolished. Four nurses, the wardmaster and eight Chelsea Pensioners died, and thirty-seven others were injured. There were also scores more trapped in buildings in Tite Street and Cheyne Place.

At around one in the morning, the six firewatchers guarding Chelsea Old Church, five men and a woman, all of them volunteers from the congregation and nearby businesses, were seen by air raid wardens proceeding along Cheyne Walk towards the Old Church. At 1.20am two huge explosions were heard close together. The wardens went out to investigate and after navigating roads littered with broken tiles, slates, plaster and lath, wood and window glass, saw in the moonlight that the Old Church, the heart of the 'village', was gone. A parachute mine had destroyed the massive tower, leaving a jagged stump of brickwork and timbers. Several of the houses on Cheyne Walk beyond it had been demolished and others were craggy wrecks. A crater was blown in Danvers Street and the gas main was alight. Five of the six firewatchers, one of them only seventeen years old, were missing.

At The 400 someone told June that the Old Church had been hit. Her first thought was for her ambulance colleagues and she insisted on leaving straight away, but when she and Sydney emerged from the nightclub they could not find a taxi.

> We walked (I was wearing a long pink and black tulle dress!). Fires were raging all around—very heavy bombing. We threw ourselves to the pavement a few times. Got a lift from Cadogan Square. Incendiary bombs all down the King's Road.

With the raid still going on overhead, the rescue parties in Chelsea worked furiously to free trapped people. That night Frances Faviell, now pregnant, was buried by a rain of debris after a bomb demolished her third-floor flat in Royal Hospital Road. When she shook off the choking dust she became aware that the warm sticky thing on her neck was a neighbour's dismembered arm. She and her husband extracted themselves from the devastated building, but three other friends in adjacent flats died. The scene at the first aid post where she was taken was 'indescribable', overwhelmed with casualties. Despite suffering panic attacks, especially when more bombs fell nearby, she started to help treat the wounded. She wrote that the 'sickening fear' she experienced was 'disgusting, degrading, nauseating'.[3]

Back in Chelsea, June and Sydney went straight to AS22.

> It [the ambulance station] was quite flat, and most of Cheyne Walk, too. Glass in windows puffed out as you looked at them. I hunted for ambulance people and found all were safe.

> One huge sheet of glass from the garage roof moved in the brilliant moonlight. Sydney pulled at it and from underneath rose a very tall policeman with a long beard, very drunk. He said he had no legs. To assure him he was standing on them, I pulled up his trousers. To his relief, he danced down the street holding Sydney's hand.[4]

3. Faviell, pp.216–7.
4. The inebriated war reserve policeman was artist Stanley Grimm (1891–1966).

While the ambulance crews were out at the Royal Hospital bombing, station officer Margaret Bridges stayed behind to answer the phones and had been in the office when a bomb shattered the glass roof and buried the policeman. Miraculously, like him, she was unhurt, although she had to pick her way out gingerly through the shards.[5] Despite the damage, the ambulance station was just about operational.

Theodora Fitzgibbon described the devastation at the Old Church: '[It] was nothing but an immense heap of timber and stone, flames licking through it; a large vaulted tomb with a stone urn on top rose up undamaged in the front. The New Café Lombard and all the large and small houses at that end of Old Church Street had been flung together into a giant mountain of shale-like destruction, all lit by the fire and the gas main. Under that fantastic mountain were people, some still alive. Heavy stones were flung aside like pebbles: the local grocer of the street, Mr Cremonosi, put his hand down through a space and felt warm flesh. A naked unhurt woman was pulled up. An old lady appeared, staggering, from the far side of the mountain, having been flung at least thirty yards and then covered with glass, wood and bricks, from which she had extricated herself. She seemed unhurt. A curious rattling sound like a time-bomb made us cautious: a battered tin was moving on a piece of stick. Below, the young woman had forced it through the bricks to attract attention. She was rescued by a war reserve policeman. A sixteen-year-old girl, pinned, only her head showing, talked to a rescue worker: she was freed, but died... several hours later.'[6]

A parachute came down. Fitzgibbon spotted a young man walking on the foreshore, and thought he was a fireman looking for unexploded bombs but he turned out to be a young German airman. An ARP warden arrested him and held him by the arm.

5. Details of Margaret Bridges' experience were published in an advertisement for Ever Ready batteries in the US magazine *Popular Mechanics*, Nov 1943.
6. Theodora Fitzgibbon, p.90. Emma Rose Mary Chandler (b. 1924) was a despatch clerk for a ladieswear wholesale business—she was tended to during the rescue by Dr Castillo (see page 94); her widowed mother, Lottie Calcott (b. 1884), later Chandler, also died in the bombing. See also Faviell, p.230.

When the airman suddenly lurched forward, a member of the public rushed up, kicked him in the backside and managed to grab the pistol he had in a pocket of his flying suit. A couple of War Reserve policemen led him away to Chelsea police station, which suffered a near-miss minutes later.[7]

June went back to Lindsey House.

> Windows out and many holes, but all was well. Sydney left. Changed—out again—amazing sight—brilliant moon—blazing wreckage—glass, glass everywhere—ambulances and cars with flat tyres. Carried a dog home.[8]

Jo Oakman listed the impact on Chelsea that night, the worst since the start of the war: a rain of parachute mines at Cheyne Place, the Royal Hospital, Old Church and Church Street, Cranmer Court and Chelsea Square; over a dozen high-explosive bombs and hundreds of incendiaries; nine fires. All the windows in Paultons Square and Chelsea Hospital were blown out. Four auxiliary firemen died at the Brompton Fire Station and three at the substation at Cheyne Place. The top floor of the nurses' home at the Cheyne Hospital for Children was destroyed. Fifty-four people died in Chelsea including the five missing fire-watchers at the Old Church.[9] Another firewatcher, 40-year-old Thomas William Sargeant, was killed in one of the yards behind Danvers Street.[10]

The raid went on for a further eight hours, with wave after

7. Theodora Fitzgibbon, pp.91-2.
8. Among the unacknowledged victims of the bombing were thousands of pets that were abandoned when their owners left London or were bombed out of their homes or that were euthanised by vets at their owners' request. Public shelters did not accept animals.
9. Yvonne Marie Green (b. 1911), previously an Auxiliary Fire Service driver. The others who died were Henry Vivian Frankland (b. 1907), carpenter; Frederick Charles Winter (b. 1905), shop manager; Sydney Robert Sims (b. 1917), optical lens maker; and Michael James Hodge (b. 1923), student. Arthur Mallett (dates unknown) was the only firewatcher to survive.
10. The Commonwealth War Graves Commission database lists fifty-two deaths in the Borough of Chelsea between 16 and 17 April 1941.

wave of bombers. After the all-clear June managed a couple of hours' sleep on a pile of cushions in the hall of No. 97.

> The dog had left... Thank God for a gloriously sunny morning. At 6am, all the skylights blown in, the sun poured through the holes in the roof. Everywhere is inches of dust and fallen plaster.

Cheyne Walk was a landscape of smoking ruins, rubble and broken glass. An acrid stench hung in the air. Frances Faviell described a 'strange dead stillness, as if the very earth had received a shock and was as numb as its inhabitants from the night's savagery'.[11] Yet, despite the dead bodies and shattered buildings, when people emerged from their shelters and homes they armed themselves with brooms, looked to the skies and began the clean-up. 'Now,' wrote June, 'everyone [was] very active and full of life.' The shock had either turned them into automatons or they were energised by the emergency. Whichever, necessity pushed them on. To continue life, the streets must be swept of glass, rubble and timbers, masonry must be stacked up or hauled away.

> Up on roof helping with the blackouts. To the ambulance station at 4—now a strange, devastating sight. No Chelsea Old Church. No Lombard Café—just a long stretch of debris. Hard to believe it is real.

> Met Alec MacTavish working with the demolition party. They had just found two more men standing on their heads—one, old Barton, who I had been looking for that morning with his son.[12] Spent evening re-equipping ambulances and 'picketing' in the street. Slept in my tin hat.

While the smell of bonfires and cordite hung in the air, emergency workers downed whiskies in the Cross Keys pub,

11. Faviell, p.97.
12. The body of Albert William Barton (b. 1876), firewood merchant and firewatcher, was discovered head down in the wreckage.

now missing a wall. Architect A.S.G. Butler, in daytime a ruin-recorder[13] for the Borough of Chelsea, emerged from firewatching duty at St Paul's Cathedral, where a high-explosive bomb had gone through the transept roof, and felt he had 'worms in his head with all the noise' and that his legs 'won't quite work'. From his vantage point, he had seen 'fire after fire' in Chelsea and feared for his home, his housekeeper and his dog.[14]

Chelsea had suffered its worst night of the war so far but the destruction across the rest of London was just as bad. The Old Church was only one of thirteen churches hit. In neighbouring Kensington a landmine fell on the Town Hall, and a German bomber was brought down in Campden Hill—one of the crew had to be rescued after he bailed out. There were major blasts at eighteen hospitals including Westminster and St Thomas's, as well as Southwark Cathedral and the Charing Cross Hotel. Paddington station, Victoria station and Victoria coach station were hit and there was a large fire in Marylebone Road. Jo Oakman gave the casualty totals across the metropolitan area as 1,179 dead and 2,233 hospitalised. The destruction of 16 April 1941 earned the date its own moniker: it came to be known amongst those who had lived through it as The Wednesday.

Even the ruin-recorder Butler, who was by then fairly inured to the impact of bombing, was moved by the sight of the Old Church when he cycled past a few days later: 'It twitched the heart to look at it; and a small group of people were standing by the barrier across the road like mourners at the grave of Chelsea's first monument.'[15] One of them may have been Ric Stewart-Jones, who made a flying visit on the 18th to see the extent of the damage for himself. June described him wandering around the ruins, salvaging artefacts and bits of masonry. 'Poor Ric,' she wrote, 'what devastation.'

There was a short raid on the 18th and on the 19th, when June was using up her leave at Odsey Corner. This attack was aimed

13. The job of a ruin recorder was to examine and report on damaged buildings.
14. Butler, pp.51–4.
15. Butler, p.78.

*June with the ruins of Chelsea
Old Church behind her.*

at the docks and came to be known as The Saturday, a twin to
The Wednesday. St Paul's was hit again, as well as both the old and
the temporary Waterloo bridges. The casualties were much lower
than on The Wednesday but they included thirty-four firemen
who died at the Old Place School in Poplar, in east London.

At Odsey, suffering with a heavy cold, June took to her
bed, but she was soon up and about, and a visit to her aunts at
the Grange produced valuable swag. They gave her a German
parachute ('unfortunately rather bloody') and from its scads and
scads of 'foaming silk' she planned to make nightgowns. She
hauled it back to London on the train.

On 25 April *Chelsea News* published death notices for two
of the firewatchers, teenager Michael Hodge and young mother
Yvonne Green, but nothing about the other casualties, and

reported the loss of the Old Church in the gossip column.[16] This apparent official insouciance was standard, designed to downplay loss and hide information from the enemy, although it must have added to the sadness of survivors and families.

Off-duty, June was back to her routine: constant activity. She skated at Queen's Club ice rink in West Kensington with Pen Gough. Alec MacTavish, June's friend in the heavy rescue squad, came to lunch, she went to see the comedy turn Flanagan & Allen, had drinks at the Ritz and dined at The Savoy, spotting Noël Coward, Lady Oxford and Robin Maugham amongst the diners.[17] She went to another lunch at PEP.

Despite the damage, AS22 was declared open. 'Spent morning peeling potatoes with Crocker (in his eye-glass and bow tie). Afternoon fire extinguishing demonstration,' wrote June. They whitened the ambulance curtains and scrubbed out the vehicles in preparation for the King's review of the Auxiliary Ambulance Service at Buckingham Palace on 6 May.

There were gaping holes in streets, crooked ruins and piles of debris everywhere but London was still beautiful. The daffodils were out and the chestnut trees were in blossom and June and some of the other women from Lindsey House had tea in their shade, sitting on the grass at the front of No. 97, where they were joined by some passing Canadian servicemen and a small gang of local 'urchins'.

After The Wednesday and The Saturday, on the quiet days, those with no sirens and no raids, June started to relax, mentally and physically—but, as so often happens after periods of great tension, instead of wellness came the opposite. She never described explicitly the symptoms that drove her to seek help—she merely noted in her diary that she had booked an appointment with a

16. *Chelsea News*, 25 Apr 1941, 2D and E.
17. Bud Flanagan (1896–1968), born Chaim Weintrop, and Chesney Allen (1894–1982) were a British singing and comedy duo; Noël Coward (1899–1973), playwright, wit, actor, director; Lady Oxford (1864–1945), widow of H. H. Asquith, Prime Minister between 1908 and 1916; Robin Maugham (1916–1981), barrister and author.

Miss Ormerod,[18] referred to thereafter as 'Miss O.' or 'Pilar', a physiotherapist or possibly a masseuse. According to June, she issued 'terrifying threats of my serious condition'. Many of those who had lived through the Blitz suffered constant aching, the result of months of pent-up anxiety, of stomach-tightening fear, of muscles deprived of oxygen. Whatever the nature of her treatment, June reported that she was feeling 'in tremendous form'. 'To bank etc, lunch at 97. Played tennis with Di, Esther and Nancy. On duty 4. Letter from George Turnbull. Work. Letters,' she wrote on Saturday 10 May, before going on duty at the ambulance station.

That night there was a full moon, with a cloudless sky, perfect visibility for enemy bombers, even clearer than the night the Old Church came down, and no one would have been surprised when at 10.30pm the sirens sounded. Along with her colleagues, June took shelter in the dugout in the corner of the ambulance station, just as she had done many times before. Above them, German planes droned. 'It seemed an ominous night,' she wrote. 'Many planes, heavy firing.' They dived and whined, flying low above the buildings.

At 11.58pm, Jo Oakman, firewatching from a roof nearby, saw a huge oil bomb drop at Victoria station, causing a major fire. She calculated that a bomb came down every minute. 'I have never heard anything like it and yet I was not afraid,' she wrote. 'It was a night of fires all round the river banks, all over the place—fires that could not be put out quickly—that just raged, forming conspicuous targets for the bombs that were still falling.' The heat and burning debris soon forced her to retreat.

Through the roof of the ambulance station, June could see that the 'sky [was] very soon dark scarlet with fires'. Thousands of incendiaries were showering down on Chelsea and, at some point before 3.30am, a 1,000 kilogram (2,200 lbs) parachute mine fell in Basil Street in Knightsbridge, a step away from Harrod's. Three ambulances went out and a fourth followed at 3.30am. Then

18. Miss Ormerod has not been positively identified. A person of that name living in Basil Street, SW3 was listed in the 1940 Post Office directory.

June and Harry Flack,[19] a chauffeur in civilian life, were called to the scene. They heard a lot of machine-gunning, which June interpreted as 'Our fighters were amongst it.' The situation at Basil Street was horrendous.

> Three houses burning fiercely. A mass of fire brigade, Red Cross wardens, Free French and us. Flack met a German nursemaid he had last met a fortnight before the declaration of war in Monte Carlo. 26 people were trapped...

> The rescue party working like mad with torches at one end of the morass and we got the first man out, gave him morphine, got him into my ambulance and the engine would not start. Got some firemen to push it over heaps of glass and rubble and off we went. Torrents of water from the hoses, boiling hot from fire, cascaded down the street. Sat on my patient to keep him still. He was bad. Found myself humming Handel's Water Music. At last, St George's Hospital [then located near Hyde Park Corner]. Met a doctor I had seen last at Queen Charlotte's Ball with Peter Vaughan.

> Back to station to change ambulance. Most of station [crews] had gone to Berkeley Square [ambulance] station. Back to Basil Street... The same firemen were still playing hoses from ladders above the buildings and overhead above them could still be heard planes, and now and then machine-gunning. Five other people had been dug out. There was no hope for the remaining 20. The fire had got hold of the wreckage and water from the hoses playing on the other side of the street had got into basements. They had filled up in spite of pumping out. We waited on until 7am. Then the fires were got under control.

> The all-clear sounded at 5am. We drank tea from the WVS [Women's Voluntary Service] canteen. Relatives of the missing

19. Harry Flack (1904–1957).

began to appear, in odd, torn garments, and with blackened faces. One or two French women very hysterical. All the rest so calm, so cheerful, ready to give anything to be of use. God, what heroes. 7.30am we left. Called for blankets at St George's and back to ambulance station. The air was thick with fog and smoke and bits of charred paper. Ambulances were still working hard.

The sour smell and the shards of blackened paper were from a burning river barge loaded with paper moored outside Phillips Mills. Frances Faviell described it as like a 'flickering curtain silhouetted against the flames... an eerie and unforgettable spectacle'.[20] It was made worse by a further fire at a paperworks at nearby Wandsworth Bridge Road, which smouldered and smoked for days. Three firemen later received gallantry awards for rescuing people in Basil Street.

At 8am, exhausted and filthy, June was released from duty.

Got into hot bath and tried to get clean. Breakfast. Bed. Slept until 4.30.

Across London, over fifteen hundred died that night and more than two thousand fires raged. The House of Commons was severely damaged. A quarter of a million books were burnt at the British Museum. The Royal College of Surgeons in Lincoln's Inn Fields was hit by a high-explosive bomb and lost thousands of specimens from the Hunterian Museum Collection. After a bomb in the stairwell at the Alexandra Hotel in Knightsbridge a hundred and forty people were trapped and twenty-four died. Three hotels in Vauxhall Bridge Road were hit. Vincent Square children's hospital in Victoria was damaged by fire and there was a huge conflagration at the Palmolive soap factory in Pimlico. A trench shelter in Eaton Square, a four-foot (1.2m) deep pit in the earth covered with a concrete or steel top, was hit. Two firemen were killed in a fire caused by a bomb striking the electricity supply station in

20. Faviell, p.234.

St Martin's Lane and igniting underground tanks filled with diesel oil.[21] At St Luke's Hospital in Sydney Street in Chelsea a bomb smashed into the operating theatre, killing two doctors and several nurses.

Apart from some small and damaging raids on London and provincial targets in June and July, this day was effectively the end of the 1940–41 Blitz. Around 43,500 lives had been lost, with a further 139,000 people left seriously injured. In the eight months between 7 September 1940 and 11 May 1941 at least three hundred and forty-four people died in the Borough of Chelsea. The next major raid on Chelsea would not occur until 23 February 1944, when the Guinness Buildings at World's End were devastated by a bomb probably intended for the Lots Road power station. About two hundred people were trapped under the rubble of eighty flats and fifty-nine people died. By then, June had long departed Lindsey House and the ambulance service, and her life had taken a completely different turn.

21. Sansom, p.84.

The Stars Go Out

Monday 12 May 1941 Much the better for sleep. Gloriously
sunny morning. Ric [Stewart-Jones] arrived in the night.
Sewed out on the roof. The workmen had mended the roof and
left the ladder. Ric and Diona came in my window and we drank
some bad sherry on the roof in the sun. Daddy rang up. Esther
came and sat with me. Saw A.P. Herbert[1] and some other sailors
down in the street. They waved and so did I. They came up the
ladder and drank sherry too, ending up in my room. A.P.H. came
down to lunch with Ric, Di and me and two crew. They went off to
sea again in the *Water Gypsy*. Later A.P.H. came ashore to coffee
and stayed until 1 o'clock.

JUNE'S ENTRY ON 12 May was the first time she mentioned
A.P. Herbert, the 50-year-old sailor, First World War veteran,
barrister, broadcaster, writer and Independent MP for Oxford
University. They must have met before this, probably introduced
by Ric. Herbert's vessel the *Water Gypsy* was often moored on the
river just below Lindsey House and his crew of veteran Lowestoft
fishermen and ex-minesweepers made use of the dining room and
the bathrooms.

Herbert, who lived with his wife the artist Gwendolyn Quilter[2]
in Hammersmith, volunteered himself and the *Water Gypsy* for
the River Emergency Service in 1938. He insisted on wearing
his own uniform, a blue peaked yachting cap, blue blazer and
grey flannel trousers, remaining a petty officer (he refused all
efforts to make him apply for a commission—and was notably
the only non-commissioned officer in the House of Commons),

1. Sir Alan Patrick Herbert (1890–1971).
2. Gwendolyn Harriet Quilter (c.1892–1986) married A.P. Herbert in 1914.

and handpicking his crew. In 1939 it included Darcy Braddell, the vice-president of the Royal Institute of British Architects; the artist Victor Pasmore; Magnus Pyke, a chemist and, later, eccentric television personality; and John Pudney, a poet and radio producer (and Herbert's son-in-law).[3]

The River Emergency Service was absorbed into the Royal Naval Auxiliary Patrol and the *Water Gypsy*, now painted grey, was kitted out with two Lewis guns, a small rifle, three revolvers, hand grenades and two cutlasses, and a new mate, Eric Udale,[4] an old comrade from Herbert's First World War days. The crew made a significant contribution to the defence of the home front by patrolling the forty-five miles of the Thames, delivering supplies and ammunition to stations between Westminster and Canvey Island, and later taking part in mine-clearance and mine-watching. Herbert's knowledge of the river was legendary and he could steer the boat perfectly to all the stages in the deepest blackout. Like her skipper, the *Water Gypsy* was a maverick. According to Herbert's commanding officer, the boat had a reputation as 'probably the untidiest ship in HM's service,'[5] an opinion endorsed by June who described a 'scene of chaos' on board. While A.P., his hair a mess, bent over a speech he was writing, she would pitch in to tidy up, wash the dishes, straighten berths and fold clothes.

The friendship between June and A.P. was swift to develop and intense. Although she had two serious romances during this period, neither of those men appeared in her diaries as frequently as A.P. did. She saw him often, for lunches, drinks and occasionally dancing, and she sought him out at the end of her shifts. She gave him a codename—November—but sometimes she referred to him as 'the old man'. On Herbert's part, he phoned June regularly and took her out to dinner. What A.P.'s wife Gwen thought of this

3. Thomas Arthur Darcy Braddell (1884–1970); Edwin John Victor Pasmore (1908–1998); Magnus Alfred Pyke (1908–1992); John Sleigh Pudney (1909–1997). By the time June and Herbert became close, all of these men were serving elsewhere in the war effort.
4. Eric Dalgleish Udale (1892–1982).
5. Pound, p.170.

An intense friendship developed between June and writer, sailor and MP A.P. Herbert.

friendship is not known. She and Herbert appear to have been living fairly separate lives, by necessity if not by choice. He slept only a couple of nights a month at their home at 12 Hammersmith Terrace[6] and she was busy with her vegetable garden and her own ambulance service duties. June did not mention Gwen at all in her diaries.

Intriguingly, on 7 November 1941, June described a party given by Esther Darlington in the ballroom at No. 96:

6. Dylan Thomas and his wife Caitlin Macnamara, who was (probably) born at 12 Hammersmith Terrace, occupied No. 13, a studio owned by A.P. Herbert, from late 1941 to early 1942.

A.P. Herbert's forehead sitting on the sofa, his youngest
daughter. Listened to long violin recital, drank hot *glühwein*
guiltily and fled.

The 'forehead' was Lavender, one of Herbert's four children,
who was then aged about 21. Why June felt guilty she doesn't
explain and the diaries give no indication that her relationship
with Herbert was anything other than platonic.

So what was behind the mutual attraction between young,
beautiful, creative June and intellectual, middle-aged Herbert?
Like many wartime friendships, it was fuelled by circumstances
of time and place—but that cannot completely explain it. Herbert
was kind, clever and funny, and a misfit. Perhaps June found
simultaneously contradictory elements of safety and illicitness in
their friendship, sparks missing from the other more conventional
men who had so far courted her.

We don't know when or how the relationship between June
and A.P. ended, whether they drifted apart or something happened
to sour it. She did not mention A.P. in her diaries after December
1942. In 1943, he was out of the country, sent by the government
to visit Newfoundland and Labrador as part of a parliamentary
commission, and by then June had left London.

Sunday 1 June Awoke 10.30. Clothes rationing!

June's exclamation came from the heart. Clothes, the design
of them, the making of them, the wearing of them, were part
of her core self. But for the war, she might have been working
full time in the bespoke fashion industry. The government had
given no prior warning of the measure, which was imposed to
ensure 'fair shares' among civilians but was also meant to prioritise
the demand for uniforms for the services. Rationing may have had,
if not an equalising, at least a toning-down effect. As Inez Holden
put it, the rich would no longer be able to 'swank about swathed

in furs'.[7] Like every other woman, June was entitled to sixty-six coupons a year; on top of the price of the item, she would have to hand over eleven for a dress, two for stockings, five for shoes; as the war progressed, fewer coupons were allocated. June was better placed than most. She already had a well-stocked wardrobe and she was in the habit of making her own clothes—much cheaper than shop-bought both in cash and coupons. During the summer of 1941, her sewing machine was busier than ever. She made a waistcoat for A.P., a gown for her friend and fellow lodger Millie Balfour (for which she was paid in precious silk stockings), and a dress for Ann, from 'yards and yards of taffeta'.

Second-hand clothes were not rationed and 'Make Do and Mend'—darning, patching, cutting down and refashioning garments into new uses—was officially encouraged. As always, when there were shortages, people innovated. Blackout material, which did not require points, was used for evening dresses, as were furnishing fabrics; cheesecloth, curtain net, butter muslin, all unrationed, were ideal for underwear. Old blankets could be turned into dressing gowns. Folded away in a corner of her room, June still had the parachute silk her aunt had given her in April. Once unpicked, the non-bloody sections would be perfect for nightclothes or even a wedding dress.

Sunday 15 June To ambulance station to hear news of it [AS22] being disbanded in two days! Great excitement. Peter Vaughan called to say, 'Come to the Derby on Wednesday.'

Monday 16 June On duty at 8. Canteened. Beat Crocker at ping-pong. Colossal fracas in the office all day. We were interviewed by Mr Smith who seemed responsible for sending us all to undesirable stations. Off duty 4. Shopping. Hat hunted. A Musical Festival in Cheyne Walk organised by Esther [Darlington]. The house filled with flat-footed sandals women scraping and chirping.

7. Holden, p.178.

Tuesday 17 June Shopping all morning. Very hot day. On duty at 4 at Ambulance Station 22 for the last time. Everyone sad at our parting. We took photographs of various things and ourselves...

June went off duty at 8am the next day, sped home and was ready to be picked up by Peter Vaughan for Pimm's at the Guards Club and a drive out to Newmarket for the Derby.[8] It was baking hot with no breeze.

For June, the closure of AS22 and the dispersal of its crews to other stations was life-changing, although she did not yet know it. A number of her closest colleagues, including Daphne Catt and John Crocker, were assigned to the Territorial Station in Riley Street (TS3), a two-minute walk west of Lindsey House, but June, to her great chagrin, was sent across the river to AS179 which was based at Bolingbroke School in Wakehurst Road, Battersea. At that time Battersea was a dreary suburb with none of the cachet of Chelsea and the school itself was Victorian, cold and impersonal, the diametric opposite of the cramped but cosy accommodation at Danvers Street. June felt like she had been exiled.

This period, after the 1940–41 Blitz ended, was strange for all Londoners. Raids were now sporadic. Since there was no pattern, the danger was ever-present. There was also the constant threat from buried delayed-action or unexploded bombs which could detonate at any time.

At AS179 June scrubbed out ambulances, cleaned toilets and worked in the station canteen, just as she had at AS22. The difference was the trek over the bridge to Battersea and the almost total lack of call-outs. It was so quiet that she would take surreptitious naps on her lilo in the playground, but by doing so she made an enemy of the station officer. 'Annoying letter from London County Council for falling asleep in the sun,' she wrote on 25 June, after she was reported to the higher-ups.

There was little routine ambulance work for the crews. The authorities vetoed expanding their duties to include transporting

8. From 1940 to 1945 the Derby was run at Newmarket rather than Epsom.

disabled children to school and running soldiers on leave to their homes because everyone, especially those involved in the defence of the home front, was required to remain as vigilant and alert as ever. Most of June's shifts were just hours of waiting around, restive and bored, increasingly frustrated that life was passing her by. Table tennis and first aid refresher courses could only go so far in breaking up the monotony. To top it all, from spring 1941, under the Civil Defence (Employment and Offences) Order, she was forbidden from resigning. Her only hope for release from the service was on compassionate or disciplinary grounds.

Mary Tolstoy, who had been at AS22 and had been assigned to AS179 with June, provided some companionship and invited her to tea at the cottage in Lister Walk she shared with Patrick O'Brian, but essentially June was lonely and missed the camaraderie of Danvers Street. She took to regularly dropping in at TS3 to see old colleagues. Then, on 30 June, came another terrible blow—the 'vile black news' of the death of sweet Harry Knight, who had courted her before the war and who had been posted with the Scots Guards to Egypt. In a rare expression of emotion, she wrote that it made her 'more frankly miserable than I could have believed'.

The lack of work meant June had more free time to network and meet new people at PEP lunches, the exiled King Zog of Albania[9] and the eccentric millionaire Anthony Joseph Drexel Biddle[10] among them. There was a drawback to these convivial gatherings, however. They made her feel out of her depth—in her words 'like a weed among the vegetables'—and she eventually 'broke the news to them that I am no celebrity!' Kenneth Lindsay's response was to invite her formally to join the group. She turned him down. In truth she felt more at home among the artists and literati of Chelsea, most of whom she met by mingling with the constant stream of visitors and friends who turned up at Lindsey

9. Zog I (1895–1961), born Ahmed Muhtar bey Zogolli, was the self-proclaimed King of Albania from 1928 until 1939.
10. Anthony Joseph Drexel Biddle Sr (1874–1948) was a theatre impresario and writer.

*June's friend Patience Clifford at No. 94 Cheyne Walk,
with Lindsey House in the background.*

House or through A.P. or her ambulance colleagues. In July,
June became friendly with the actors Judith Furse and Constance
Cummings[11] at a summer party at the Chelsea ARP post (they
performed a cabaret for the wardens); afterwards they invited
her, A.P. and Patience Clifford back to their home in Old Church
Street to drink in the garden under the stars. 'We sat among
the high lime trees on the sweeping lawn,' wrote June. 'Judith
and Cummings played and sang an old song and we drank until
1am. Back to the river with A.P., shimmering silver, unbelievably
lovely.' The evening yielded promises: Cummings's playwright
husband Benn Levy offered her a job designing costumes for his
next production and the head ARP warden at Cook's Ground
School supported her plea to be moved from Battersea. Within a

11. Judith Furse (1912–1974) was a British actor known for her androgynous
looks; she often played baddies. Constance Cummings (1910–2005), US-born
British actor, was married to Benn Levy (1900–1973), a British playwright and
screenwriter, who was elected an MP in 1945. In the 1939 Register, Levy was
listed as living at 66 Old Church Street, Chelsea.

couple of days she was composing her request for a transfer and making plans to apply for membership of the London Library to research costumes for Levy's play. For the first time in months she felt energised and hopeful. A new direction was possible.

Friday 11 July   Back over the river to that barracks by 8.
After scrubbing ambulances spent rest of day avoiding the most unpopular girl in the school! [June does not say who this is.]
And doing my own things. Off duty at 4. Very jaded. Went to see Peter Ustinov[12] at Players Club. Very good.

The Players, a cramped theatre club in a deep basement in Albemarle Street, was an odd and uniquely British experience where the audience was entertained with nineteenth-century burlesque and goaded into participating by a master of ceremonies dressed as a Regency beau. June, entranced by the performance of 20-year-old Peter Ustinov doing his sketch 'The Bishop of Limpopoland', paid little attention to the man sitting next to her.

Saturday 12 July   Thunderstorm and heavy rain, in which I got thoroughly soaked in going over bridge at 4. Took everything off and remained inside with Patience and Ann until 6.30.
To party with Mike Streatfeild...

We were the only English there and became more so. Russian, French, Egyptian. Funnily enough the little fat man who had sat next to me at Players the night before [was] introduced as 'Ustinov', Russian. Greeted me as an old friend, much excited as he had studied me and wanted to tell me all he thought he knew, which was amazingly accurate!

---

12. Multi-talented Peter Ustinov (1921–2004) was a British performer, writer, raconteur, academic.

Jona, Baron von Ustinov,[13] also known as Klop—meaning 'little bedbug'—was Peter Ustinov's father. A former German army conscript, journalist, diplomat, he had been recruited as an MI5 spy. Despite his unprepossessing appearance (very short, with bulging eyes), he was known for his ability to charm and cajole into bed any woman he set his sights on. He undoubtedly identified June as a mark and his attentions to her were fully in line with the skills the British secret services appreciated in him.

June was having none of it, and she was saved from having to repel Ustinov's predations by the arrival of Mike Streatfeild and his friend Harry Morton Colvile,[14] a 36-year-old Swiss-born divorced artist now working for the BBC, who lived a ten-minute walk from Lindsey House at Glebe Place. He was instantly attracted to June and on 1 August he surprised her by turning up at the end of her shift at AS179 and insisting on accompanying her home across the bridge. Before long, they were seeing each other almost every day. June's diary became a litany of lunches out with Harry, teas in her room with Harry, visits to Lindsey House from Harry. Sometimes he stayed the night in the office or in Cad's Alley, the section of Lindsey House set aside for young men, and took breakfast with her in the dining room. He painted in her room and asked her to sit for him.

> *Monday 18 August* [After a shift] back to breakfast in pouring
> rain. Bathed. Breakfast with Harry. To Harrod's etc... Worked
> at Millie's taffeta. Collapsed. Slept. Harry came in at four, having
> had hair cut. We had large tea in my room and sat there until 8.
> Terrence[15] came up. Very cold and we terribly tired. Staggered
> to supper at Roma's and drink in Black Lion. Staggered back
> to sleep. A.P. rang up.

13. Jona Freiherr von Ustinov (1892–1962), Peter Ustinov's father, flew for the Germans in the First World War. In 1935, when working as a journalist attached to the German Embassy, he refused to 'prove' his Aryan credentials (he had Jewish heritage) and secretly became a British subject.
14. Harry Claud Rudolph Morton Colvile (1905–1992).
15. Possibly Terrence Elwyn Morris (1911–1986), an architecture student.

Harry had joined the RAF and been assigned to 'special duties'. 'I knew it couldn't go on like this,' she wrote on 19 August. 'One of the few stars in my life. They go out like a dream just when I was coming to love them.'

Their romance did not change the fact that she was unhappy at AS179. Even with Harry to distract her, June's life was stuck running along the same dull tracks. Now, though, she was not above taking the occasional sick day. So far there had been no response from the LAAS administration to her request for a transfer, so she continued to lobby hard, writing to ask for an interview with Major Harding-Newman,[16] staff officer to the town clerk of Chelsea.

In reality, she was utterly exhausted ('terrible tired') and for the first time Odsey Corner failed to restore her. On one of her now infrequent overnights there she was pampered with breakfast in bed ('crisp omelette, coffee, brown melba toast') and spent the afternoon alone walking in the woods, but she found her beloved mother 'a bit overpowering', and came away feeling like 'a heavily licked kitten'.

Relief came at just the right moment. Her friend Arthur Dorrien Smith,[17] also known as A.D.S., Adie or Froggy, whose family had lent June their flat in Lowndes Street before she moved to Lindsey House, invited her to spend some time with him at the family seat in Tresco on the Scilly Isles. She did not hesitate. The prospect of a break on a subtropical haven of woodland, lush greenery and pristine sandy beaches was too good to turn down, even if it meant temporarily parting from Harry.

In the afternoon of 23 August Harry saw June off at Paddington station.

> We couldn't find a taxi. H. ran with my bag for nearly a mile.
> We caught one at Town Hall. Getting to Paddington 10 mins

16. Thomas Harold Harding Harding-Newman [sic] (1976–1953) was appointed in March 1939 and was later Chief, and then Deputy Controller (Operations) in Chelsea. *Chelsea News*, 29 Aug 1941, p.2E.
17. Francis Arthur Dorrien Smith (1921–1944).

to spare. Frightfully packed smelly train. Eventually found
a seat. H. found a better one, out came the luggage. 3 mins
to 5 train. We extracted from stupid porter that train would
not connect to boat to Scilly. So out everything came for 3rd
time! And we dashed to another platform and at last tracked
down a seat. My beloved H. Could any man go through so much
and still be smiling!

She would be away for twelve days. Both she and Harry
promised to write. At last she was experiencing what felt like a
real romance—but just as it seemed to be blossoming it was put
to the test.

A New World

Saturday 23 August 1941 The respectable family in my carriage,
which Harry had carefully selected, adopted me and insisted on
my eating their sandwiches. When I awoke with frightful cramp
it was deluging outside. The brakes of the train broke in the night
and we stopped for 3 hours. Arrived 4 hours late at Penzance.
The torrential downpour continued… A youth in the Navy [was]
also stranded and I tried all sources of transport to the island.
He left me to go over in a motor launch with the Navy. I found
a bed in a boarding house. Telephoned to Tresco. They were
charming about it all. Ann gave me Paul Ziegler's number in
Penzance. I rang up, and we arranged to meet at Queen's Hotel.

Arrived soaked to the skin at the hotel and found, to my
surprise, a bellboy paging me. A strange woman said, 'I hear you
are stranded. Please come and stay. The car is just arriving.'
It came, with Paul inside, and we drove quickly through the rain
out towards Land's End, up a beautiful drive full of flowering
shrubs and hydrangeas. The arching of the trees—it reminded
me of something I had seen before. Through the mist and rain
were old pine trees and lovely lawns with a stone house full of
Victorian things and wallpaper. Lovely china and pictures.
I met Mrs Poulsen. Very small and dark. And Lady Swinfen,
who I was to share a room with. I bathed and was immediately
put to bed in Paul's room, where I slept until dinner.

AS THE CAR drove through the two sturdy granite pillars marking
the entrance to the enclave of Boskenna, down a dark colonnade
of trees, and round a series of bends to the house, June had little
idea of the world she was about to enter. She had a sense of *déjà vû*,

and she was probably thinking of the dramatic opening sequence of Alfred Hitchcock's film of Daphne du Maurier's novel *Rebecca* starring Laurence Olivier and Joan Fontaine, which she had seen the previous August. A few days after she arrived at Boskenna, she wrote confidently but wrongly that the film had been made there.[1]

The decidedly unromantic seventeenth-century house at the centre of Boskenna, built of unadorned granite with a solid square porchway, was the ancestral home of Mrs Poulsen's father, the widowed 77-year-old Colonel Paynter,[2] who ran his two-thousand-acre estate as an independent fiefdom, masterminding a black market in food and petrol, and, it was rumoured, like his forefathers, exercising *droît de seigneur* on his female tenants.[3] Betty Poulsen[4] was his only legitimate child.

In the Twenties and Thirties Boskenna was a revolving door of famous visitors, hangers-on and charity cases. Paynter encouraged Betty to bring a cosmopolitan and unconventional set of people to Boskenna, including her lifelong friend Mary, Lady Swinfen[5] who, when June met her, had separated from her barrister husband Charles Eady, 2nd Baron Swinfen. Betty later remembered life at Boskenna: 'Lawrence of Arabia would roar up and down the drive on his motorcycle... Einstein would come over from Sennen and explain his complicated theories to me, D.H. Lawrence would come here from Zennor. Augustus John was a regular visitor and one night he brought a baby that some woman had given him... We had marvellous parties. It was not the thing to invite the trade, but artists were always welcome.'[6] During

1. The inspiration for Manderley was actually Menabilly near Fowey, Cornwall. The 1940 film was shot almost entirely in the studio with a few exterior scenes around California.
2. Camborne Haweis Paynter (1864–1949).
3. Marnham, p.42. Much of the information about the Paynters is from Marnham's biography of Mary Wesley.
4. Elizabeth Narcissa Marie Paynter, later Poulsen, later Hill (1907–1980).
5. Mary Aline Mynors Farmar (1912–2002), later Eady (Lady Swinfen), later Siepmann, known as Mary Wesley.
6. Quoted in *The Wedding Detectives*, BBC Radio 4, broadcast 20 Oct 2020. Sennen Cove and Zennor are on the north coast of Cornwall, six and thirteen miles respectively from Boskenna.

the war numerous child evacuees arrived at Boskenna, and, at times, groups of serving officers and men on leave, and while June was there, Betty's current admirer Alec Beechman,[7] the Liberal MP for St Ives.

Neither Betty Poulsen nor Mary Swinfen was 'respectable' in the accepted sense. Betty's baby daughter was not her husband's (although she was at pains to make it appear that she was), and Mary's second son was similarly the result of her affair with Heinz Ziegler, the brother of Ann's lover Paul, which was also covered up. The group was a sexual merry-go-round. Paul had been Betty's lover before he moved on to Mary, and many others, including Ann Channer. June would not have been especially shocked by Betty and Mary's private lives—she always took other people's unusual domestic arrangements in her stride. She did not blink when faced with Mary Tolstoy and Patrick O'Brian's extramarital relationship and had nothing to say about Ric and Jim's 'close friendship'.

June and Mary had much in common. Both were beautiful, intelligent and popular with men, and unafraid to express their mind. They moved smoothly through a social sphere encompassing both the conventional and the bohemian. June probably exchanged ambulance experiences with Mary, who had joined the service in Kensington in 1939 but became bored during the Phoney War and jumped at the chance to decipher German and Russian radio call signals instead, a project later absorbed into the work of Bletchley Park.

June's two-day stay at Boskenna was idyllic, filled with breakfasts in bed, walks through the voluptuously flowering gardens, lunch on the rocks watching the sea, fresh food (cream teas, lobster for dinner) and sweet, restoring sleep. The estate included thirty-two farms, scores of houses and much of the coastal land between Land's End and Penzance. The Colonel invited June to accompany him on a morning drive to meet some of his tenants. He was known for his eccentric and perilous driving

7. Neville Alexander Beechman (1896–1965).

style, and June wrote of flying along in his Baby Ford 'at breakneck speed, down the long twisty hills into hilly wooded valleys'.

'He had a joke with everyone and discussed their latest problems, however small and personal,' she wrote. 'We ended the round amongst the gooseberries in the walled garden at Boskenna. He remarked how much he loved dancing but couldn't find the partners, only schoolmistresses nowadays.' To June, he was 'an adorable spiky little cavalier,' and if he made sexual advances to her, she did not record them.

To crown her contentment, Ann arrived with Paul Ziegler, the two of them obviously in love. They all dashed through the rock gardens down to the sea to watch the passing convoys bound for America, and June and Ann gossiped about their hosts and Betty's oddly attractive appearance—'gooseberry eyes and black hair and miniature form' in June's words.

> We came back and picked sweetcorn on the way to large tea
> of Cornish cream, jam and saffron bread, pineapple cake etc.
> I delved among books with oranges and gin and early supper.
> Mary Swinfen drove Ann and Paul to the night train to London.
> The most gloriously lovely evening, wonderful views softened
> by pale mauve black clouds and the brilliant sky. Back in the
> moonlight. Walked through the pine trees to the lookout post
> to watch the evening. The crickets were cricketing all round.
> A telegram from Harding-Newman [the ARP staff officer at
> Chelsea town hall to whom June had applied for a transfer]—
> how on earth did he know I was there?[8]—which I was able
> to answer by Ann... Bed.

Before dropping off to sleep, she listened to the prime minister on the radio and tried to write to Harry, but the words would not come. Early in the morning, she was driven to Penzance to catch the boat to Tresco, where her friend Adie Dorrien Smith and his family were awaiting her.

8. Someone at Lindsey House must have forwarded it.

Ghastly moment before going aboard—had forgotten identity card, managed to wangle with ration book. And so I left England. Unfortunately overcome after a few moments and later drastically ill. Taken below by steward. Three hours of misery and I came to the light feeling very ashamed, never having been amongst so much sickness before.

A startling sight in that blue and green sea. Masses of islands. Heavenly transparent sea. As we got near Tresco the grey walls of the Abbey House rising out of the trees. Climbed out onto the pink seaweed and silver sand. Met by Mrs [Eleanor] Dorrien Smith[9] with white pony and trap. So we proceeded to the Abbey down a winding track. Huge tropical flowers growing wild on either side and palms, flamingos... paddling about in little pools.

Into the courtyard where cactuses and strange flowers were growing out of the walls very well. 11th-century archways. Relics of the Vikings. Down to the silver sands with Helen, the little daughter. Adie was fishing. Nursery tea on the terrace. Adie came back with the Mayor. Adie began to show me the garden flowers. In no way a European garden; huge varieties of trees, one which grows downwards. Mad. A summerhouse made entirely of figureheads from beached sailing ships. Ten acres of enormous rock garden. Adie thought I looked green and insisted on my going to bed before dinner which couldn't have suited me more. Out of my window—sea, sea and little islands. 4 Hurricanes guard the island and shoot down any straggling invader. The Spitfires sounded busy and there was some AA firing.

Tresco is the largest of an archipelago of a hundred and fifty craggy granite islands, only five of which are inhabited. It was

9. Eleanor Salvin Bowlby (1887–1978), later Dorrien Smith; Helen Dorrien Smith (1932–2015). At the time June visited, the family had already lost two sons in the war: Algernon Robert Dorrien Smith (b. 1910), a captain in the Royal Armoured Corps, and Lionel Roger Dorrien Smith (b. 1918), a pilot officer in the Royal Air Force Voluntary Reserve, both of whom died in France on 20 May 1940.

here that Adie Dorrien Smith's ancestor, Augustus Smith, built Tresco Abbey and cultivated an astonishing collection of plants which thrived in the almost subtropical climate. The Scillies historically acted as the gateway for sea traffic from France or Spain heading for Ireland and the north of Scotland—the islands are littered with centuries-old fortifications—but in 1939 there were no anti-aircraft guns and no significant naval presence, just one independent company of troops.[10] On 29 August 1940 the Germans bombed a military installation on Peninnis Head, and more raids followed, some of the pilots probably dumping bombs rather than targeting civilians or military installations. As June noticed, Hawker Hurricanes were now defending the islands[11]; troops had been doubled to about a thousand and anti-aircraft guns had been installed, but about half the population, feeling their vulnerability and perhaps with an eye on the fate of the Channel Islanders now living under German occupation, evacuated to the mainland.

June and Adie sailed the short distance over to the bleak island of Bryher, climbing over to its furthest side to sit on the high rocks and watch great breakers crash onto the shore; back on Tresco they rode ponies through the woods and up to the highest peaks, seeking 'glorious wild views to the sea and uninhabited islands' and then down through the heather; she went crabbing, helped with the lobster pots and fished for pollock. At her request, she was landed on the uninhabited island of Annet and left alone to explore for a couple of hours. After the frenetic months under fire, the ambulance shifts, the mad socialising, the dispiriting boredom of Battersea, and most recently the romance with Harry, which was exciting but strangely disruptive, she had at last found stillness and solitude.

It had to end, of course. On 1 September, clutching flowers from Adie, she was taken by pony and trap back down to the boat. Betty Poulsen had rung up the evening before and invited her to

10. A temporary expeditionary formation of the British Army.
11. See Mark Bowden and Allan Brodie, *Defending Scilly* (2011). Swindon: English Heritage.

spend a few more days at Boskenna before her return to London and, on her behalf, had sent a 'wild' telegram to the ambulance station to excuse her absence.

June spent her twenty-fifth birthday at Boskenna feeding the chickens, lunching with the colonel and fishing at Mousehole. There was more chat with Mary Swinfen, who 'threw some light onto some of Betty's past', including the fact that at the age of 17 she had for a brief time been engaged, or almost engaged, to 50-year-old Italian radio pioneer Guglielmo Marconi,[12] and amused her with tales about Betty's disastrous wedding to Olaf Poulsen De Baerdemaecker, a Dane from a Ghent shipping dynasty, who was then serving in the RAF. Mary told her each had married thinking the other's family was minted and had given lavish wedding presents, but it turned out that both were broke. The marriage lasted only two years. June wrote that she found Mary's stories 'hysterically funny' and 'tried to persuade her to write a book about it'.

Many decades later, Mary did write a book, a novel about the complex relationships between five cousins and their friends, from golden days spent at a beautiful estate in Cornwall overlooking the sea to the privations and absurdities of wartime life in London. *The Camomile Lawn* was published in 1984 under the name Mary Wesley.

Wednesday 20 August Off duty 8. Bathed, washed my hair. To hairdresser. 10.30 set out with Harry [Colvile] to look for his uniform until lunch in Soho... Ended at Harrod's for shirts, both completely exhausted. Back home to Cheyne. We parted, I to drink with Dugdale who had been painting the now famous crew of *Target for Tonight* (Ministry of Information film), also one picture of A.P. Herbert... Arranged to sit as an auxiliary driver in September.

12. Guglielmo Marconi (1874–1937).

*Dugdale's portrait of June appeared
on the cover of 'Woman's Journal'.*

A.P. had introduced June to Tom Dugdale,[13] who immediately suggested June join him for a drink the next day—he had an idea he wanted to discuss. In 1941 Dugdale was among the many artists who had been commissioned to create works for the War Artists' Advisory Committee (WAAC). This body, headed by art historian Kenneth Clark,[14] aimed to create imagery for use in propaganda and information campaigns and to provide employment for the country's artists. The WAAC portrait artists working on the home front were directed to choose factory workers, firemen, shipbuilders, nurses and civil defence workers as subjects rather than figures of authority, and to show them in informal poses. The underlying message was that the war effort was a unifying project,

13. Thomas Cantrell Dugdale (1880–1952).
14. Sir Kenneth Clark (1903–1983), art historian and director of the National Gallery.

a joint effort by the entire population, irrespective of class, gender and age, and that ordinary citizens who showed fortitude in stressful conditions were the heroes and heroines of that effort.

Sixty-one, bespectacled, down-to-earth and avuncular, Thomas Cantrell Dugdale was not born into privilege. He started life in Blackburn, Lancashire, the son of a law stationery salesman, and went to Manchester Municipal School of Art, afterwards embarking on a career as a book illustrator. During the First World War he served as a staff sergeant in the Middlesex Yeomanry in North Africa, the Middle East, Gallipoli and the Balkans. His artistic talents were recognised and he was given permission to make official visual records of incidents.

After the First World War, Dugdale increasingly specialised in portraiture: captains of industry, politicians and actresses (among them Vivien Leigh, Jessie Matthews and Wendy Hiller), but he also showed a sharper edge. His 1936 'The Arrival of the Jarrow Marchers in London, Viewed From an Interior' was a comment on society's divisions: an upper-class woman in a lamé evening dress, a cigarette holder in hand, stares out of the window at the hordes of unemployed and hungry working-class protesters who have arrived at Hyde Park Corner, while her uninterested male companion ignores them, smoking.

Wearing her navy blue ambulance service greatcoat (but not the cap) June sat for Dugdale at least five times between September and November. According to his obituary in *The Times*, Dugdale was an 'impulsive, emotional man, greatly liked by his associates'.[15] June would have found him easy to confide in. His portrait perfectly captured the tension within her: the end of the Blitz, which had brought terrible, traumatising excitement, created a vacuum in which June was now stuck, unhappy, frustrated and directionless. He showed her in three-quarters profile, gazing out into the middle-distance, her expression contemplative, on the verge of world-weary.

The portrait was finished in January 1942 and in the following

15. *The Times*, 14 Nov 1952, 8E.

October Dugdale showed it at the Royal Academy. Whether June bought it or was given it afterwards by Dugdale is not known, but she acquired it somehow and it remains in her family.

While June was away in Cornwall she had received no word from Harry. 'H. hasn't rung up,' she wrote simply on 2 September, her birthday. Her own emotions were blocked—she had felt unable to find words to write to him. By the time she got off the Penzance train at Paddington she had descended into melancholy. She and Ann talked into the night. 'H.'s picture in my room. Slight comfort,' she wrote acidly, probably referring to his own portrait of her. It was another five days before she heard from him—'Letter from H.' She said nothing about its contents. Worse, almost: despite her efforts there was still no word from Harding-Newman about her transfer from AS179.

In an effort to bat away her disappointment, she saw friends—her ambulance colleagues John Crocker and Mary Tolstoy, and A.P., who was always available to comfort and mentor. She alternated between monotonous shifts at AS179 and evenings at the Hungaria or the Mirabelle and the Players Club, but it all seemed pointless.

There was also stunning news from her old AS22 colleagues: 'Heard to my amusement and bewilderment how I had been accused of being the thief of 22 Stn.' She had never been directly confronted and the culprit had been identified in February as 'Morris', but to have grown close to a set of people in circumstances of extreme stress, to crouch together in the dugout while bombs whined and exploded nearby, only to find out that she had been distrusted and whispered about behind her back was crushing and intensified her symptoms. She suffered 'crashing headaches' and tense muscles, and booked further appointments with Miss O.

Harry was not much help and was still sporadically incommunicado. He phoned on 21 September. '[He's] on leave,' she wrote miserably. 'He spent the morning with me. Left all too mysteriously before lunch.'

❖

Wednesday 15 October Feeling frightful. Up with difficulty and
eventually left for Odsey on a motor-bicycle. Exciting quite new
experience. First 10 miles terrifying, forgot how to stop.

June had spent the previous day drinking at the Café Royal,[16] the
Ritz, the Berkeley and the Antelope, and had had little sleep—she
had been woken at four to be introduced to Ann's friends Frank
Waldron and Murrough Loftus,[17] who were staying in Cads' Alley.
It was not the best preparation for her journey to Hertfordshire
on a borrowed motorbike.[18] 'With all the luck arrived at Odsey
Corner in two hours and as I thawed the hangover came back.'
The return journey was, if anything, more dangerous.

Glorious sunny morning. Little on the roads but army convoys.
At Stevenage the thing gave a quiet chuff and faded. Five garages
in Stevenage didn't touch such bikes. Fat motherly man came
to the rescue. Took the thing to pieces and put it together again.
Took an hour. Off again. Stopping every 100 yards. Knebworth
at last. 'Don't touch motorbikes.' After struggling for 2 hours in
front of 4 empty-handed tough mechanics embarrassed them.
They took it to bits again in spite of my protesting that that was
done a mile back. Continued to London. Seemed so frightfully
remote and distant. Discovered the trouble was no petrol.

June managed to fill the tank with the help of mechanics at
another garage and continued her journey.

Alas forgot completely the oil. It happened. The nightmare of
years past. It seized up suddenly. I didn't do a handstand or
catapult over the front. Pushed the thing a mile. Got some oil
and at last I got to the metropolis... Telephoned Daphne [Catt].

16. The Café Royal is at 68 Regent Street.
17. Frank Arthur Lovegrove Waldron (1916–1988); Maurice Pierce Murrough
Loftus (1912–1991), the son of the Conservative MP Pierse Loftus. Both served
in the Scots Guards.
18. June did not give a reason for not going to Odsey by train.

More enjoyable were her river jaunts with A.P. On 19 October she wrote of her elation after a 'night of adventures' when she returned to Lindsey House covered in mud, with rips in her trousers. The *Water Gypsy* had lost the dinghy when it barely scraped under Battersea Bridge in an exceptionally high tide and A.P. had had to dive into the water to retrieve it. There was no time to change her clothes before she was due to meet a new acquaintance, Randall Gough,[19] a US naval attaché. 'He was rather taken aback by the sight of me (fisherman's jersey, old trousers). I was an exhibit of war in London.'

As her male friends disappeared into the services, June filled their places with new ones, many of them from overseas. Through the PEP lunches, she became acquainted with the Canadian journalist and socialist Graham Spry and Claude Mowbray Berkeley, a translator for the League of Nations, who was now serving in the army, as well as a group from the American diplomatic community. She also mentioned Humphrey Brooke, an art historian and archivist, and the historian Felix Markham.[20]

Harry had not quite disappeared from June's life—he still occasionally wrote or phoned—but in his absence others came in hot pursuit. Murrough Loftus tried to romance her with drinks at L'Apéritif and dinner at the Lansdowne, but she was not interested, describing him a 'crazy Irishman'. He was 'too odd' and she was unimpressed when he 'announced loudly in the hall by the light of the nightlight that he was madly in love'.

On 22 November, June bumped into Humphrey Brooke who was walking by the river with the artists Anthony Devas[21] and Augustus John. June actively avoided John, who had expressed an interest in painting her but had a reputation for horrible lechery.

19. Randall Gough is unidentified.
20. Graham Spry (1900–1983), became personal assistant to Sir Stafford Cripps 1942–45 and travelled with him to India; Claude Mowbray Berkeley (1906–1973) was born in Lausanne, Switzerland; Thomas Humphrey Brooke (1914–1988); Felix Maurice Hippisley Markham (1908–1992).
21. Thomas Anthony Devas (1911–1958) and his wife Nicolette Macnamara (1911–1987), were both artists. Nicolette's sister Caitlin was married to the poet Dylan Thomas.

She must have written to Harry about it because he replied, 'frankly warning me against old disgusting John', but she became fond of Devas, who was also a portrait painter, and visited him and his wife Nicolette and their newborn son. She began sitting for him in late January.

Despite Harry's concern for June's safety, his interest in her was fading. While Loftus eventually took the hint and moved on, Humphrey Brooke frequently trekked across Battersea Bridge to visit June at AS179. He gamely played her at ping-pong, inviting her to join him at the Berkeley and to dine and dance at the bohemian Pheasantry Club in the King's Road.[22] He did not realise that he was soon to have a rival, whose zest for life, and for her, June found an exhilarating change.

22. The Pheasantry is at 152 King's Road; the Pheasantry Club was in the basement and closed in 1966.

Love, Possibly

Wednesday 26 November 1941 Bicycled to West End. Charged to speaker lunch at PEP on bicycle, buying cream cheese on the way and arriving with eyes full of grief in bad temper. Sat next to Felix Markham and Fred Hurday (USA). The speaker did not arrive... A good substitute on Industry (reorganisation taking the place of production). Claude [Berkeley] and Papandreou sat opposite me. Good roast duck.

Dashed back to Cheyne. Humphrey [Brooke] arrived with Maggie Teyte records and with apologies for spilling beer on me. He walked over bridge with me... Bill Batt, Averell Harriman's secretary, wanted me to go on to a party.[1]

IN WAR THERE was no time to lose. If something was to be done, it must be done now. If you delayed, the situation might change and you would lose out. In love, you saw your chance and grabbed it. Twenty-five-year-old Harvard graduate William Batt[2] was posted to London in April 1941 as an executive secretary to the Lend-Lease mission of American industrialist and diplomat W. Averell Harriman,[3] which was based at the US embassy in Grosvenor Square. Bill was seated at the table at PEP when June

1. 'Fred Hurday' is unidentified. June's spelling veered between Hurday, Howday and Hoday. Probably Andreas Papandreou (1919–1996), Greek socialist politician. Maggie Teyte (1888–1976) was a British operatic soprano.
2. William Loren Batt Jr (1916–2004).
3. William Averell Harriman (1891–1986), US businessman, diplomat and politician, went on to be US ambassador to the Soviet Union. After the war he was ambassador to the UK, Governor of New York and served in various offices under multiple US presidents. Under the Lend-Lease policy, the US supplied the Britain (and other states) with food, oil and war material, including hardware, free or on loan.

arrived in her ambulance service greatcoat, and was instantly smitten, and although June turned down his invitation, she gave him her phone number. He rang the next day: 'We had a strange conversation for the first-ever. I said I would dine on Saturday. He said, he couldn't bear it, he didn't deserve it etc!' She was rather nonplussed by him. His strangeness—unlike Murrough Loftus's—was appealing. 'So tall, so wonderfully odd, like some tree, almost from another planet!'

Batt, the son of a prominent mechanical engineer and industrialist, was a serious young man with ambitions for a career in government, but he had a youthful expressiveness quite unlike the stiffer, more formal British manners June was used to. She agreed to meet him at the Embassy club in Old Bond Street on Saturday evening; they went on to the Park Lane Hotel, 'milling with Americans,' where they bumped into Batt's colleague Fisher Howe,[4] an intelligence officer. 'Joy!' she wrote in her diary as she described Fisher and Bill dancing in their socks at a nightclub. Encouraged by Bill's enthusiasm for one of her favourite occupations, dancing, June began to reciprocate his feelings.

The next few days were a proverbial whirlwind. Everything was congenial and fun. Bill came to see June at No. 97 bearing a gift of silk stockings, and then they headed off to the Queen's Club for lunch.[5] They walked back to Lindsey House beside the river in the grey fog and Bill accompanied June across the bridge to her shift at AS179, where he dutifully played her at ping-pong. She extended her friendship to his friends. When she came off shift, Fisher Howe rang up: 'Hello, is that Whistler's mother?' he joked. He had last been at 'Whistler's House' when his grandfather, an art collector, had taken him there as a child.

If June and Bill had known how little time they were to have together perhaps they would have packed in even more. June spent two nights at Odsey Corner, her visit marred by the onset

4. Fisher Howe (1914–2015), an executive officer with the US Office of Strategic Services (OSS), a predecessor to the CIA, in London.
5. The Queen's Club, a private sporting club with multiple tennis courts, is in Palliser Road, West Kensington.

of a debilitating cold, and arrived back in London 'feeling like death', not helped by reading William Shirer's account of the Nazi occupation of the Rhineland.[6] It had made her weep on the train. She was cheered later by a letter from George Turnbull, who was stationed in the Syrian desert, in which he had enclosed a pressed flower, which she pinned carefully into the back of her diary. It meant he was alive, at least up until the time of writing, which is all you could know about loved ones serving abroad.

Bill insisted they dine at La Belle Meunière[7] in Fitzrovia, which she managed, propped up with painkillers, but paid for her pleasure in the morning ('golf balls in the neck, beehive head, feeling awful'). All that day, alternately shivering and sweating, she sheltered in bed under her eiderdown, while Claude Berkeley and her fellow lodgers Millie Balfour, Ann and Patience ministered to her. Humphrey Brooke, Paul Ziegler, Esther Darlington, John Perfect and even Harry Colvile, wearing the RAF uniform June had helped him buy, paid court the next day and she set some of her guests to work unpicking the German silk parachute her aunt had given her.

Friday was slightly better, although the circus of visitors did not abate. Humphrey Brooke returned, bearing Champagne and a book of Augustus John's drawings. He played a recording of *Don Giovanni* on June's pride and joy, her new electric gramophone.

Saturday 6 December In bed all the morning. Harry was in and out, mostly out. Got up for tea party in my room. Graham Spry arrived with box of drawing pins which he pinned into the sole of his shoe, tap dancing furiously at intervals. Harry took his leave. Paul, Ann and Terrence [Morris] and Claude [Berkeley] arrived... I found Harry returned and bathed in his room. Fisher rang up... asking me to high tea with him before he left for Scotland. B. Batt rang at last, dining with his 2 substitutes just come up from Lisbon. Dinner at White Tower, Dorset House.[8] Packed.

6. *Berlin Diary*, published in New York in June 1941.
7. La Belle Meunière was at 5 Charlotte Street, W1.
8. The White Tower was at 1 Percy Street in the West End.

Feeling much better, June spent Sunday drinking port, working on the parachute and taking leave of Harry, who was returning to his station 'full of hopes [the war] was ending next year and painting again, hating going'. They had succeeded in building a friendship from the ashes of their romance.

That evening, at a few minutes after 6.15pm, while it snowed heavily and thunder and lightning crashed in the skies, June and Bill were ordering dinner from the waiter at the Mirabelle in Curzon Street. Seven thousand miles away in Honolulu, the Imperial Japanese Navy launched a surprise attack on the US naval base in which eighteen ships were destroyed or crippled and almost two and a half thousand men were killed.

After dinner, June walked with Bill through the blackout to the US embassy in Grosvenor Square.[9] Bill, who had responsibility for the building, which was largely deserted because Churchill had invited the higher-ups to Chequers for the weekend, went up to the roof to check on the firewatchers, leaving June in his office. According to the story June told her family years later, the phone rang and June did what was natural—picked it up. In what seems to us now an astonishing disregard for protocol, the White House official on the other end of the line gave her a message to pass on to Bill: the Japanese had attacked Pearl Harbor and President Roosevelt would soon be making an announcement about it in Congress.[10]

For Bill, there was no question over what he should do next. Roosevelt was bound to declare the US at war. As he walked June home he told her that he would return home immediately to enlist in the army. He called her the following afternoon.

9.   In 1941 the embassy was at 1 Grosvenor Square. In 1960 it moved to a new building at No. 24. It has since moved again, to Nine Elms in south London.
10. This was the seven-minute speech delivered on 8 December in which Roosevelt said that the previous day was 'a date which will live in infamy.' Congress declared war on Japan thirty-three minutes after he finished speaking.

Monday 8 December Could I dine? Joy. Got there at nine.
Together we listened to the news. Churchill speaking and then the
President. PM so long and drawn out. Bill so enthusiastic, nice
about him. Roosevelt short, to the point, better, sounded tired.
Terrific applause. Endless news, endless islands declaring war on
each other. China declares war on Germany, Italy and Japan!

They ate in Soho and danced for the last time at the Embassy,
and then it was time to get a taxi to Euston station for Bill's train
to Liverpool and the boat home.

Together we walked down dark, almost misty deserted platforms,
played with the electric trucks and at last there was no time so he
went slowly away to America. How unnecessary it seems, another
star has gone out. Waited ages for a taxi, talked to nice policeman
and felt better. Home alone to Cheyne.

Tired, still suffering from her cold and bewildered at the
speed of her loss, June felt 'pretty desolate'. A letter from Bill,
written at the dock as he waited to embark for New York, arrived
at Cheyne Walk in the morning. 'It wasn't easy leaving you at the
train last night. It was ever so grand of you to come down. Did
you get home all right? Little things to worry about, but it's the
little things you remember, the way you looked when the train
pulled out, your eyes shining. Goodbye, Sweetness. We'll see each
other again soon. 'Ole 'itler can't keep us apart, not yet.' They had
known each other for a total of thirteen days.

During the tempestuous voyage across the Atlantic—'this
little cockleshell of a boat has alternated between lying on its sides
and standing on its ends'—Bill wrote June long, chatty letters. He
was 'damn glad' the US had finally joined the war, 'and can stop
frightening each other and start in on Hitler and the Japs'. He
had heard that Germany and Italy had declared war on the US.
'We haven't heard yet whether Congress has reciprocated but
presumably it has,' he wrote. 'That's too marvelous for words.
Now it's all but on the table. Them against us... Of course I

Bill Batt wrote to June after his return to the
US following the attack on Pearl Harbor.

won't know till I get there, but I bet you the morale at home is magnificent. Mine is.'

He expounded on the need for the US to take the offensive in the war and to launch another expeditionary force in Europe. He wrote about his visions, 'castle-building' he called it, for a postwar new world order. 'Whatever the solution is, it must be along the road of greater security and economic opportunity for the masses of the people of the earth. The victory we earn must be for the people, for the have-nots. Suddenly I remembered that we had never discussed these things together, you and I... I want to know what you feel—not only this but about everything.' He also pleaded for the 'mugshot you're going to send me of yourself in the uniform you had on when I met you—hat and everything'.

❖

Christmas 1940, when June was stranded in a blitz-torn London with Di and her mother, had been dreary. This year was quite different. June spent Christmas Eve lunching at the Café Royal with Harry Colvile ('in tremendous form, gay, happy I believe') reminiscing about his Swiss childhood, followed by Disney's *Dumbo* ('which we loved') at the cinema. She allowed herself the luxury of a fire in her room and spent the evening cosily drinking *glühwein* with Claude Berkeley and listening to the joint broadcast by Churchill and Roosevelt from the White House in which they addressed their 'fellow workers for freedom' and praised the efforts of all involved in the 'very great cause'. It would be a 'strange Christmas,' said Churchill, but he hoped that young people would be able to enjoy an 'evening of happiness in a night of storms'.

Thursday 25 December On duty 8 in grey dawn, greyer Battersea... Harry came to church with me at the Georgian church by the river[11] which is lovely but the vicar was hopeless. Had 2 hours off—a present from the LCC.

Murrough Loftus arrived 'like a fairy dogmother [sic]' and whisked her off to the Hyde Park Hotel for a five-course lunch complete with flaming Christmas pudding and then it was back to Lindsey House to prepare for the ball.

The ballroom looked so lovely, the lighted trees, candles, buffet. Great having Harry there. It was a beautiful dance, a strangely gentle stiffness about it. Mrs Mary and Claude Berkeley played waltzes on the two grand pianos. There were about 50 Greeks. Americans, Canadians very well represented. Afterwards Harry, Humphrey [Brooke] and I sat by the dying embers and discussed the party. Everyone had had presents from the tree. Humphrey gave me Elgar's *Enigma Variations*.

11. St Mary's Church, Battersea.

June received a telegram from Bill, sent from his army training camp in Pennsylvania: 'Dearest girl one thing on earth could make me happier this Christmas Day that would be you.' Buoyed up by transatlantic love and the warmth of her life at Lindsey House, she was able, at least for now, to forget her dilemma. She abandoned the effort to get a transfer and now sought to step off the treadmill and leave the ambulance service altogether, but until that happened, she intended to throw herself into entertainments and diversions.

While she spent the 26th assisting a midwife 'in grey fog' in Battersea, June made plans for another ball at Lindsey House and she enlisted her new friend Canadian journalist Graham Spry to help organise it as a fundraiser for the Royal Canadian Regiment. When Spry left London—he was appointed personal assistant to Sir Stafford Cripps[12] and went with him on his diplomatic mission to India—she continued the project without him.

On 1 January 1942 when June attended the Pageant of the Empire and her Allies at the Royal Albert Hall, she noticed the Russian ambassador, Ivan Maisky,[13] looking pensive, and yearned to discuss this with Bill. None of her previous boyfriends had affected her this way. Harry was friendly but diffident and distant, and she had been unable to feel close to him. She liked to see George Turnbull when he was in London on leave, and enjoyed his letters, but he was now simply a friend to her. Similarly, she kept Peter Vaughan at arm's length. Bill was different. She missed his boundless energy and enthusiasm for politics. Their connection had been short and intense, and their conversations had provoked new questions in her.

There was no indication in June's diaries that she and Bill had sealed their commitment to each other with intimacy. During wartime some people seek love as both a solace and a confirmation that life continues alongside danger and death; in that search

12. Churchill considered Labour politician and cabinet member Sir Stafford Cripps (1889–1952) a rival and sent him to India to negotiate an agreement with the nationalist leaders that would keep India loyal to the British war effort.
13. Ivan Maisky or Maysky (1884–1975).

many mistake lust for love. Keeping a lid on sexual desire could be a struggle. The blackout offered myriad opportunities for illicit assignations or chance encounters. 'As soon as the bombs started to fall, the city became like a paved double bed,' Quentin Crisp famously wrote in *The Naked Civil Servant*.[14] From 1939 to 1942 births outside marriage increased by over forty-three per cent and there was a seventy per cent rise in sexually transmitted diseases.[15] Colleagues facing danger together, especially where they shared sleeping spaces or shelters, such as in the ambulance service, could become emotionally close in a short period of time.

With Bill thousands of miles away, Humphrey Brooke, who had been in pursuit of June from the time he first met her, considered his next move. If she recognised that he sought something more than friendship, she may have chosen to ignore it. They became frequent companions; they went shopping and to the ballet at Sadlers Wells, and he helped her pass the time by playing ping-pong at AS179. She regularly called on him at the Public Records Office, where he worked. Humphrey assumed that their feelings for each other were building to a crescendo.[16] June, meanwhile, was receiving long, effusive letters from Bill—one begins 'Girl that I love with the love that passeth all understanding'—and she was also immersed in preparations for the ball in aid of the Canadians.

The day of the ball, 24 January, was chaotic. 'A hundred things' went wrong, according to June. The band was terrible. There was not enough food. Harry, home on leave, went off in a huff. June didn't explain the reason for it, just that his behaviour was 'too ghastly'. 'Why must good men be such temperamental fools? Such a waste of time,' she complained. Still, there was much to celebrate. The ballroom was packed. The wine flowed. 'So many people to see, so little time,' wrote June. 'Wonderful miscellany of persons, young and old. Professors, historians, actors, playwrights, Americans, Greeks, of course, Canadians.

14. Quentin Crisp, *The Naked Civil Servant* (1997). New York: Plume. p.154.
15. Levine, p.213.
16. Unbeknown to his friends and probably to himself at this stage, Brooke had bipolar disorder.

A.P. anchored the *Water Gypsy* outside and came in on great form. Kenneth Lindsay was there.'

Not everyone was happy with how things went. After the ball, June noticed that Ric's sister Di seemed preoccupied, not realising that this was a sign of the increasing tension between Di and the Lindsey House boarders, and especially June herself. It was no small job keeping such a large property clean, sourcing the coal, organising the kitchen, managing the cleaners and cooks, and dealing with the myriad problems that arose from housing forty single people—even without a big, noisy party to contend with. All Di really wanted was peace and quiet, especially now that she was in the early stages of pregnancy.[17]

To Di, parties in the ballroom at No. 96, which was essentially in the Stewart-Joneses' private domain, must have felt like an invasion. Under her management, the freewheeling come-what-may bohemian everyone-is-welcome atmosphere cultivated by her brother came to an end. Running up and down stairs, nipping in and out of each others' rooms, slamming doors, laughter and loud conversation stopped. Now everything had to be spoken *sotto voce*. The ever-loyal, ever-protective Christiana Sams became Di's enforcer. Her standard mantra to anyone who transgressed in some way was 'We don't do that in this house, Miss Smith' and so on. The lodgers must have thought they had been transported back to boarding school.

June was suffering her own dissatisfactions. The ball was an enjoyable interlude but she was in the 'depths of gloom' and felt that her life was in the doldrums. None of her many attempts to be granted a transfer from AS179 had borne fruit and even Kenneth Lindsay's letter to County Hall had had no effect. Her despair was obvious to her ambulance station colleagues. 'The firemen were sweet and tried to cheer Miss Spencer by making faces, playing and singing favourite tunes and drawing very cleverly on the blackboard,' she wrote. She envied her brother David who was about to be posted abroad with his regiment. In desperation,

17. Lees-Milne, *Ancestral Voices*, p.8.

she consulted another fortune-teller, the third since the start of the war, and Ann helped her fill in applications to work for the Foreign Office and MI5.

Then her best friend Ann Channer revealed that she was being posted to Sweden to work for Sir Victor Mallet, the British ambassador.[18] June was devastated. Ann was her 'prop and spur'—especially now that the easygoing atmosphere at Lindsey House had gone. There would be no more convivial times at PEP. 'Kenneth Lindsay sat next to me at lunch and pretended it was an accident! Smoked the last cigar in PEP,' she wrote on 26 January, although it turned out not to be. Bad weather delayed Ann's departure and she and June squeezed in another lunch on 4 February. At King's Cross two days later, June saw off her friend on the night train to Scotland to take the plane to Stockholm.

To crown things, she had to fend off Humphrey Brooke. He had tried to embrace her and she had pushed him away. 'I don't want this, I only want you as a friend,' she had told him. 'I don't want my friends to be lovers.' Stung and annoyed, Humphrey wrote to her a few days later, to explain why they must now see less of each other. 'Your attitude is to build a wall around yourself,' he wrote, perhaps not unfairly, but he went on to insult her. 'Your relationships with men are dominated by a repugnance of things physical... You are satisfied with less than a real friendship and actually prefer the casual, hollow relationships, where no feelings are involved, cardboard-puppet affairs.' He refused to be one of her 'stuffed sort of dining-out companions,' he said. In a particularly insulting passage, he claimed that her refusal to accept his 'very gentle' advances meant that their friendship would be 'a horrible stunted sub-human affair, tolerable only among cretins'. June, stunned, did not mention the letter in her diary but did not destroy it, preserving it amongst her papers.

June and Humphrey seem to have made no attempt to avoid each other after this, carrying on much as before; they met as part of larger groups but also *à deux* for meals out in the West End,

18. Sir Victor Mallet (1893–1969), envoy to Sweden 1940 to 1945.

expeditions to the ballet and visits to art exhibitions—they went to see Jacob Epstein's new bronzes 'Jacob and the Angel', 'Two Heads of Maisky' and 'Haile Selassie' at the Leicester Galleries in Mayfair. He regularly rang her at Lindsey House, made her suppers at his flat in Markham Square and gave her presents of roses and jewellery, which she recorded in her diary without comment.

Tuesday 10 March The usual succession of half-asleep nightmares—finally waking at 2pm to find I had been asleep all the time and all the intruders were nightmares. Walked to the King's Road. Noticed grey look on most faces.

In the early part of 1942 June's physical ailments multiplied. She suffered a string of illnesses: temperatures, toothache and sleep problems. The 'paralysingly cold' weather, the misery of the ambulance shifts, anxiety about the war—British defeat in Java was imminent—and separation from Bill brought her lower than ever. Finally, however, on 14 March, came a small victory. 'Big news. The Foreign Office offered me appointment, letter by the afternoon post. Hurrah at last!' She wrote at once to LAAS HQ at County Hall to request her release.

Her hopes were dashed as quickly as they were raised. Gates,[19] the station officer, was furious when she found out, pulling June up on her failure to follow correct procedure and inform her first. She made it clear that until she received an explicit instruction from Harding-Newman at head office, June would have to continue to do her shifts at AS179. There would be, it seemed, no end to the dull make-work and endless ping-pong.

Perhaps it was June's fixation on leaving the ambulance service that blinded her to a threat coming from a completely different direction.

19. Gates is unidentified.

The Menagerie

Friday 10 April 1942 On duty all day until 4. Wrote to Ann,
Patience etc. Posted parcel to [Ann in] Stockholm. Off 4, to
West End to shop. Like a thunderbolt from the blue that night
Betty Stucley arrived, a great splendid mass of energy, to take
over from Di and run the Menagerie... Talked for hours to
Betty—she's fun. Feeling lousy with a cold.

DI STEWART-JONES HAD recently suffered two blows: her pregnancy had miscarried—in the circumspect way of the times,
June wrote, 'Poor Di. News of her hopes fallen through'—and
her mother Eva had been diagnosed with terminal cancer. At the
same time, Di's relationship with the residents of Lindsey House
was disintegrating and she asked Ric to find someone else to take
over the running of the house. As luck would have it, the cavalry
arrived in the shape of his friend Betty Stucley, who was looking
for a place to live in London.

Years later, Betty reported her conversation with Ric in
her (second) rollicking autobiography, *Life Is For Living*. 'So
there you are, Betty! I've been asking all over London what had
happened to you. I think you would be just the person to run the
place when I'm away. It needs livening up. Can you start today?'
said Ric. 'But you know nothing about my capabilities,' replied
Betty. 'I know quite enough,' said Ric. 'You'd make the house
cheerful. Do come!'[1]

In her own words Betty was 'six feet tall, impetuous, excitable,
and optimistic' and able to 'drive, cook, type, sew, organize,
public speak'. 'I have always had a boundless confidence in my

1. Stucley, p.202.

own abilities, and usually plunge in and do the job first, and find out how it should have been done afterwards,' she wrote. Born in 1906 in Devon, the daughter of a baronet, Betty had dutifully made her debut at court, but the world of society parties where she might be expected to catch a suitable husband was not for her. She later studied at the London School of Economics (where, coincidentally, she made the acquaintance of Mary Swinfen) and by the time she turned up at Lindsey House she was already the author of two novels, a children's guide to economics and her first autobiography, and had worked as a cook for her local regiment, a children's therapist and a village schoolteacher. She joined the Motorised Transport Corps early in the war, had served in France and made a dramatic escape from advancing enemy forces.[2]

After settling in to her new accommodation at No. 94, Betty made her way to supper in the dining room at No. 96. In keeping with Di and Nanny's strictures, the atmosphere was hushed. The boarders spoke to each other in monastic whispers and after eating slid away to their rooms. Her attempts to converse in a normal tone of voice—'I think it's going to rain,' she said to her neighbours at the table—were greeted with alarm, or ignored. Ric was not wrong. The place did indeed need 'brightening up'.

When the meal was over, 'a very lovely girl came and invited me to coffee in her room,' wrote Betty in her memoirs. This was June. 'We climbed to the top of the house to where [she] lived. She had a huge attic with a sloping ceiling and a magnificent view. It must have been the nursery I think. As she shut the door behind her, she turned and fixed her beautiful blue eyes on me—her skin was pure alabaster—and said: "Thank goodness you've come... You're just what we need. You can see what it's like here. We all sit and whisper... You said something banal in a normal voice. That's not done here."'[3]

Within a couple of days, the icy silence at supper was thawing, replaced with real conversation and a little laughter. Residents who had previously avoided the dining room started to appear.

2. See page 58.
3. Stucley, p.204.

The change in management did not meet universal approval. June reported that there were 'great undercurrents in the house over the new arrival'. Betty ignored these and instead threw herself into getting things done—she took over all of Di's household tasks and, according to June, started 'distempering [the walls] madly'.

Betty's arrival lifted June's spirits but the pain of having to serve at AS179 remained. While she waited for permission to leave she was frequently unwell, by turns feverish and exhausted, unable to do her shifts, fit only to take gentle strolls, unpick the parachute and watch the river roll by from her bed. As the weeks went on, she took intermittent breaks at Odsey Corner, until she was sufficiently improved to go back across the bridge and resume her obligations. 17 April, the day of June's return to duty at the ambulance station from sick leave, was also the first day that civil defence workers were rostered to do 24-hour shifts rather than the more usual eight. It was also her last day of service. 'My release papers arrived, causing chaos in the office,' she wrote. 'Never had they heard yet of an application for release being granted... [I had] an odd feeling of a convict who has served his term...' When she got back to No. 97 there was 'great rejoicing' and she felt 'bewilderingly free... Everyone so pleased for me'.

She was so happy that she failed to notice that Humphrey Brooke was building up to another emotional scene. His awful letter had not persuaded her to submit and neither had his carefully angled gifts. He 'once more lay his heart on the table'. June was unimpressed. 'Oh dear, what an egotistical old bore,' she wrote. He hung about for a few weeks, occasionally turning up at Lindsey House to be put on parachute-unpicking duty, but either gradually drifted away or was pushed out of the circle by June. His name appeared in her diaries for the last time on 6 July 1942, when she described him as looking like a 'large pink mass'. He was in the reserve of the King's Royal Rifles and before long left to serve as a 'monuments man' working on the rescue of artworks and historic buildings in Europe.[4]

4. Monuments men (and a few women) mitigated the damage done to works of art and other artefacts and found and recovered artworks stolen by the Nazis.

At Lindsey House, galvanised by Betty's project to liven things up and bring the house together, the boarders brainstormed ideas for an event that would lift the mood and raise money for a good cause. In the end it was decided that they would hold another party—the Inter-Allied Dance—in the ballroom. Everyone was encouraged to invite their friends and to contribute to the cost of food and drink. Nanny Sams disapproved but Betty managed to talk her round.

June, exhausted by yet another viral infection, was due to start work at the Foreign Office in Whitehall, and needed to be properly well. After a restorative weekend at Odsey, she felt ready and in the mood to start networking.

> *Tuesday 28 April* Began new job. Arrived at HM Foreign Office at 11am! Met Rosemary Adams.[5] What a joyous new day. Adams and I lunched at National Gallery Service Canteen and met friends in common.

June never divulged, in the diaries or to her children, exactly what she did in a basement at the Foreign Office, except to say that it involved encrypting messages from the government, including from Churchill, whose handwriting she found difficult to read (I wonder what he would have made of her own scrawl). Given her difficulties with spelling, it was perhaps not an ideal role for her, and from the start she doubted her own abilities, constantly 'in fear and trembling of being kicked out'. To her surprise and intense relief, she managed to pass her probation period.

The party at Lindsey House on Saturday 9 May turned out to be a success, just the confidence boost June needed. Guests arrived in droves—Betty estimated that there were two hundred people of eighteen different nationalities—the house looked spectacular, 'wonderful galaxies of flowers... glorious lilac, rhododendrons (a wine dark red), all flowering shrubs and scented' and it was only Nanny's insistence that stopped the dancing at midnight.

5. Elizabeth Rosemary Adams (1914–1983), née Dale.

Success or not, the day had been stressful for June, who had had to fit in an early morning hairdresser's appointment and a day's work in Whitehall beforehand. If anything, the day afterwards, Sunday, was better fun. 'Lovely sun. Wandered about the Cheynes,' wrote June. 'We danced reels before lunch in the ballroom! Played ballet on the grand piano. Delicious lunch. Rum and coffee, a photograph album with the Darwins.[6] We climbed on the roof and took photographs of the river among the chimneys, wrote letters. More people to huge tea party in my room, pounds of cream cakes.'

That evening June listened to Churchill address the nation on the radio: 'This latest chapter, universal war, confronts us with many difficulties and immense complications,' he said. 'But is there any thoughtful, sensible person who cannot see how vastly and decisively the awful balances have turned to the advantage of the cause of freedom?' Despite the setbacks in the Far East, the Allies would 'drive on to the end and do our duty, win or die; God helping us, we can do no other.'

The ball secured Betty's acceptance by the boarders, barring a few of the 'old regime', and a new feeling pervaded the dining room. 'Meals became lively. We all talked a lot and giggled a great deal, retiring to one or other of the rooms afterwards to finish the conversation,' she wrote in her memoirs.

A few weeks later, it became clear that radiotherapy was not helping Eva Stewart-Jones's cancer and she was moved from her nursing home to Lindsey House to spend her last days tended to by nurses and surrounded by her children. When June returned to London after a weekend at Odsey Corner, she found Ric 'making a passageway of my room to Cads' Alley through my cupboard' in order to reroute 'traffic' away from Eva's room at No. 96. He did

6. Artists Robert ('Robin') Vere Darwin (1910–1974), a great-grandson of Charles Darwin, later Rector of the Royal College of Art, and Yvonne Darby (1909–1984). During the war Robin worked at the camouflage directorate of the Ministry of Home Security.

not want lodgers tramping past and making a noise. Jim Lees-Milne returned to the house to support him.

Eva died in the early hours of 31 May, but in keeping with the muted atmosphere, the news was slow to permeate through the house. 'At breakfast there was no reference to what had happened so that I wondered if indeed it had,' wrote Jim in his diary.[7]

June was working nights at the Foreign Office, napping there on the cold leather sofas and arriving home exhausted to snatch moments of unsatisfying sleep. In desperation, she took a sleeping powder that Bill had given her before he left for America and woke disoriented and thick-headed.

> *Monday 8 June* Home rejoicing that inhuman work over.
> Slept. A hideous black day. Betty broke the news to me that
> I must leave my room by the next day.

We don't know the nature of the Stewart-Joneses' complaint against June. She did not explain it in her diaries nor mention it in later years to her children. Perhaps her confused state had led her to say something for which Di and Ric could find no forgiveness; perhaps Di and Nanny saw the Inter-Allied Ball, with its noisy aftermath, as an infringement too far. Whatever it was, June was suddenly and brutally *persona non grata*.

> *Tuesday 9 June* All one's foundations seem to have been
> swept away, leaving immense misery... Slept for the last time
> in my room. Jim [Lees-Milne] and John [Perfect] brought tea
> to my room. Betty and Ric [Stewart-Jones] dashed in and swept
> my bed out into the street and into the basement of No. 93.

It was not that she was put out in the street—Ric had acquired No. 93 Cheyne Walk the previous year—but the hurt was profound. She had been evicted from her beloved 'studio' and marked out as a delinquent. She was stunned, unable to express herself. Her

7. Lees-Milne, *Ancestral Voices*, p.63.

diary entries were exceptionally clipped, even for someone who was not often expansive, the short sentences speaking of deep unhappiness. Everything looked bleak. She wrote of 'misery' and of days being 'grey', 'glum' and 'gloomy'. Unnamed ailments plagued her. She reported feeling 'extremely ill for no reason' and 'miserable, numb'. There was further pain when her friend Phil Scott,[8] a captain in the King's Royal Rifles, was reported killed in Libya: 'more misery in the house'.

June was still permitted to eat in the dining room but now had to knock at the front door of No. 96 like a visitor. 'Nanny let me in... I think she looked slightly guilty, which made me absurdly happy again,' she wrote. Later she discovered that 'Dragon Nanny' had given away her most treasured possession, her electric gramophone, to an untraceable guest. She assumed this was on purpose.

She spent hours moving her remaining belongings down the stairs of No. 97 and into the basement of No. 93, after which she retreated to Odsey Corner for the weekend, joined by Betty Stucley, but remained dejected and exhausted, and slept badly. The heat ('boiling hot') did not help, nor was there much joy in writing to Bill. 'Oh help, the bottom has fallen out,' she wrote in her diary on 17 July.

Alarmed by June's state, Benn Levy, who had reappeared after spending time in America, urged her to see a doctor, as did Ric, perhaps feeling guilty about the way she had been treated. She took herself off to see Miss O. but 'emerged after a long session feeling lower than bottom, with not a vestige of hope or faith in myself'. Things were terrible at the Foreign Office, too. Her new friend Rosemary Adams was leaving for a posting to Cairo. They had got 'tight' together on her last night and the next morning Rosemary stopped by at No. 93 to 'say what fun it was last night and to say goodbye and off she went on her bicycle—wonder where we shall meet next'. At the office, she was given very little work to do and, armed with a doctor's note, handed in her resignation.

8. James Philip Edmund Scott (b. 1915), brother of June's friend and fellow ambulance driver Katharine Scott. See page 39.

'So strange to be free,' she wrote, but there was none of the elation she felt when she was released from the ambulance service. There was nothing for it. It was time to give up London and return to her parents.

Four days later, June packed her day clothes, evening gowns, shoes, books, diaries, the parachute, belts and sewing machine into borrowed trunks. With the help of a friend's army batman she loaded them into a taxi and headed for King's Cross. The train guard told her she had more than twice the permitted weight but then took pity on her and let her put her things in his van. At Ashwell, she was met by the family gardener, who drove her the short distance to Odsey Corner, where she swiftly retired to the nursery to sleep. She was utterly depleted.

She was also unemployed. She had no civil defence duties, although she began to help out at her mother's Red Cross canteen and painted posters for it, so when in late August she was invited for another two-week break with the Dorrien Smiths at Tresco she did not hesitate. She took a slow train packed with dogs and babies, read Arthur Bryant's *English Saga*[9] until she reached Penzance, and crossed to Tresco. 'Oh joy, to see the sea again,' she wrote.

This time there was no adventure at Boskenna with the Colonel, Betty Poulsen and Mary Swinfen—just quiet days exploring the islands, bird-watching, shrimping and swimming, although without the companionship of Adie, who was serving in the Middle East. On her twenty-sixth birthday, the second that June had spent in Cornwall, she picked apples and hunted for shells on the beach. Most of the time, Lindsey House, Di, Nanny Sams and the Menagerie felt a million miles away but she did not succeed in hiding her sadness from her hosts. 'Pa said you looked very much down when you went to Scilly,' Adie wrote to her a few months later.

Back at Odsey Corner, June stuck to simple pleasures. She spent the days sewing, drawing, walking the dog, writing letters

9. *English Saga, 1840-1940* by Arthur Wynne Morgan Bryant (1899–1985) was published in 1940 and celebrated British patriotism.

and perusing the bookshops of Cambridge. As summer turned into autumn she made scattergun efforts to find work. She half-heartedly pursued the chance of a job painting filmsets; she took typing lessons and then lost interest; she applied to join the Women's Royal Naval Service (WRNS); she went for interviews at the Ministry of Information; she signed on at Letchworth Labour Exchange; she tried Universal Aunts again.

On visits to London, she stayed at No. 94 with Patience and Betty, and dined with Graham Spry at the Allies Club in Piccadilly and with A.P. at the Good Intent on the King's Road, but it was awkward and dispiriting to be there. In late September she went to see Ric to discuss the 'misunderstandings' leading to her eviction, emerging 'a thousand times relieved', although she did not detail their conversation and Ric did not invite her to move back in. On later trips, when she came up to London to look for jobs, she avoided Cheyne Walk and instead opted to stay with Eleanor McCaw,[10] whose brother Dick was a friend of her sister Janet's, at her bijou apartment in Cottesmore Court in Kensington.

London had lost much of its allure. Her old beloved nightclubs and restaurants were now crowded with people she did not know ('strangers everywhere'). One comfort, although it made her feel guilty for her inability to reciprocate at a similar rate, was the regular correspondence from Bill: words of encouragement and adoration, as well as gifts of silk stockings. By October, however, she was having serious doubts that their relationship would survive. She was unforthcoming in the diaries, merely stating 'Posted bad letter to William' on 6 October.

Tom Dugdale's portrait of June was hung at the Royal Academy in October as part of a show by the Royal Society of Portrait Painters. 'Bad painting of me in Burlington House,' she wrote, half joking, after she and her mother went to see it. Perhaps it reminded her of a difficult time when she was unhappy in the ambulance service. In passing, she noted that Harry

10. Eleanor Mary MacCaw (1916–1987), later MacInnes; Richard Eric McCaw (1920–1942).

Colvile had married one of his old friends, Geraldine Fitzgibbon.[11] 'How extraordinary,' she wrote and left it at that. She may have wondered if their own romance had been, for Harry, merely a diversion from his relationship with Geraldine.

Gradually her depression started to lift. The news from the Eastern front was good, which helped. 'Marvellous thrust forward by Russians holding the Germans back. Everywhere we advance,' she wrote, but she remained on guard. 'Trying to fortify myself at the same time "that some great blow might be waiting".' The safety of her brother David was a constant worry and it was a relief to receive a telegram from him ('Very fit and well') from the Middle East. Their sister Janet was once more at a loose end, having left the Land Army; she was now terrified of being called up. She and June went to Ashwell to enquire about factory work, without success.

In late November June was asked to attend an interview with the WRNS, who recommended she persevere for a job with the Admiralty, but when she got back to the flat, she found that John Postlethwaite[12] from the Ministry of Food (MoF) had left a message offering her a position. Here, at last, was something to do. The MoF was then the largest government department, with a remit covering every aspect of food supply from animal feed to brewing. Its offices were scattered across the country from central London to Colwyn Bay on the north Wales coast. June was to work in Portman Square, two blocks behind Oxford Street, on the British Restaurants project, and driving would be part of her duties. Her new boss, Herbert van Thal,[13] who sported a monocle

11. In the 1939 Register Frances Geraldine Dillon Fitzgibbon (1908–1969) was recorded as living with her mother Georgette and brother Robert in Hurley, Berkshire; Harry Colvile was listed at the same address. Geraldine was the sister of Constantine Fitzgibbon, whose *Winter of Bombs* includes a first-hand account of the 1940–41 Blitz in Chelsea, and sister-in-law of Theodora Fitzgibbon, whose memoir *With Love* covers her time living in Chelsea during the Blitz.
12. John Rutherford Parkin Postlethwaite (1883–1952), Divisional Officer at the Ministry of Food.
13. Herbert van Thal (1904–1983). After the war van Thal edited the 24-volume *Pan Book of Horror Stories* series.

and bow tie, had been a publisher, agent and author before the war and was entertaining, creative and urbane, with what he described in his memoirs as 'a ready liking for women'. Van Thal's job was to balance the competing demands for manpower of the food trades and the services, and to that end he and June visited scores of factories making everything from cotton bags to gin.

He was also helpful in finding June a new place to live. She was happy in the flat with Eleanor McCaw. It felt safer to share with just one other person than with a host of others, any one of whom might stab you in the back, but she needed a place of her own. Van Thal put her in touch with his erstwhile publishing partner Lady Margaret Douglas-Home,[14] whose small flat in Eaton Place would be available for six weeks. In the meantime, June and Eleanor spent some evenings with a new friend, Captain Charles Schlegel,[15] the Swiss military and air attaché, who entertained them with drinks, dinners, trips to the theatre and home movies of skiing in the Alps.

Then the hopeful mood was abruptly shattered by a telegram. Eleanor's 22-year-old brother Dick had been killed at Benghazi in Libya. 'Oh, how bloody life can be,' wrote June. Another star extinguished.

By 13 December June was installed in the Eaton Place flat, which came complete with Lillie, a live-in maid who brought her breakfast in bed, made fires in the grate and had supper ready for her when she came in from work. Brigadier General Robert C. Candee,[16] an American in charge of the Eighth Ground Air Support, lived downstairs and offered her lifts to work and gave her gifts of oranges.

Wednesday 16 December To the office. Drove [John]

14. Alexandra Margaret Elizabeth Spencer, later Douglas-Home (1906–1996).
15. Charles Schlegel was dispatched to London to keep Berne abreast of the latest developments in air warfare.
16. Robert C. Candee (1892–1963) .

Postlethwaite... to open the new British Restaurant at Ilford [Essex]. Lunched with the Mayor and Corporation and wasted a lot of time in his parlour. Great ideas of my painting posters. We then opened the Good Advice Centre, took tea with the Mayor and left.

In London there was a project to 'brighten up' British Restaurants with pictures and murals. 'It is well known that more benefit is derived from food if a person is happy and at ease while eating it,' commented the *West London Observer*.[17] It would be satisfying to think that this is what June meant by 'painting posters' and that her duties were not confined to driving.

As welcome as it was, the job did not assuage her low spirits. The black cloud of depression had returned. 'Feeling in the depths all the afternoon,' and 'Feeling miserable, despondent,' she wrote on 18 and 19 December. It did not help that she was moved to a new section, Manpower, based in Cork Street, and that on her occasional visits to Lindsey House she found it 'very empty and sadly unfriendly'. The romance with Bill Batt, foundering for weeks, was now shipwrecked. She rarely replied to his letters.

Christmas 1942 at Odsey Corner was a boost. She arrived on Christmas Eve to find her parents and Janet 'in high spirits'. 'Lovely to be there,' she wrote simply. There was goose for Christmas dinner and five days of pottering, visiting family, teas and dances with American officers at Royston Hospital. New Year's Eve was spent in London in the old style: in full evening dress, drinking and dancing with Robin and Yvonne Darwin at the Players club and the Embassy.

Thursday 31 December And so the year went out and in that haze and heat among such very pleasant company the New Year came in. We danced our way out at 5am, when the car arrived to take us home.

17. *West London Observer*, 6 Nov 1942, p.7H.

Destinations

Thursday 14 January 1943 Dined at the Mirabelle.
News of Tony's death in France. Hard to realise.

ANTHONY EUSTACE HILL,[1] brother of June's friends Robin and
Sukie and son of Barbara Hill, who had sponsored her debut
at Court in 1938, was shot down while on a reconnaissance
mission in France and died three months later, on 12 November.
He was 28. June took the train to Odsey after work on Friday,
and on Saturday sat with her family in the church at Ashwell for
the memorial service. 'The church was very full,' she wrote. 'The
service was difficult.' To say more risked allowing a flood of grief
to overwhelm her, so she did not.

She was grateful for distractions. Herbert van Thal's brother
Dennis[2] asked her to become involved in a project to make a
film about the London Philharmonic Orchestra in wartime, and
invited her to lunches with his friend the sculptor and writer Peter
Lambda[3] to discuss it. In the end nothing came to pass. Although
Battle for Music, a film about how the orchestra was kept together
during the war, was made, neither van Thal nor Lambda appeared
in the credits.[4]

Away from Lindsey House, June was living her life in brief
episodes; she made a series of short-lived friendships kindled

1. Anthony Eustace Hill (b. 1914), a squadron leader in the Royal Air Force
Volunteer Reserve.
2. Dennis van Thal (1906–1998) was a music arranger, theatre impresario and
film producer.
3. Peter Lambda (1911–1995), born in Budapest. During the war he worked for
the Crown Film Unit and wrote propaganda scripts for the BBC.
4. *Battle for Music* (1943) was directed by Donald Taylor and starred Joss
Ambler. The musicians played themselves.

briskly by circumstances and ended in the same serendipitous way. In November while playing squash at the Lansdowne she acquired a new friend, Pamela Ellis,[5] and discovered that she had also been an ambulance driver and that she had been born at Newham Hall, near Ashwell. With Pamela's husband William they went to the Ritz to join the Ellises' friends, a trio of theatre greats—Noël Coward, Ralph Richardson and John Gielgud.

A jolly dinner with famous and stimulating acquaintances was certainly an enjoyable diversion, but that was all it was. For June, everything felt wrong. Every hope that was raised was dashed. Even the crocuses pushing through in February managed only to induce melancholy and thoughts of what might have been. 'Dear Belgravia looked so stunning,' she wrote. 'There is something about its ghosts—all so silent and deserted but for a few cries of children with nurses. Bomb-chipped and damp but what a tale of past synthetic splendours.' She was drinking more and often woke with a hangover.

All around her, friends and colleagues were moving on, to marry, have babies, join the services or take new and purposeful jobs. June was delighted to hear that Ann, still in Stockholm, was now engaged to Swedish businessman Stig Kempe, but the news also felt like a blow.

> *Sunday 17 January* Back to London after tea. Lillie [the maid] cooked my dinner and the sirens sounded. The guns made a terrific noise, far louder than ever before it seemed. Everything shook. It seemed funny for the first time to have no tin hat... There was another burst in the early hours and Patricia Lloyd-Dolbey[6] [a neighbour] and I descended.

It had been six months since June mentioned a raid in her diaries and this one must have reminded her of the darkest days

5. Evelyn Pamela Hine, later Green, later Ellis (1916-?).
6. Evelyn Mary Patricia Stock, later Lloyd-Dolbey, later Stransky (b. 1913), a debutante and model who married the exiled Jan Stransky, son of the Czech Minister of Justice, in 1944.

of the Blitz and pointed up the changes in her circumstances. Not only was the tin hat gone, but also a hands-on active role in the war. She had to take her turn firewatching on the roof of her office block like everyone else, but that just meant hours of tedium, often in the cold, and a cricked neck from staring skywards.

❖

Thursday 25 February Back to breakfast. Lunched with Pen, feeling frightful, like the old days of 1941. Bed early.

Just as June was beginning to sink into despair she was invited for a medical by the Women's Royal Naval Service (WRNS), only to be informed that it had been postponed. She lost herself in an endless social round. She went out almost every night, to the theatre, to the cinema, to the Café Royal and the Lansdowne Club, and for drinks with the Ellises, but the humiliation of the Lindsey House *débâcle* still hurt. She went to a party given by Betty Stucley, who had moved out of Lindsey House, but found the 'Cheyne mass' who were also there 'slightly terrifying'.

Saturday 6 March Packed and by taxi to office. A bad morning for work. Ate sandwiches and chatted… Caught 1 train to Baldock, lorry to Odsey… Country deliciously soft and fresh. Mum and Dad read Ann's letter of her betrothal and welcome into Swedish nationality. Bed.

The last few diary entries June made in 1943 were barely coherent notes, dashed down at speed. Things were not going well at the Ministry of Food. The factory visits were boring, and the atmosphere in the office was, in her word, 'indescribable'. We are left to guess the reasons for this. Van Thal's film project had failed. There were further bittersweet reminders of past times when *Woman's Journal* magazine used Tom Dugdale's portrait of her for a full-colour cover. So much had happened since she sat for Dugdale: friends had departed, some of them for ever, and friendships had ended.

*June served in the WRNS at HMS Vulture
from late 1943.*

The 6 March diary entry was almost the last June wrote until after the war. While it is not possible to know the exact reasons for this hiatus, we can speculate that her acceptance into the Royal Navy and the events that followed prompted a final break with her journal.

On 28 July she arrived at the solid brick gates of HMS Pembroke III,[7] the Navy's huge college at Mill Hill in north London. As instructed, she carried a small suitcase in which she had packed a travel rug, gas mask and torch.[8] June's training

7. HMS Pembroke III was based at the requisitioned headquarters of the National Institute of Medical Research.
8. The WRNS was reformed in 1939—the service had been disbanded after the First World War—but, in common with the other services, did not allow women to be combatants. Their role was to free up men for fighting by performing clerical or domestic duties; they also worked on AA units, Radar stations, as pilots delivering planes to airfields, and in the secret communications units.

started immediately. Dressed in her probationer's navy blue overalls, she and the three hundred other women in her cohort attended lectures, drilled, route marched, cleaned and canteened, all very familiar duties from her LAAS days. It must have been water off a duck's back. She was nearly 27, had plenty of life experience and did not suffer from homesickness, unlike many of her teenage comrades. When the two weeks were up, those not up to the required standard bowed out or were sent packing. The rest, June included, were interviewed, given a medical, issued with proper uniform, welcomed into the service and posted.

Sunday 14 November 64mph blast off the briny! Hail, rain and brilliant sunshine. Lights fused. Morning spent chasing engineer. To Rock with Angus and Joan R. to take glider. Lovely wild autumn skies and moor. Ten in the M/T [Motor Transport] yard and A showed us his films. Very cold, back on 7 transport. Bathed. Read *Times* aloud.

Monday 25 November Brighter gale but still blasting winds. Letters David and Mum. Rocket shells go off. Pheasant pâté for tea. Fencing 1/2 hour. Treglos. Thunder and lightning. Very wild. Cold night.

Tuesday 16 November Enormous 10 o'clock coffee with Chubs in Padstow. Commandos barefooted walking about and swimming in full kit in the sea!

June was assigned to the Motor Transport division and, under orders, returned to Cornwall, this time to HMS Vulture at St Merryn, on the north coast, fifty-five miles and a world away from the eccentricities of Boskenna.

As a training base for airborne observers and aircraft carrier fighters, Vulture was crucial to the war effort. It was here that men from dozens of naval units and RAF squadrons learned to fly gliders, dive bomb, and land and take off from the four short runways. It is possible that June had duties at the satellite site Vulture II, the air-to-ground bombing and gunnery practice range run entirely by the WRNS—but we don't know. Apart from her brief official record, all that survives to document her service are the three diary entries from November and the draft of a note to the station master at Padstow to apologise for damaging some guttering with her lorry.

We can be sure that June would have known of the trainee pilots' frequent and, at times, deadly crash landings on Gulland Rock and of enemy attacks on the base. On 20 February 1944, the news came through that the destroyer HMS *Warwick* had been torpedoed by a German submarine fifteen miles off the north Cornwall coast with the loss of sixty-six lives. Six of those rescued from the sea who later died were buried in the churchyard at St Merryn—a sharp reminder, if anyone needed one, of the brutal serendipity that comes with war.

The pace and tenor of life in Cornwall was utterly different to London and to Odsey Corner. Here she had little autonomy. There were no impromptu shopping jaunts, no congenial lunches, and no popping home to recuperate from life's slings and arrows with Mum and Dad. Instead, there was camaraderie and parties, and she had the good fortune to be stationed near the home of some family friends, the Rhodes-Moorhouses, who lived six miles away at Hardings in Constantine Bay. It is likely that here they introduced her to Lady Milbanke, an Australian socialite born Sheila Chisholm,[9] who was to become a lifelong friend.

The connection to Lady Milbanke brought June into the purview of Lewis George Anselan Buchanan[10]—'Buck' to his many friends—an almost impossibly handsome RAF pilot, tall, lean, 31 years old, with shiny blue-black hair and long dark eyelashes. He had joined No. 278 Squadron which was stationed at RAF Davidstowe Moor, twenty miles north of Padstow, to take part in

9. Sheila Chisholm (1895–1969) married three times: Francis St Clair-Erskine, Sir John Charles Peniston Milbanke and Prince Dmitri Alexandrovich of Russia. She was probably the inspiration for the Australian term 'good-looking Sheila'.
10. Lewis George Anselan Buchanan (1912–1989).

*'Buck' Buchanan, a Pilot Officer in the RAF,
was stationed in Cornwall.*

air–sea rescue. His upper-class roots in Omagh, County Tyrone, faint Irish lilt and reputation as a risk-taker only added to his romantic allure.

Buck and Lady Milbanke, who was between marriages, would take walks on the beach together to watch the sunset and to talk about Sheila's youngest son Peter, an RAF recruit who was killed in a flying accident only a few days after start of the war. There was a deep mutual attraction between Buck and Sheila, despite the age gap, and they remained close even after the spark between them fizzled out.

As it did so, it became clear that Buck and June were falling in love. Soon they were taking their own intimate walks together on the beach.

❖

While June was serving with the WRNS in Cornwall, what became of Chelsea? Lots Road power station continued to be a target for occasional but deadly raids by the Luftwaffe. A German bomber narrowly missed it on 23 February 1944, killing eleven people in nearby streets and then dumping four high-explosive bombs on the Guinness Trust estate near the King's Road. If June had stayed in the London Auxiliary Ambulance Service, she would have been sent there and seen chimney sweep Anthony Smith of the heavy rescue squad squeeze through a gap in the rubble to reach a man trapped in the basement. Smith, who was later awarded the George Cross, dodged a falling wall, but then went back to the basement with a colleague to retrieve a woman who was about to drown in flood water. Fifty-nine people died at the Guinness Buildings. Jo Oakman, the ARP warden, survived because she was on duty and not at her flat in E block, where most of the casualties occurred. 'You can look at pictures of destruction and be shocked,' she wrote in her journal. 'It's quite different to look at the destruction of buildings you have known every single day of your life. Different to understand that the men moving over the huge mound of rubble were searching for people you knew, with names you can name.'

On 13 June 1944, a week after the D-Day landings, the Luftwaffe started sending over the notorious 'doodlebugs'—also called buzz bombs or V1s (the V standing for *Vergeltungswaffe* or 'vengeance weapon'), which opened the second phase of bombing, the so-called Baby Blitz. On 3 July seventy-four US servicemen and three civilians were killed when a V1 exploded in Turk's Row, just south of Sloane Square station, the single greatest loss of American military personnel on the UK mainland. On 3 January 1945, Chelsea suffered again when the Royal Hospital took a direct hit from a V2 rocket. Nineteen people were injured and a further five died, the last fatalities of enemy bombing in the borough.

About 43,000 civilians were killed by bombs that fell in the Blitz in 1940 and 1941, when June was driving her ambulance, and a further 17,000 in the period after to 1945, with half of all the deaths taking place in London. Eighty-six thousand people were seriously injured and went to hospital, and 151,000 were slightly injured. Chelsea was hit by 321 missiles and innumerable incendiaries. Four hundred and fifty-seven civilians were killed.[11] Per capita, only Bermondsey and Westminster suffered more.

On 2 May 1945 ARP services were stood down, as victory in Europe looked increasingly secure. A month later a final rally, attended by the King and Queen, was held in Hyde Park. Across the country 2,379 civil defence workers died in the line of duty, of whom 204 were ambulance workers for the various services. Thirty of those served with the LAAS, including four in Holborn, who were blown to pieces in September 1940 when two ambulances were hit, and four whose ARP station on the Isle of Dogs was destroyed (twenty-two other civil defence workers also died). In Chelsea, the only death among LAAS workers was Eleanor Foxall at Cheyne Row.[12]

Buck was nothing like June's previous boyfriends: he had none of the uprightness of George Turnbull or Peter Vaughan nor the nerviness of Harry Colvile, and although he was outgoing and affectionate, just as Bill Batt had been, he did not blanket June with effusive declarations. June's friend Patience said, years later, that when June fell in love with Buck it 'seemed to light her up'.

Buck had been a cadet at RAF College Cranwell in Lincolnshire in 1932 and joined the RAF at the end of 1938. Shortly after the declaration of war the following year he was posted to No. 217 Squadron to help protect shipping on the western coast of the UK. He seemed born for the RAF, and was much appreciated by his commanding officers. Before long he was assigned to duties as an instructor in navigation at a number of RAF stations around the country and sometimes was chosen to fly senior officers to meetings all over Britain. In July 1944, when Buck's squadron was posted to operations in East Anglia, on the other side of the

11. Commonwealth War Graves Commission, *Civilian War Dead in the United Kingdom, 1939–1945* (1954-1957). London: Peter Singlehurst, pp.1031-47. .
12. See page 108.

country, June may have found herself wondering if another of her stars had gone out, but Buck would purloin planes in order to be with her within hours, his commanding officer turning a blind eye. Occasionally, he was caught out. Years later, she told her children that when Buck borrowed a training plane marked as a target for Spitfire pilots and took June to lunch in a pub, a bewildered local policeman turned up asking if anyone could explain the presence of an alien craft on the local landing strip. Buck took June on at least one of his missions to escort a squadron of US Flying Fortress bombers out over the Channel on their way to Germany and to hang around over the sea to guide them back. After landing, June won the discretion of the American airmen by handing out chocolates and charm.

By August, she and Buck were engaged and hastily planning a wedding. 'Just so long as you are sure of yourself and him, then nothing else matters,' wrote her father. Arthur was almost as smitten with the blue-eyed Irishman as his daughter. 'I took a fancy to Buck the moment I saw him for no reason that I seem able to explain,' he continued. Even so, Arthur could not hide his suspicion that, despite Buck's venerable antecedents, he might not prove the rock the family wanted him to be. The Spencers, while not poor by any stretch of the imagination, were feeling the pinch and their estate could not support June and Buck and any possible children. 'I am quite sure,' wrote Arthur, without sounding it, 'but I do hope that he will be able to keep you in comfort without your having to slave and so that you will be able to develop your great artistic tastes to some extent at all events.' He knew that his daughter's happiness would not reside in a life of submissive domesticity.

On 19 September 1944 June Spencer and Buck Buchanan were married at the parish church of Bradwell-on-Sea in Essex with Buck's Squadron Leader, Ben Bowring,[13] a Battle of Britain pilot, as best man. Their wedding night was spent in a room at the Dorchester Hotel on Park Lane celebrating with members of a

13. Benjamin Harvey Bowring (1918–1994).

Pathfinders squadron who were about to take part in the Battle of Arnhem, which none of them would survive.

June was released from the WRNS when she discovered she was pregnant and after her first baby, Anselan, was born and the war had ended, the Buchanans settled at 36 Old Church Street in Chelsea. James was born in 1953 and Fenella arrived the following year. Buck remained in the RAF reserve but joined civilian life, taking a job as a furniture-buyer for Fortnum & Mason. He later became managing director of Lady Milbanke's travel agency, which operated from the same store until the firm folded. June modelled for the *Vogue* fashion photographer Norman Parkinson[14] and appeared in the magazine several times. The marriage ended in 1964.

What happened to June's erstwhile fellow lodgers and Chelsea friends? Some months after the destruction of Chelsea Old Church, Ric Stewart-Jones organised a concert in the ballroom at Lindsey House to raise funds for iron railings around the ruins to keep out pilferers looking for wooden beams to burn and artefacts and scrap metal to sell. Benjamin Britten and Peter Pears performed and Cecil Beaton and Kenneth Clark were among the audience.[15] Ric was determined that the church he loved would be rebuilt. After the war, by facing down trenchant opposition from the diocese, he succeeded. A restored Chelsea Old Church was reconsecrated in 1958 in the presence of Queen Elizabeth and the Queen Mother, but Ric was not at the ceremony. The year before, his heart had given out and he died on 22 September, aged 47. His widow Emma Smith[16]—they had married in 1951 after a four-week romance—was left to bring up their two young children.

14. Norman Parkinson (1913–1990).
15. Edward Benjamin Britten (1913–1976), composer, conductor and pianist; Peter Neville Luard Pears (1910–1986), tenor, Britten's personal and professional partner; Cecil Beaton (1904–1980), fashion, portrait and war photographer, diarist, painter, and interior designer; Kenneth Clark, see footnote page 184.
16. Emma Smith (1923–2018), novelist and children's writer.

Ric's soul-mate James Lees-Milne carried on working for the National Trust and wrote a number of pioneering architectural works. Twelve volumes of his personal diaries have been published. He died in 1997, aged 90, after a life devoted to beautiful buildings, and struggling, at times, with the tension between his marriage, his homosexuality and the Catholic church.

June and Ric had reconciled in the months after her eviction from Lindsey House and she achieved her peace with the rest of the Stewart-Jones family. She returned to the house many times for reunions and Christmas drinks. In the early 1950s, Ric had managed to reunite Nos. 97 and 98 and handed it over to the National Trust, who also took over Nos. 99/100. In the 2020s the once crumbling seventeenth-century palace is a row of well cared-for town residences leased to the uber-wealthy.

June remained friends with Ann Channer, who lived in Sweden until her death in 1984, and with Patience Clifford, who pursued her career in architecture and went on to work with Maxwell Fry and Neville Conder on designs for new schools; their work was exhibited at the 1951 Festival of Britain. Patricia married Henry Bayne-Powell and died in 2008. Charlotte Waterlow, of Lindsey House and PEP, was awarded an MBE in 1950 for services to the Foreign Office, wrote history books and was a peace campaigner, dying in 2011 at the age of 96.

Betty Stucley, with whom June remained friends, produced two more novels, a play and seven children's books, including *Magnolia Buildings* in 1960, at the time considered groundbreaking for spotlighting the lives of 'ordinary' families. She married at the age of 49 and adopted a child. June's children remember visiting Betty in Clapham, where she was known for unofficially mentoring local teenagers. She died in 1974.

Humphrey Brooke became deputy director of the Tate Gallery in London and secretary of the Royal Academy. Mental ill-health led to his early retirement, after which he became an expert on growing roses. He died in 1988. Harry Morton Colvile disappeared from June's life after his marriage. He died in 1992.

Peter Vaughan made a career in the army, retiring as a

lieutenant-colonel of the Worcestershire and Sherwood Foresters. George Turnbull died in 1998, aged 86.

In the 1945 general election, in which Labour won a resounding victory, A.P. Herbert was returned once more as an Independent MP for Oxford University and was knighted in Churchill's resignation honours. Before his seat was abolished in 1950, he campaigned on various reforms including legal aid for the poor and fairer voting, while continuing his career as a writer. He died aged 81 in 1971, his wife Gwen in 1986, aged 97. Their house in Hammersmith Terrace now bears a blue plaque.

Kenneth Lindsay of PEP became the Independent MP for the Combined English Universities in 1945. He died in 1991 at the age of 93. In 1978 PEP merged with the Centre for the Study of Social Policy and became the Policy Studies Institute.

After the war, journalist Graham Spry returned to London as the Saskatchewan representative of the Ontario Co-operative Commonwealth Federation government. In 1968 he founded the Canadian Broadcasting League.[17] He died in Ottawa in 1983.

June stayed in touch with Bill Batt, whose family continued to send her copies of his letters from the European front even after she had met and married Buck. Bill went on to play a key role in President Harry S. Truman's re-election campaign and pursued a career in the Labor Department, never losing his enthusiasm for building a better world. He died in 2004.

Adie Dorrien Smith, who had invited June to Tresco to recuperate, became the third of Eleanor and Arthur Dorrien Smith's sons to die in the war, killed in action in France on 20 June 1944.[18] The family's descendants still live at Tresco.

On the death of her father in 1949, Betty Poulsen inherited the Boskenna estate but she and her second husband, solicitor Paull Hill,[19] ran it into the ground and it was sold off in 1957. Betty died in 1980, a few months after Hill was tried for, and acquitted

---

17. A non-profit whose aim was to fight increasing commercialisation and direct US investment in Canadian broadcasting.
18. See footnote page 181.
19. Stephen Paull J. Hill (1912–1985).

of, murdering Betty's 36-year-old lover. Mary Swinfen divorced her husband and married journalist Eric Siepmann. After she was widowed in 1970 and found herself with no means of support, she wrote *Jumping the Queue*, published under the name Mary Wesley, and then *The Camomile Lawn*; she based the character Max Liebermann on Paul Ziegler. She died in 2002, aged 90.

Paul Ziegler, inamorata of Ann Channer and countless others, became a Catholic monk and died in 1986. His brother Heinz, the secret father of Mary Swinfen's second child, served as a pilot in Bomber Command and was killed when his plane was shot down in May 1944.

June's father Arthur died, aged 80, in 1950; her mother Helen outlived him by nearly forty years, dying at the age of 98 in 1988. June's siblings David and Janet died in 2004 and 2012.

Damage should not be measured only in broken bodies and smashed walls. Although June was not injured in the Blitz, she shared with every other person who experienced the home front an assault on her peace of mind. She and her friends may not have had to worry about income or food but they went through the same emotional dilemmas as anyone else, especially the question of how, or whether, to express anxiety or fear and the same grief for friends and family lost to war.

Innumerable members of the civil defence services performed acts that were at least as brave as George Goshawk and driver Bertram Matthewman, who took their ambulance through a 'sheet of flame' and loaded it with casualties just before a nearby building collapsed, for which they were awarded the George Medal[20]; or Betty Leverton, Mabel Anne Armitage, Philip Davey, Ruby Sandford, Joseph Slipman and George Tindall[21] who drove to the docks on the night of 7 September 1940 and under heavy bombardment evacuated people in their ambulances in relay. They were only different to June in that they were awarded medals

20. *London Gazette*, No. 35117, 28 Mar 1941, p.1778.
21. *London Gazette*, No. 35174, 27 May 1941, p.3066.

and she was not.[22] June showed an astonishing cool-headedness when she drove through London under a shower of bombs. She could have been killed at any time, yet she continued to report for duty as required, ready to do it all over again.

June never wrote of terror or disgust while on ambulance duty, although she would certainly have felt it. How did she cope with the scenes of suffering and pain, with severed heads and limbs, with her patients' searing grief and trauma? She stepped back, as many did. Often outwardly brittle, inside she was a mass of vulnerabilities: to depression, physical illness and unfeasible relationships. The dizzying two-week romance with Bill Batt, who may have mistaken June's thundery demeanour at a PEP lunch for spirited single-mindedness, could never have succeeded. For June, it was a simple step from that state of mind to the thrill and thrall of speed and daring with Pilot Officer Buck Buchanan.

In 1942 June struggled to get a release from her service with the LAAS and eventually succeeded. She was not unusual in wanting to leave civil defence services. Some of her colleagues served only a few months before leaving. Many of June's ambulance colleagues went to jobs more suited to their skills and personalities. Patrick O'Brian joined the French section of the Political Warfare Executive (PWE), a secretive government organisation co-ordinating an ideological war against Nazism. Mary Tolstoy continued to work for the ambulance service, divorced her husband in 1942 and then joined Patrick at PWE. John Crocker, who had peeled potatoes with June at AS22 and discussed their mutual friends, joined the Maritime Artillery as a gunner, defending British ships in the Atlantic from U-boats. Daphne Mulholland left the ambulance service and went into the Auxiliary Territorial Service, rising to the rank of Senior Commander.[23]

22. Other LAAS recipients of medals: Edward Morrison (George Medal, 1941); Rosemary Campbell (BEM, 1941), Vera Cowper-Smith (BEM, 1941), Hilda Watts, BEM, 1942).
23. In 1942, she married Sir John Guthrie Ward.

After her divorce from Buck, June remained in Chelsea. Determined to give her children a happy and stable home, she made a living as a window dresser for her good friend the fashion designer Laura Ashley[24] and offered couture dressmaking to the rich and famous. The Duchess of Windsor and Sarah Frances Croker Poole, the wife of the Aga Khan, were among her customers.

In 1985 June contributed her memories to a London Weekend Television documentary series *London at War*.[25] 'The bombs would be falling all around, but you felt better out doing something to help rather than waiting for them to drop on you,' she said. 'But my life off duty was like another world. I'd be shopping in the West End, dining at the Ritz, wearing smart dresses, going to balls, generally enjoying the social scene that I'd just been introduced to after I was presented to the King.'

At the age of 70, June bought a flat with a large picture window overlooking the Thames. It was on what she once considered the 'wrong' side, at Battersea, near the bridge, close to where we imagined ourselves standing at the beginning of this book—and it was an inspired choice. Here, from her sitting room, not only could she paint the river she loved so much but she could look directly across at Lindsey House. How often did she recall those difficult, dangerous war days, diving under the ambulance while incendiaries came down, playing cards in the dugout, hosting teas in her freezing attic bedroom, heading out for a night of dancing at The 400, sewing satin frocks by a dim yellow light, crammed like sardines into the hall at Lindsey House while above her a rehearsal for hell played out?

I met June only once. She was then in her late eighties and still strikingly beautiful, bright-eyed, with perfect white hair. She sat on the sofa at her daughter Fenella's house, upright and assured, and greeted me with a restrained but friendly smile. I was instantly in awe, but perhaps I should not have been. Years later, as I inched my way through her diaries, I met another June Spencer. Unprecedented horror, destruction and peril forced to

24. Laura Ashley (1925–1985), née Moutney.
25. Produced by Steve Humphries.

manage her emotions, even within the pages of her diary, but the descriptions of the path she carved showed her to be daring, stalwart, witty, compassionate and brave and, like most of us, a mass of contradictions. As I remember June in that sitting room, I wonder whether, even then, a layer of self-doubt sat beneath her confidence or, after the shock of her dramatic rejection by friends she had trusted, she had been left with an abiding fear of its repetition.

Her wry sense of humour certainly stayed with her. June died on 14 November 2013, at the age of 97. By then she was in a nursing home, where, towards the end, the staff would ask her every morning what plans she had. She always played their game. 'I don't know. I haven't decided yet. I may go out. Let's wait and see what happens.' She knew that neither she nor anyone else could predict what life would bring.

Bibliography

Anon. *Chelsea Old Church* (1957). Fulham, London: Buckenham and Son.

Alexander, Eileen (2020). *Love in the Blitz: The Greatest Lost Love Letters of the Second World War*. London: William Collins.

Atkins, Peter J. (2011). Communal Feeding in War Time: British Restaurants 1940–1947. In: Rachel Duffett et al (eds), *Food and War in Twentieth Century Europe*. Abingdon: Routledge.

Barsley, Michael (1940). *Ritzkrieg: The Old Guard's Private War*. London: The Pilot Press.

Beardmore, George (1984). *Civilians at War: Journals 1938–1946*. London: John Murray.

Bell, Amy Helen (2002). *London Was Ours: Diaries and Memoirs of the London Blitz 1940–1941*. PhD thesis, Queen's University, Kingston, Ontario.

Bell, Amy (2009). Landscapes of Fear: Wartime London, 1939-1945. *Journal of British Studies*, Vol. 48, No. 1, pp.153-175.

Bowden, Jean (1963). *Call an Ambulance! The Story of the London Ambulance Crews*. London: Robert Hale..

Braybon, Gail & Summerfield, Penny (2013). *Out of the Cage: Women's Experiences in Two World Wars*. Abingdon: Routledge.

Bridgland, Tony (2001). *Waves of Hate: Naval Atrocities of the Second World War*. Barnsley: Pen & Sword.

Burke, Thomas (1941). *English Night-Life: From Norman Curfew to Present Black-Out*. London: Batsford.

Butler, A. S. G. (1942). *Recording Ruin*. London: Constable & Co.

Calder, Angus (1969). *The People's War: Britain 1939–45*. London: Jonathan Cape.

Clapson, M. (2019). *The Blitz Companion: Aerial Warfare, Civilians and the City since 1911*. London: University of Westminster Press.

Cockett, Olivia (2008). *Love & War in London*. Stroud: The History Press.

Collier, Richard (1960). *The City That Would Not Die: The Bombing of London May 10–11, 1941*. New York: E.P. Dutton and Company.

Conekin B.E.(2009). 'Magazines are essentially about the here and now. And this was wartime': British Vogue's Responses to the Second World War. In: Levine P., Grayzel S.R. (eds), *Gender, Labour, War and Empire*. London: Palgrave Macmillan.

De Courcy, Anne (2006). *Debs at War: 1939–1945 How Wartime Changed Their Lives*. London: Phoenix.

Essex-Lopresti, Tim (2005). *A Brief History of Civil Defence*. Matlock: Civil Defence Association.

Faviell, Frances (2016). *A Chelsea Concerto*. London: Dean Street Press (reprint).

Feigel, Lara (2013). *The Love-charm of Bombs: Restless Lives in the Second World War*. London: Bloomsbury.

Field, Geoffrey (2002). Nights Underground in Darkest London: The Blitz 1940-41. *International Labor and Working-Class History*, No. 62, pp.11–49.

Fisher, Katherine E. (2014). *Writing (in) the Spaces of the Blitz: Spatial Myths and Memory in Wartime British Literature*. PhD thesis, University of Michigan.

Fitzgibbon, Constantine (1957). *The Winter of the Bombs: The Story of the Blitz of London*. New York: W. W. Norton.

FitzGibbon, Theodora (1982). *With Love: An Autobiography 1938–1946*. London: Century.

Foley, Victoria (2013). *'Make Do and Mend' – An Evaluation of How Women Lived and Worked in World War II England and Wales*. PhD thesis, Southern Connecticut State University.

Foot, M.R.D. (1984). *SOE: The Special Operations Executive 1940–46*. London: BBC Books.

Foss, Brian Frederick (1991). *British Artists and the Second World War. With Particular Reference to the War Artists' Advisory Committee of the Ministry of Information*. PhD thesis, University College, London.

Glinert, Ed. (2007). *West End Chronicles: 300 Years of Glamour and Excess in the Heart of London*. London: Allen Lane.

Godfrey, Walter H. (1913). Lindsey House, Nos. 95-100, Cheyne Walk. In: *Survey of London*. Vol. 4, Chelsea, Pt. 2. London: London County Council.

Goodall, Felicity (2006). *Voices from the Home Front*. London: David & Charles.

Graves, Robert & Hodge, Alan (1940). *The Long Weekend*. London: Faber & Faber.

Harris, Carol (2010). *Blitz Diary: Life Under Fire in World War II*. Stroud: History Press.

Harrisson, Tom (1978). *Living Through the Blitz*. London: Penguin.

Heiligman, Deborah (2019). *Torpedoed: The True Story of the World War II Sinking of 'The Children's Ship'*. New York: Henry Holt & Company.

Hodgson, Vere (1999). *Few Eggs and No Oranges: A Diary Showing How Unimportant People in London and Birmingham Lived Through the War Years 1940–1945*. London: Persephone Books.

Holden, Inez (2020). *Blitz Writing: Night Shift & It Was Different At The Time*. Bath: Handheld Press.

Jesse, John (2014). *A Fridge for a Picasso*. London: Muswell Press.

King, Dean (2000). *Patrick O'Brian: A Life Revealed*. London: Hodder and Stoughton.

Kroyer, Peter (1956). *The Story of Lindsey House, Chelsea*. London: Country Life.

Lambert, Angela (1989). *1939: The Last Season of Peace*. London: Weidenfeld and Nicolson.

Leatherdale, Duncan (2017). *Life of a Teenager in Wartime London*. Barnsley: Pen & Sword.

Lees-Milne, James (1975). *Ancestral Voices*. London: Chatto & Windus.

Lees-Milne, James (2000). *Another Self*. London: Faber & Faber.

Levine, Joshua (2015). *The Secret History of the Blitz: How We Behaved During our Darkest Days and Created Modern Britain*. London: Simon & Schuster.

Longmate, Norman (2002). *How We Lived Then: The History of Everyday Life During the Second World War*. London: Pimlico.

Mackay, Robert (1999). *The Test of War: Inside Britain 1939-45*. London: UCL Press.

Mackay, Robert (2002). *Half the Battle: Civilian Morale in Britain During the Second World War*. Manchester University Press.

Marnham, Patrick (2006). *Wild Mary: A Life of Mary Wesley*. London: Chatto & Windus.

Maclaren-Ross, Julian (1984). *Memoirs of the Forties*. London: Cardinal.

Macaulay, Rose (1942). *Life Among the English*. London: William Collins.

Macaulay, Rose (1962). *Letters to a Sister*. New York: Atheneum.

Malcolmson, Patricia and Robert (2013). *Women at the Ready: The Remarkable Story of the Women's Voluntary Services on the Home Front*. London: Abacus.

Nixon, Barbara (1943). *Raiders Overhead: A Diary of the London Blitz*. London: Lindsay Drummond.

Nott, James (2017). 'The Dancing Front: Dancing, Morale, and the War Effort in Britain during World War II.' *Journal of Social History*, Vol. 51, No. 2, pp.387–406.

Panter-Downes, Mollie (2017). *London War Notes 1939–1945*. London: Longman.

Pearsall, Phyllis (1990). *Women at War*. Aldershot: Ashgate Editions.

Piratin, Phil (2007). *Our Flag Stays Red*. London: Faber & Faber (reprint).

Potvin, Rose (1992). *Passion and Conviction: The Letters of Graham Spry*. Canadian Plains Research Centre, University of Regina.

Pound, Leonard (1976). *A.P. Herbert: A Biography*. London: Michael Joseph.

Pulford, Elizabeth, ed. (1980). *Richard Llewellyn Stewart-Jones: As remembered by his friends*. Privately printed.

Raby, Angela (1999). *The Forgotten Service: Auxiliary Ambulance Station 39*. London: Battle of Britain International.

Roberts, Hannah (2017). *The WRNS in Wartime: The Women's Royal Naval Service 1917–1945*. London: Bloomsbury.

Rothwell, Stanley (1981). *Lambeth at War*. London: SE1 People's History Project c/o Morley College.

Sansom, William (1947). *Westminster in War*. London: Faber & Faber.

Scharff, Virginia (1992). *Taking the Wheel: Women and the Coming of the Motor Age*. New York: The Free Press.

Shaler, Tracy L. (2009). *Frenchy: I Wanted to Get Back at Hitler*. Bloomington, Indiana: iUniverse.

Shute, Nerina (1945). *We Mixed Our Drinks: The Story of a Generation*. London: Jarrolds.

Sitwell, William (2017). *Eggs or Anarchy: The Remarkable Story of the Man Tasked with the Impossible — to Feed a Nation at War*. New York: Simon & Shuster.

Stucley, Elizabeth (1959). *Life is For Living: The Erratic Life of Elizabeth Stucley*. London: Anthony Blond.

Sweet, Matthew (2011). *The West End Front: The Wartime Secrets of London's Grand Hotels*. London: Faber & Faber.

Tolstoy, Nikolai (2004). *Patrick O'Brian: The Making of the Novelist*. London: Century.

Van Thal, Herbert (1971). *The Tops of The Mulberry Trees*. London: George Allen & Unwin.

Wainwright, Robert (2014). *Sheila: The Australian Ingenue who Bewitched British Society*. London: Allen & Unwin.

Walkowitz, Judith R. (2012). *Nights Out: Life in Cosmopolitan London*. New Haven and London: Yale University Press.

Wheal, Donald James (2005). *World's End: A Memoir of a Blitz Childhood*. London: Century.

Wiggam, Marc Patrick (2011). *The Blackout in Britain and Germany during the Second World War*. PhD thesis, University of Exeter.

Woon, Basil (1941). *Hell Came to London: A Reportage of the Blitz During 14 Days*. London: Peter Davies.

Wyndham, Joan (1985). *Love Lessons: A Wartime Diary*. London: William Heinemann.

Ziegler, Philip (1995). *London at War 1939-1945*. London: Sinclair-Stevenson.

Index

Adams, Rosemary 205, 208
Ainsworth, Josephine 35, 39, 47, 135
Alexander, Eileen 78
Ambrose, Bert 113
Ambulance service: *See* London
  Auxiliary Ambulance Service
  (LAAS).
Ames family 114–15
Antisemitism 113–14
Air Raid Precautions (ARP): *See* Civil
  Defence
AS22, AS179: *See* London Auxiliary
  Ambulance Service (LAAS)

Barsley, Michael 30–2, 48
Battersea 103, 170, 196, 229
  bomb incidents 81, 120, 152
  Bridge 1–2, 59–60, 188
  Park 1–2, 53, 70, 80, 120
  power station 62, 84, 135
Batt, William Jr (Bill) 190–213, 222,
  226, 228
BBC 9, 22, 27, 52, 102, 109, 127,
  129, 174
Benson, Theodora 51
Berkeley, The 23, 26, 28, 33, 36, 37,
  76, 112, 151, 187, 189
Berkeley, Claude Mowbray 188, 190,
  192, 196
Blackout 11, 24–5, 27–31, 42, 45, 49,
  53, 55, 96, 169, 193, 197–8
Blitz
  7 September 1940 1, 76–8
  8 September 1940 83–94
  10 September 1940 95–99
  11 September 1940 99–101
  13 September 1940 102
  14 September 1940 102,
  105–108
  18 September 1940 109
  17–18 September 1940 108–9
  24–27 September 1940 114–16
  7–11 October 1940 118–21
  15 October 1940 121-3
  12 November 1940 124–5
  8 December 1940 128–9

  29 December 1940 131–3
  19–20 February 1941 135–6
  8 March 1941 146–150
  19 March 1941 151
  16 April 1941 152–60
  18–19 April 1941 158
  10 May 1941 161–4
  anti-aircraft (AA) guns 26, 77,
  78, 80, 88, 100–101, 104,
  133, 135, 181, 182
  emotions about 71–2, 102–5,
  110–11, 118–19
  shelters 10, 71–4, 86–90, 105–8,
  112–13, 126–7
  sleeplessness during 77,
  100–101, 116–17, 150, 201
  total casualties 221–2
Boskenna 177-80, 182-3, 226-7
Bowring, Ben 223
Bridges, Margaret 49, 155
Briggs, Irene 48–9, 84–6, 92–3,
  95–9, 101, 103
British Restaurants 145, 211–13
Brooke, Humphrey 188–9, 190, 192,
  196, 198, 200–201, 204, 225
Buchanan, 'Buck' (George Lewis
  Anselan) 6, 219–20, 222–4, 228
Butler , A.S.G. 7, 158

Café de Paris 26, 33, 34, 148–50
Café Royal 187, 196
Catt, Daphne 47, 86, 109, 114, 134–5,
  137, 170, 187
Chamberlain, Neville 10, 19, 37, 124
Channer, Ann 57, 68, 76, 84, 93–4,
  119–20, 125, 128, 130, 132–3,
  135, 137, 138–9, 141, 145–6, 150,
  169, 173, 177–80, 186, 192, 200,
  202, 215, 225, 227
Chelsea. *See also* Lindsey House.
  ARP post (Cook's Ground School
  viii, 79, 133, 152–3, 172–3
  Basil Street 161–3
  Beaufort Street viii, 73–4,
  86–95, 115
  Carlyle Laundry 122

Chelsea *continued*
  casualties in Blitz 221–2
  Chelsea Manor Buildings 102
  Cheyne Walk: *See also* Lindsey
    House.
    No. 93 207–8
    No. 94 62, 64, 68, 71, 92, 172,
      203, 210
  Church of the Most Holy
    Redeemer viii, 107–8
  Danvers Street viii, 44, 46, 50,
    51, 73, 75, 79, 81, 85, 86,
    135–6, 153, 156, 170, 171
  Glebe Place 108, 174
  Guinness Trust estate 7, 164, 221
  King's Road viii, 46–47, 61, 71,
    86, 96, 108, 116, 133, 135,
    146, 147, 154, 189, 201, 210,
    221
  Lots Road power station viii, 62,
    63, 84, 107, 108, 135, 153,
    164, 221
  Old Church viii, 1–2, 60, 83,
    122, 126, 131, 152–60, 224
  Paultons Square viii, 85–7, 101,
    135–6, 156
  Peabody Trust housing 73, 115
  Peter Jones viii, 3, 36, 61, 110,
    125, 127. See also John Lewis
  Riley Street 47, 122, 170
  Royal Hospital viii, 20, 60, 84,
    153–6, 221
  Shawfield Street 123
  Sloane Gardens 122
  Sloane Square 38, 60, 61, 124–5,
    127, 142–3
  Sloane Square station 124–5
  St Luke's Hospital 164
  World's End 1, 7, 73, 164
Chester, Peggy: *See* Finlayson, Tulip
Churchill, Winston 33, 37, 39, 71,
  101, 108–9, 132, 144, 193–4,
  196, 205, 206
Civil Defence 10–11, 38–41, 82.
  See also London Auxiliary
  Ambulance Service (LAAS);
  Shelters.
  Air Raid Precautions (ARP) 10,
    36, 41–5, 51–2, 56–7, 82, 83,
    84–91, 93, 100–1, 107, 123,

    147, 152, 180, 222
  ARP wardens 2, 78, 79, 86, 100,
    101–2, 104, 105, 107, 110, 115,
    122, 133, 153, 155–6, 221
  Fire Services 45, 78, 81
  heavy rescue 2, 53, 84–8 , 94,
    140–1, 160, 221
Clifford, Patience 68, 137, 141, 150,
  172, 173, 192, 202, 210, 222, 225
Olivia Cockett 118
Colvile, Harry Morton 4, 8, 174–7,
  180, 182–3, 186, 188–9, 192–3,
  196–8, 210–11, 222, 225
Coward, Noël 160, 215
Crocker, John Delamain 75, 87, 124,
  160, 169, 186, 228
Crowther, Marguerite (Peggy) 90
Cummings, Constance 4, 172–3
Cuthbert, Sydney 152, 154

Dall, Evelyn 113
Darling, Jean 90
Darlington, Esther 40, 65, 68, 69, 73,
  74, 109, 122, 124, 129, 161, 165,
  167, 170, 192
Darwin, Robin and Yvonne 206, 213
Devas, Anthony 4, 188–9
Dorchester, The 32, 127, 143, 224
Dorrien Smith family; Adie 14,
  175–6, 180–2, 209, 226
Dugdale, Tom 4, 183–6, 210, 216
Dunkirk 38, 40, 58, 75, 108–9, 140

East End 7, 43, 52, 62, 70–1, 76–7,
  81–4, 100, 102, 105–8, 109, 113
Edgcumbe, Piers 40, 75
Ellis, Pamela 215
Elmhirst, Dorothy and Leonard 138
Emary, Barbara 42–3, 147
Embassy Club 21, 33–4, 191, 194, 213

Faviell, Frances 7, 90, 112, 125, 154,
  157, 163
Finlayson, Tulip 45, 49
Fitzgibbon, Theodora 7, 80, 83,
  155–6
Flack, Harry 161
Foxall, Eleanor 108, 222

Friends Ambulance Unit (FAU)
    126–7, 128
Fulham hospitals
    Fulham Hospital 95–102
    St Stephen's 135
Furse, Judith 172

Gambier-Parry, Gill 74–5, 126, 131–2
George VI 3, 16, 19, 27, 63, 102, 222
Gielgud, John 215
Gilliat-Smith, Sybil 43, 84, 115
Good Intent, The 143, 146, 210
Gough, John 26, 57, 72, 127
Gough, Penelope 26, 57, 66, 69, 70,
    72–3, 114–5, 126, 160, 216
Green, Yvonne 156, 159–60
Grosvenor House Hotel 20, 33, 36,
    106, 129, 130, 134, 146–9

Harding-Newman, Thomas Harold
    Harding 175, 180, 186, 201
Harrod's 13, 17, 72, 108, 115, 161,
    175, 183
Haslewood, Irene 88, 123
Hatchett's 33, 106, 143
Hedges, Geraldine 48
Herbert, A.P. viii, 4, 165–8, 172–3,
    175, 183–4, 188, 199, 210, 226
Hill, Anthony Eustace 214
Hill, Barbara 15, 18-19, 214
Hill, 'Robin' 18-19, 35, 214
Hodgson, Vere 101, 131, 147, 152
Holden, Inez 70, 102–4, 117, 169
Howe, Fisher 191–2
Hungaria, The 106, 186
Huxley, Julian 138–9
Hyde Park Hotel 196

Jesse, John 86
Jews. See Antisemitism
John, Augustus 4, 63, 178, 188–9,
    192
John Lewis 61, 109–10
Johnson, Ken 'Snakehips' 34, 148
    See also Café de Paris
Junior Carlton Club 33, 143

Knight, Harry 21, 171

La Belle Meunière 192
Lambda, Peter 214
Lansdowne, The 106, 127, 143, 188,
    215, 216
L'Apéritif 33, 188
Lees-Milne, James (Jim) 7, 63, 65,
    67, 72, 124, 125, 127, 141, 199,
    207, 225
Le Suivi 126, 127
Levy, Benn 4, 172–3, 208
Lidderdale, David 151
Lindsay, Kenneth 4, 137, 139, 172,
    199–200, 226
Lindsey House viii, 1, 7, 14, 27, 39,
    46, 48, 51, 54, 59–66, 71, 72–3,
    92–4, 103, 107, 112, 114, 117, 119,
    122, 123, 125–8, 130–1, 143, 146,
    150–1, 156, 160, 164, 165, 170,
    172, 174, 175, 180, 191, 196–7,
    199–200, 202–209, 213, 214,
    216, 224–5, 229
    No. 96 1, 20, 59–60, 63–4, 72–3,
        126, 167–8, 199, 203–9
    No. 97 1, 59, 64–6, 84, 92, 99,
        100, 108, 112, 115, 121, 124,
        130, 134, 135, 139, 151, 157,
        160, 161, 191, 204, 208
    See also Chelsea: Cheyne Walk
        No. 93 and No. 94
Loftus, Murrough 187, 188, 189, 191,
    196
Lombard, The 57, 70, 143, 155, 157
London Auxiliary Ambulance Service
    (LAAS) 7, 8, 25, 40–55, 68, 81,
    108, 116, 171, 175, 201, 221-2,
    227, 228
    See also Civil Defence.
    AS22 (Danvers Street) viii, 2,
        44–55, 85, 92, 95–6, 98,
        108–109, 122, 130, 135–136,
        153–5, 160, 170, 186, 228
    AS104 (Adelphi) 52, 82–3
    AS179 (Battersea) 1, 170–1, 174,
        175, 186, 189, 191, 199, 204
    TS3 (Riley Street) 47, 170, 171

Macaulay, Rose 7, 25, 43, 52, 87–8
MacTavish, Alexander (Alec) 140–1,
    157, 160
Markham, Felix 188, 190

May Fair Hotel 32, 106, 112–114
McCaw, Eleanor 210, 212
Milbanke, Sheila 219–220, 224
Mirabelle, The 142, 143, 186, 193, 214
Morrison, Herbert 107, 132
Morris, Terrence 175, 192
Mulholland, Daphne 101, 133, 228

Nagle, Pauline 89
Nicholson, Max 139
Nicol-Smith, Marjory 48–9, 52
Nixon, Barbara 78, 80, 82, 110

Oakman, Jo 79, 81, 86, 90, 102, 104,
    107–108, 115, 118–119, 120, 133,
    153, 156, 158, 161, 221
O'Brian, Patrick 49–50, 171, 179, 228
    See also Tolstoy, Mary.
Odsey Corner, Hertfordshire 3,
    10–12. See also Spencer, June: at
    Odsey Corner
Oppé, Fred 65, 114

Panter-Downes, Mollie 55–7,
    100–101
Paynter, Betty. See Poulsen, Betty.
Paynter, Camborne Haweis 178–80
Pearsall, Phyllis 82, 105
Perfect, Janet 68, 72
Perfect, John 57, 69, 112–15,
    192, 207
Pheasantry Club, The 189
Phoney War 22–39
Piratin, Phil 105–107. See also Savoy
    Hotel.
Players Club 173–4, 186, 213
Political and Economic Planning
    (PEP) 4–5, 57, 69, 137–9, 160,
    171, 188, 190–1, 200, 225, 226,
    228
Postlethwaite, John 211, 213
Poulsen, Betty 177–9, 182–3, 209,
    226–7

Quaglino's 31, 33
Queen Charlotte's Ball 20, 37–8,
    146–147, 162
    Blitz Ball 129–130
Raikes, Lisel 38, 114

Rationing
    clothes 168–9
    food 30-2, 116, 120, 142–6
    petrol 42, 45, 121–2
Restaurants 30–2, 58, 106,
    143–5, 210-13. See also British
    Restaurants.
Richardson, Ralph 215
Ritz, The 30, 33, 46, 112, 121, 144,
    160, 187, 215, 229
River Emergency Services 165–6
    See also Herbert, A.P.
Rothwell, Stanley 91

Sams, Christiana (Nanny) 27, 64, 66,
    69, 72–3, 124-8, 134, 199, 205,
    207–9
Sansom, William 78, 91–2, 99, 105,
    122, 164
Savoy Hotel 20, 28, 32, 52, 105–108,
    143–4, 160
Sayer, Honour 68, 75, 84, 150
Scott, Katharine 38–9, 48–9, 68,
    208
Scott's restaurant 33, 70
Spencer, Arthur 10–12, 223, 227
Spencer, David 10, 12, 36, 45, 72,
    130, 199, 211, 218, 227
Spencer, Helen 5, 8, 10–12, 14, 18,
    150, 175, 210, 227
Spencer, Janet 9–12, 26, 35–8, 40,
    135, 211, 213, 227
Spencer, June
    antecedents 11, 15
    upbringing 12–14
    presentation at court 14–21
    during Phoney War 22–39
    joins ambulance service 40–5
    in summer 1940 59–75
    witnesses first day of Blitz 76–83
    at Beaufort Street bombing
    86–94
    drives under fire to Fulham
    Hospital 95–102
    nights in West End 112–16
    meets Ziegler brothers 119
    attends Diona Stewart-Jones's
    wedding 125–6
    consults fortune teller 128, 200
    goes to Blitz Ball 129

Christmas 1940 at Lindsey
House 131
tries out for *Vogue* 137
attends lunches at PEP 138–9
night of bomb at Cafe de Paris
146–51
bombing of Old Church 152–64
attends Basil Street incident
161–3
friendship with A.P. Herbert
165–8
service at AS179 170–1,
173
in Cornwall, Scillies 175–83
at Boskenna 177–80, 183
sits for Tom Dugdale 184–6;
relationship with Bill Batt
190–5, 197–8
takes call about Pearl Harbor
193
organises party at Lindsey House
198–9
works at Foreign Office 200–1,
205–209
leaves Lindsey House 207–208
joins Ministry of Food 211–16
serves in WRNS 211, 216–20,
224
relationship with 'Buck'
Buchanan 219–20, 222–3
death 230
Spies 32, 108–109
Spry, Graham 4, 188, 192, 197, 210,
226
SS *City of Benares* 116
Stewart-Jones, Diona 27, 64, 66,
72–3, 99–100, 115, 121, 125–7,
128, 129, 131, 161, 165, 199,
202–7, 209
Stewart-Jones, Edward 66, 125
Stewart-Jones, Eva 62, 64, 125, 202,
206–207
Stewart-Jones, Michael 64
Stewart-Jones, Richard (Ric) 1, 14,
20, 26, 58, 59–67, 72, 114, 125–7,
129, 158, 165, 202–3, 206–8,
210, 224–5
St Paul's Cathedral 132, 158–9
Streatfeild, Michael 137, 173–4
Streatfeild, Yvonne ('Eve') 17

Stucley, Elizabeth (Betty) 58, 202–8,
216, 225
Swinfen, Lady. *See* Wesley, Mary.
Tennant, Alison 134–5
The 400 Club 21, 28, 33, 35, 37, 46,
134, 149, 150, 153
Thomas, Dylan 80, 167, 188
Tolstoy, Mary 49–50, 171, 179, 186,
228
Turnbull, George 9, 15, 18, 22, 24–5,
28, 36, 161, 192, 197, 226

Ustinov, Jona and Peter 173–4

van Thal, Dennis and Herbert
211–12, 214
Vaughan, Peter 142, 146, 150, 170,
197, 225–6
Venturette, Hélène 13, 16
Vereker, Sandy 139–40
Vogue magazine 32, 119, 137–138,
224

Waldron, Frank 187
War Artists' Advisory Committee
184–5
Waterfield, Honor and Tony 116, 124,
126, 137, 146
Waterlow, Charlotte 68, 137, 139, 225
Wesley, Mary (Lady Swinfen) 5, 43,
177–83, 203, 209, 227
Wheal, Donald 7
Whistler, James McNeill 1, 60, 66,
191
Wyndham, Joan 7, 81, 112, 122,
131–132, 148
Woodard, Joe and Jean (The Joes)
64, 126, 143, 146

Ziegler, Heinz and Paul 119–20, 124,
179–80, 192, 227

SPONSORS

These sponsors have been paramount in getting this book into the public sphere, and I offer them my special thanks.

Dolly Bantry
Jane and Adrian Brewer
Amanda and Ken Brown
James Buchanan
Tommy Candler
Michele and Martin Colyer
Jane Cook
Ginny Dougary
Rosemary Ellis
Judy Ewens
Nell and Simon Gatehouse
Christine Keiffer
Frances and Frank Kitson

Simon and Suzy Frith
Mandy Glass
Pamela and Doug Grau
Diana Gregory
Alison and Tony Guest
Robin Harold-Barry
Lucy and Ian Hawkins
Ben and Claire McCreanor
Leonardo Paz
Barbara Segall
Dudley and Sarah Winterbottom
Mark Winterton
Andrew Zajac

THE AUTHOR

Naomi Clifford is an acclaimed author and history writer. She is a host of The Door History Podcast and co-editor of Vauxhall History website.

Naomi was born in London, the child of US emigrés. 'My family had no experience of the Blitz,' she says, 'but my father served in the US Air Force, and by the mid-50s he and my mother had settled in north London. The Blitz was still a raw and vivid wound. I have clear childhood memories of playing in bomb sites and sifting through the rubble looking for "treasure". When I look back I wonder if this infantile archaeology pointed to my later fascination with the world evoked by June Spencer's thought-provoking diaries.'

Naomi is available for interviews and talks. Contact her via hlaagency.co.uk.

Thank you for reading this book.
We really value your opinion
so please leave a review on
Amazon or GoodReads or your favourite
book site, and spread the word amongst
your friends and family.

Printed in Great Britain
by Amazon